S0-BOK-735

An ITALIAN JOURNEY

*Celebrating the
Sweet Life
of Tuscany*

CAMPAGNA Books by JAMES ERNEST SHAW

AN ITALIAN JOURNEY
A Harvest of Revelations in the Olive Groves of Tuscany

AN AMERICAN JOURNEY
Travels with Friday in Search of America and Americans

An
ITALIAN
JOURNEY

Celebrating the
Sweet Life
of Tuscany

JAMES ERNEST SHAW

Copyright © 2013 James Ernest Shaw
Published in the United States of America
All rights reserved.

First Edition

ISBN 978-0-9846585-3-4

The text in this book is composed in Giovanni

Cover by Roger Morgan
Cover design by George Foster
Interior design by Susan Knopf
Illustrations by Jonathan Edward Shaw
Photographs by James Ernest Shaw

Publisher's Cataloging-in-Publication Data
Shaw, James Ernest, 1946 – An Italian Journey: A Harvest of Revelations in the Olive
Groves of Tuscany / James Ernest Shaw 1. Tuscany (Italy) – Description and travel.
2. Italy – Traditions, social life, and customs.   3. Farming – Italy & United States.
4. Local Food – Italy & United States. 5. Farmers – Italy & United States. 6. Christianity
– Roman Catholicism. 7. Science – History.

Campagna Books, Wisconsin
http://www.facebook.com/Campagna

Printed in the United States of America

10 9 8 7 6 5 4 3 2 1

Dedication

I dedicate this book to my wife, Mardi Shaw, who has for the past three years certainly, and often throughout our forty plus year marriage, had to shoulder a large burden because of the enthusiasms of her husband. *Grazie per Grazia.*

I also dedicate this book to the people of my hometown, Hayes Center, Nebraska, because they first taught me the importance of shared work on the land.

I dedicate it also to the Ross and Sarah Peters Family and to Rossy and Cathy especially, because they first opened my eyes to the idea that Italians are truly marvelous people.

I want to also dedicate this book to all the wonderful people of Italy who taught me the true meaning of *Ciao*, especially the Tuscan farmers who welcomed me to their farms, and most especially to Aurora and Pietro, Joshua and Annamarja.

Ciao!

Acknowledgments

Thank you to all who assisted me on these travels, whether you have been mentioned in this book or not. I recall countless folks who aided me, whether with directions, advice, translations, or just a drink of water—check that, especially a drink of water. *Grazie per la ospitalità.*

For those who noticed a big man pulling a suitcase with an odd-looking bicycle, I thank you for your smile, your wave, your *Buongiorno* as I biked by, your curious questions about my mode of travel, my family, and my itinerary.

I thank those of you who provided me a place to sleep and a seat at your table, who offered your time to answer my many questions. A traveler is in need of many friends, especially when traveling by bicycle, and I found more than a person has a right to expect on my Italian journey.

I also want to express my heart-felt appreciation and admiration: for the work of George Foster who designed the cover for the book; for the knowledgeable and ever vigilant sharp-eyed copyediting, interior design, and typesetting of Sue Knopf; for the superb editing of Ellen Tarver; for the beautiful and evocative drawings of Jonathan Shaw; and for the advice of my agent Ed Breslin, who gave me the confidence to keep working these many years to bring this journey to the printed page.

It was a joy and an honor working with everyone of you.

But don't blame any of them for the word choices, grammar, spelling, or oddities in English and Italian that remain. Sometimes I prefer the quirky—or maybe I just overlooked their good advice.

Contents

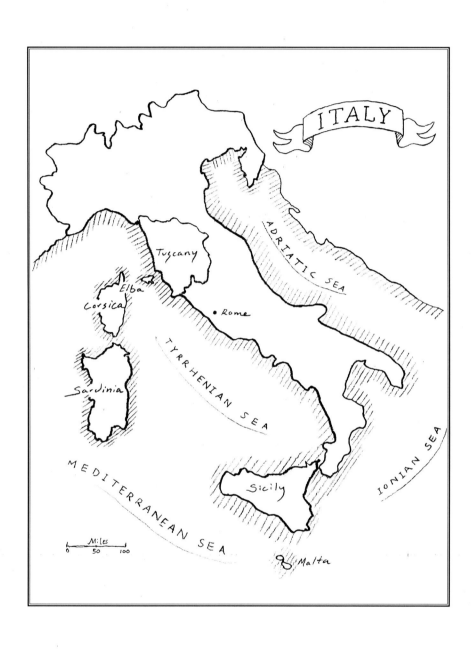

An

ITALIAN
JOURNEY

Celebrating the
Sweet Life
of Tuscany

Photos by
JAMES ERNEST SHAW
Illustrations by
JONATHAN EDWARD SHAW

Introduction

Love and understand the Italians,
for the people are more marvelous than the land.
E.M. FORSTER

Do I love Italy because of my sweet memories of childhood,
or is there something about Italy that sets it apart for everyone?

A Pretty Girl

I didn't know it at the time, but I was smitten by things Italian when I was eleven years old. I thought she was just a pretty girl. Her skin was olive, her hair dark, her figure slender, her face divine. One hot August day, she lured her best friend's cousin under the low-hanging branches of an apple tree on the pretense that the coolest and sweetest fruit was to be found there. She then proceeded to teach that impressionable young boy how to kiss—not a May-Day-basket peck of a kiss, but a real kiss—a wet, chills-down-the-back-of-your-neck kind of kiss. I didn't tell Dad about the kiss, but I did ask him about Cathy. He was the one who told me she was Italian. Her brother, Rossy, was my best friend, and always had been. Dad told me he was Italian too.

Their mother and father owned my favorite restaurant. I guess I didn't know they were Italian because they didn't advertise their Italian-ness. Heck, they didn't advertise anything. They just served good meals and called the place White Café. I loved their food. I loved that whole family. I especially loved the times they invited me to join them for Sunday dinner at their home. They seemed more like a family than mine. I didn't know exactly what I meant by that, or why I loved it, but I sure knew what being with that family felt like.

Back then I attached little significance to the fact that they were Italian. When you're a kid, things just are. You don't question how they got that way. I was not then raising children or grandchildren. I was just being a kid. Reasons weren't so important to me then.

But now I want to know more. I want to know why I love Italy. I know I'm not the only one to fall under the charm of things Italian. What is it about the way Italians eat and the way they live that is so appealing? Do I love Italy because of my sweet memories of childhood, or is there something about Italy that sets it apart for everyone? I'm convinced there is only one way to find out.

When I was fifteen and over six feet tall, my best friend's sister was no longer teaching me about birds and bees and apple trees. Even though I would have loved advanced schooling, to her I was still "little Jimmie Shaw." She was dating young men her age. I wished she would have seen me as more of a man, of being worthy of continued attention, but seniors don't date freshmen. The best I could hope for was that the men who worked for my dad would quit treating me like a boy. I wanted to get to know them and I wanted them to get to know me. Working alongside them in a Nebraska wheat field one suffocatingly hot July day, they first saw me do the work of a man. That evening, they invited me to eat with them at their table, a table that just happened to be in the restaurant of my best friend's parents. That's when I first learned that sharing work brings people together.

I have come to Italy with the hope that if I am willing to pick their grapes and their olives, if I am eager to work alongside them, Italians will invite me to sit with them at their tables, just like the men who worked for my father. I hope that by eating with Italians, I will discover why people began falling in love with Italy long before I first succumbed to her charms. I'm convinced that if I break bread with Italians, they will share not only their food and their wine with me, but their lives, their stories, and maybe even a few of their secrets as well.

Chapter One

Tuscany is a state of grace.
The countryside is so lovingly designed that
the eye sweeps the mountains and valleys
without stumbling over a single stone.
The lilt of the rolling green hills, the upsurging cypresses,
the terraces sculptured by generations that have
handled the rocks with skillful tenderness,
the fields geometrically juxtaposed as though
drawn by a draftsman for beauty as well as productivity;
the battlements of castles on the hills,
their tall towers standing gray-blue and golden tan
among the forest of trees, the air of such clarity that
every sod of earth stands out in dazzling detail...

IRVING STONE

*We were at the lane's end, at Aurora's farm,
at her truly Tuscan farmhouse, a simple large rectangle,
perfectly proportioned, terraces of olive trees
stepping up the hill behind it.*

Why Tuscany? Why Italy?

A stone-walled farmyard framed by the dark green of cypress trees was creating the foreground of a Renaissance composition and drawing my eyes toward a man getting on a motorcycle. Out of place and time, the anachronism was in the driveway, only a few feet from the road. In the distance, shimmering olive groves and the rhythmic, geometric patchwork of vineyards surrounding the walled city of Cortona completed the masterpiece of form and color. As I entered the foreground the picture changed. The motorcycle became a motorbike. Seconds later I realized he was not getting on the bike, but leaning over it. My eyes focused on his movements. The haze of distance and presumptions cleared and the man became a woman. She grabbed a screwdriver and bent down to adjust the carburetor. I quit pedaling.

Any woman working on a motorbike would have intrigued me, but what drew me in, as she straightened up and our eyes connected, was the strength of her movements. Wearing knee-high muck boots, a long bright-yellow slicker covering well-worn work clothes, and just a hint of a smile, she glowed with the confidence of a healthy old age—a vibrant woman with short, gray-streaked hair ready for whatever the day might throw at her.

The farmyard too was aged and just as robust as she was—nothing out of place but that motorbike. She looked as if she had been taking care of herself and her farm all of her eighty-plus-year life and had no intention of turning either job over to others. If I had ridden by a day earlier, my guess is that I might have seen her gutting a wild boar, *un cinghiale,* or heaving straw bales into her barn.

I wanted to go back and ask if I could take a portrait of her standing next to that dry stone wall that was itself a work of art. I wanted to capture the lines in her face, to hear the story of her life, to learn of her hard-earned wisdom, to see her riding her little red putt-putt across the fields, her yellow coat flapping in the breeze. But I could find neither the courage nor the brashness. The scene looked just right without me. Maybe some other day. Another farmer, twelve kilometers down the road, was expecting me. I resumed pedaling. But my mind would not leave her. Her steel gray-blue eyes, filled with light, were still piercing me.

In that brief moment as our eyes locked, she became for me an icon of healthy, productive old age—a lasting memory of what a life well spent looks like. But I was wondering how she saw her life. Was she thankful she was still caring for herself and her farm? She most likely saw herself less heroically than I did. If I'd had the courage to ask, she would probably have said she was just a farmer, a *contadina* who joined her life to the gift of good land to create a healthy life for her family.

Or maybe, because she was old enough to have suffered through World War II and the way things used to be in Italy, she might have spoken of the pain of being seen as a *cafona,* a disparaging word, a curse linked to farming and the land, but which emphasizes poverty, a lack of formal education, and a willingness to suffer. If any of that formed her, grace now covered it. In that moment when we looked into each other's eyes she became for me a vision of a self-reliant life to celebrate.

And I rode right on by her.

The road that day had been faithfully following the lay of the land, twisting and turning over rounded hills and clear-running streams, slicing through darkened, sweetly scented woods and into the light of rolling fields of wheat and oats bordered by sunflowers following the sun. I was pedaling comfortably. The hills were gentle, the temperature mild, the pavement was playing out before me like a sweet-sounding symphony, and had been all morning. Feeling the rhythm of the land, I crested a small hill, checked my mirrors for cars, saw an empty ribbon of road and gathered speed, using the whole lane to sweep through a series of gentle curves that began with a melodious chord, but came out sounding the discordant note of a long straight line thrust into the heart of the rolling countryside. No longer in tune with the land, the superimposed efficiency did, however, offer an unexpected benefit. I could now see where I was going.

I had almost given up finding a farm like the one I hoped was awaiting me. While the phone was ringing, I glanced one more time at the description included on the World Wide Opportunities on Organic Farms (WWOOF) website: "Aurora (63) needs help pruning." Just as I was rehearsing the message I would leave on her answering machine that would convince her to call me, she answered. She told me a bit of her story. I told her a bit of mine, that I had been in Italy picking olives for a week, but I was looking for a farm that placed a higher value on tradition. I told her I had bicycled away from my first farm at daybreak, and was calling from Pienza. I didn't tell her she was the last farmer on my list, my last hope. I also didn't mention I had spent the whole morning compiling the list, and all afternoon calling. I felt a drop of sweat trickle down my arm. After a few minutes of back and forth, she mentioned she lived near Cortona and thought her olives would be ready the next day. *Ah good, she needs help right away.*

We kept talking and I kept hoping. A few moments later she said, "I am going to put my son on the phone. He is better at giving directions."

Wonderful. And it's a multigenerational farm too. But when Pietro began talking, my certainty that I had found a traditional farm became a bit less certain. For starters, his English had a Down Under twang. Even though I had once lived in New Zealand, I couldn't say whether it was a Kiwi or Aussie accent. Nothing against those who celebrate Christmas at the beach and go skiing in July, but I wasn't looking to be picking olives with a Crocodile Dundee type. Something else was not quite right, but I had already committed. Besides, Aurora sounded like a good person, a good farmer. How could her son be any different?

Pietro seemed to know precisely how far I was from Cortona. He was also certain he knew the best route for me to follow. He didn't seem surprised that I was biking. I took that as a good sign. But he was not sure I could make the fifty-some kilometers to his farm yet that day. He suggested noon the following day. I made a quick calculation and realized that meant just about equal amounts of daylight, whether I started riding right away or waited until the next morning.

I asked Pietro for his address, but he told me my GPS would not find his farm, even if it had steered me down little-traveled roads to my first farm. He suggested that I meet him on Sodo Street in the village of Camucia at noon the next day. I asked for a cross street, but he said that would not be necessary. He told me to just call him when I got to the first gas station I saw on Sodo Street. That seemed less than ideal, but what the heck, I rationalized, we have cell phones.

Recalling that Aurora had told me she intended to start picking olives the next day, I suggested again that I could bike to his farm before dark. I had programmed Camucia, which Pietro said was Cortona's train station stop, into the GPS and discovered I had an hour to spare. However, Pietro still seemed certain it was too far, so the next day it was.

The first photograph I took in Italy—just outside the train station in Chiusi. The picture reminds me of the excitement I felt as I pulled the parts out of the suitcase and assembled Friday and the trailer and decided how best to pack everything. I pulled off the road not far from Chiusi to take Friday's first portrait in Italy.

I was pinching myself as I bicycled my first kilometers in Tuscany—looking out across vineyards and olive groves to see farmyards and villages perched on top of every hill—and everywhere the iconic cedar trees. Even though I was enjoying the Tuscan landscapes I wasn't sure I was on the right road—I didn't yet have faith in my GPS. It kept telling me to turn onto "unpaved road" after "unpaved road." I wondered how it could be possible that every unnamed road in Italy could be in the system. But that little technological marvel led me down these gravel strewn roads to my first farm.

I was practicing Italian greetings as I topped yet another hill and saw Cortona once again covering the mountainside now only eight kilometers in the distance. The cypress-lined road pointed right at the center of the town, framing the village perfectly on the hillside. Kilometer after kilometer I had been riding toward the walled city trying to recall how I had heard of Cortona. Finally I realized it was the town Frances Mayes brought to the attention of the world with her book *Under the Tuscan Sun*. She had described it well. Cortona did look enchanting, a storybook town in a beautiful setting. But then just about every town I'd seen in Tuscany was a gem in a gorgeous setting.

I tried to imagine where Aurora's farm was on the hillside. Or did it lie protected in a valley? Would the farm be close enough that she walked to Cortona or Camucia for her bread, her vegetables, her wine? Pietro had said that the farm was only a few kilometers from the center of the village. I wondered if the shopkeepers missed her when she didn't show up for a few days? I wanted to feel the pulse of the town—to get to know her butcher, her baker, her vegetable vendor.

I had not been able to tell from the WWOOF website whether Aurora was the widow of a farmer or not, but somehow I sensed she was. I hoped she had a lifetime of experience with the farm—that hers was not just a century farm, as many are in America, but that it had been in her or her husband's family for centuries.

I knew from the website that she was a retired teacher and was willing to give Italian and Latin lessons. If this farm, like my first one, proved to be less than I was hoping for, at least I would leave Aurora's place speaking Italian much better than when I arrived.

Pietro had told me I would see the walled city high on the hill long before I got to it, and that I wouldn't have to climb into the old city. I was carrying a morning of hopeful thoughts down that arrow-straight road to a roundabout that dropped me unprepared into snarled, midday traffic.

With Sodo Street as its destination, the GPS was displaying ".7 km." But right in front of me was a street so steep, I swore it was only a few degrees off plumb. I would have been smart to turn around and suffer the GPS's HAL-like, slightly snide, and somewhat irritating voice saying, "Recalculating." But I rationalized that at least I was no longer weaving around double-parked delivery trucks and turning cars. Pushing my bike and trailer straight up the hill and reproving Pietro with each step for not giving me a cross street, I tried to reconcile his instructions with the clues in front of my eyes. He had been very explicit. *You won't have to climb into Cortona.* And I thanked him for that. But with my next gasp, I wondered why he hadn't mentioned that I would be clambering into Camucia to get to Sodo Street.

When at last I got to the top of the hill, I had two choices. One was to turn right on Sodo and climb even higher. But that would take me toward Cortona, perched high above. The other choice was to turn left and go down Sodo. I shuddered at the thought that I had climbed this high for no reason. Even worse, what if I biked down and found out that Pietro's gas station was indeed still above me. Then I'd have to climb back up again. Neither option looked good or clear.

I called Pietro but had to leave a message: "I know I'm a little early, but I wanted to let you know I'm on Sodo Street, still looking for a gas station. *Ciao.*"

I looked up and down the street hoping for a clue that would solve my dilemma. I saw nothing but houses above and houses below. My only hope was that Sodo Street was extremely crooked and that somewhere down the hill the road took a huge left turn and headed back out into the valley toward the highway I could see far below me—back to where a gas station most likely would be.

I started coasting down Sodo, still uncertain if I had made the right choice. I was hoping to hear my phone ring any second before I lost too much of what I had struggled so hard to gain. The area seemed prosperous; the gently winding road led past comfortable but moderately sized houses. I was riding the brakes, hoping as I rounded each corner that I'd see a gas station, even though I knew it would look totally out of place. Sodo, more smooth, wide boulevard than street, dropped lower and lower, sweeping gently in curves, never turning sharply enough or long enough to head back into the valley. I coasted a kilometer and a half, maybe two, and saw not a hint of a gas station.

The boulevard narrowed at a cross street and turned ninety degrees left. At that corner I saw the only business I'd seen since summitting Sodo Street—a nice-looking inn, a bed and breakfast, on the uphill side, right at the bottom of the hill. I stopped, called Pietro, and left another message: "On Sodo Street, still no gas station. I'm in front of *Il Sole del Sodo*, sitting on a large rock, basking in their sun."

I pulled a sandwich from my backpack. I was eating the first half of it when a little car screeched to a halt behind me.

"Aha! I have found you. Wait here. Don't go anywhere. I'll turn around and lead you the rest of the way." Pietro was leaning out the window of a Fiat. He looked to be in his late thirties, with Italian hair, a square face, and much confidence. Without waiting for my reply—and without another word—he disappeared up the narrow road behind me.

I don't remember exactly what kind of person I thought Pietro would be when Aurora told me she was going to put her son on the phone to give me directions, but I'm pretty sure the expectation would not have lined up with the person I had just met. He seemed rushed, driven, rather un-Tuscan, maybe more big-city Italian. He was definitely different from anyone I had yet met in Italy.

Before I had finished wrapping what was left of my sandwich and stuffing it into my pack, he was back. He had changed his mind. "Here, James," he said as he flung open the hatchback, "throw everything in here."

But everything didn't fit in there—it wasn't even close. But by laying the seats down we shoehorned my backpack and trailer inside, the hitch projecting at an odd angle into the front passenger seat. "Follow me, James—it is only two kilometers." And with that Pietro sped off.

I was not yet riding a lean, mean Italian racing bike, but I *was* seventy pounds closer. My bike had been set free. I was thankful we didn't retrace my route, nor did we pass a gas station, and for what remained of the downhill I was able to keep up with Pietro. At a roundabout, we grabbed the first exit, crossed a small creek, then the road leveled. We breezed along at a good clip among olive groves, stone houses, meandering walls, and overhanging chestnut trees. The rush of the wind thrilled me—I was feeling the speed and the freedom of riding light. My little-wheeled Bike Friday, with Pietro's Fiat as its rabbit, was zipping around corners, catching air over stone bridges, and streaking past elegant cypress trees.

The land surged upward and the road with it. Pietro now had the advantage. He continued zipping around corners and over hills. I, on the other hand, was struggling. Each time I crested a hill or rounded a bend I would look off in the distance just in time to see Pietro disappear around a corner or over the top of yet another hill. I wished I would have noted the mileage at the roundabout. *Surely we've gone two kilometers.* The road narrowed, more like a lane now, hardly wide enough for even his little car. Fifty meters ahead, I saw him drive under an arch. The road cut right through the middle of a farmhouse. He disappeared.

I rode through the narrow gap, expecting to see his car parked at the back of the house, but instead saw only a road leading ever upward, now strewn with boulders. I wondered how he had kept from getting his car high-centered on the big rocks, and how I was going to get up the road. As a point of pride, I was not going to let him catch me pushing my bike; something in Pietro was bringing out the competitiveness in me. I dropped into my granny gear and put as much weight as possible on the front wheel, but even that was not enough. I had to ride wheelies around the huge rocks to remain on the bike. I got to the top, found a fork in the road, and had to guess which way to go while maintaining enough momentum to stay upright and moving forward.

I guessed right and soon saw Pietro's car waiting in the distance. The road leveled, then passed within inches of another farmhouse. I was sweating, keeping up as best I could. I took my focus off the rocks and deep holes in the road and glanced at the countryside. We had circled around the valley. The lower walls of Cortona were now below us on the distant hillside. On the near hillside some of the olive groves lining our path were well tended. Others looked as if they had not been pruned for decades.

Pietro had disappeared. Only one choice lay before me and it was filled with puddles. I navigated the least muddy route. The lane climbed for a few tenths of a kilometer, then hugged the hill, leading me around a bend where I found Pietro leaning against the back of his car, arms folded. "Not bad, James. Hot little bike you have there."

I smiled, drew in desperately needed oxygen and said, "Beautiful place you have here." We were at the lane's end, at Aurora's farm, at her truly Tuscan farmhouse—a simple, large rectangle, perfectly proportioned, terraces of olive trees stepping up the hill behind it. How could anyone not love it here? I parked my bike on the sunny side of a small stone building. "Not bad, Pietro."

"You like, James?"

"I do."

Pietro turned. I followed him into the house. "I got your *wwoofer*," he announced to his mother.

Aurora popped out from behind a sheet covering a doorway to a room that I presumed had to be the kitchen, but from what I could see from the position of the walls, seemed to be unusually small. She too was smaller than I expected, not much more than five feet tall. Her smile was open, her eyes direct, her voice solid, her skin weathered. She reached for my hand with both of hers.

"Welcome, James. Oh, you are a tall one. Good for picking the high branches, but I am afraid you will not like it here. I am sorry. The *wwoofer* website is wrong. Did I tell you I have no room for you in the house?" she asked me, mostly in English. She seemed overly apologetic. I did not yet know of the other things on her mind.

I would, she said, be sleeping in a loft that she and a workman had just finished in what used to be a garage—a loft with a ceiling so low she feared I would have to crawl to my bed. "And also James, you will have to use the outdoor bathroom. We just finished it—you will be the first to use it," Aurora added. She glanced in the direction of Pietro. He was looking through his mail. "Pietro is here from Australia looking for a job. He and his son, Joshua, have been living with me a couple of months—and Pietro's wife will be arriving soon, so we built it rather quickly. I hope you like it."

I was beginning to understand the situation a little better. At least I thought I did, but I didn't want to pry so I just said, "I'm sure it will be just fine."

"*Fame*, James?" Aurora asked me. "Are you hungry?"

"*Si*," I said, remembering the half-eaten sandwich in my backpack, but to be polite I added, "*Piccolo fame*," hoping that might mean something like, "I'm a little bit hungry."

"Pietro, please show James where the bathroom is and help him get his things into the loft," Aurora said and ducked back into the kitchen. I followed Pietro outside. He gave me a quick look at the *bagno esterno*, then led me across the parking area to the garage. I crawled up the almost vertical stairs and stretched out on the floor. Pietro tossed the bags up to me. "Remember James, no sleepwalking," he said as he turned to go.

Aurora was right. I couldn't stand up except under the peak of the roof. But the space was comfortable, especially the bed. It had been built by the loving hands of a craftsman and was charming and private. The same could be said for the outdoor latrine and shower wrapped in slab wood and camouflaged by lush plants. I liked showering outdoors so much I began upgrading my plans for an outhouse near the cabin on my farm to something more like Aurora's out-in-the-bushes bathroom. Before I'd gotten around to unpacking my suitcase, Aurora was at the front door yelling, "*Pranzo, pranzo.*" I had been on the farm less than thirty minutes when Pietro, Aurora and I sat down to eat.

The first course was pasta. We ate and we talked. Then Aurora got up and slipped into the kitchen. When she parted the sheet to bring us the second course, I saw that the kitchen was even smaller than I thought—about the size of a large closet—very un-Tuscan. But the food was definitely Tuscan—fresh, local, and lots of it. Every few minutes she got up, went to the kitchen and quickly reappeared with another course, another pleasant surprise—cheese, bread, *prosciutto*, olives, fruit, another bottle of wine. We were seated around a table just big enough for four,

squeezed in front of a small TV that was in the corner but not turned on.
With each course we got more comfortable with each other. We passed
by the small talk and began joking and laughing as though we had been
friends for years—relaxed, except for occasional lapses from Aurora. As
she brought the salad to the table, which turned out to be the last course,
she again mentioned the loft. "Oh, James, I am worried about your knees.
You are not so young as most *wwoofers.*"

"No, please don't worry. My knees are fine. I like it up there. It's very
cozy."

Pietro jumped in. "When I got here from Australia I took one look
around at what my mother had done to the place. I told her I could
take care of her worries, all her problems, if I had but two bombs." He
paused, turned from looking at his mother and looked straight at me.
He drew out the sound of my name, "Jaaayyymes, one is for where you
sleep, the other for where you take a crap."

Trying hard to suppress a nervous laugh, I looked toward Aurora. She
was holding her head in her hands. "Oh, *Babbo,*" she said quietly. She
sat there—not moving—and then with more force she said, "Oh, *Baa
booo*"—it sounded like a plaintive cry, a sigh to her father, or a prayer to
God—I wasn't sure. The mournful tone made me uncomfortable.

"What kind of work did you do in Australia?" I asked, attempting
to change the subject.

Pietro said he was in business, that he sold something. He was talking
very fast and I didn't catch what it was, or why he was leaving Australia.
I did find out that he had an MBA, but before I could learn more, he
was again railing at his mother. "I don't know why you had to put that
crapper right in the front yard."

I was trying hard to not take sides, but my sentiments were with
Aurora. It wasn't in the front yard, more like at the side, and there was no
street, so no one would be driving past—a footpath through the woods
yes, but who would ever see the structure, especially since it was hidden
by bushes and plantings until you were right on top of it. And besides,
a son shouldn't talk like that to his mother.

But I liked Pietro. He was quick witted. He was funny and surprising. I asked him how his search for a place to live was going. But because he was still talking very fast, I didn't catch what he said—what kind of place he wanted or how near it would be to his mother's farm. Before I could ask more of him, he had excused himself from the table. Maybe it was a question he couldn't answer or saw no need to until he had found a job—until he knew where he would be working, or maybe I had misunderstood the situation.

Aurora and I remained at the table, sipping red wine from nearby Montepulciano (a name I loved hearing Aurora say) and telling more of our stories. World War II was an important part of her life. Her father had fought in the war. Story-telling molded her childhood; she told stories of the war almost as though she too had been fighting at the front. The passion with which she told her stories revealed that the war and its aftermath affected her deeply and was still affecting her. Her admiration and her love for her father were clear, but she turned her attention back to Pietro.

"He is a good boy. He just has a bad habit. He says bad things about his mother. It has always been that way. If I say 'this,' he says 'that.' If I say 'cold,' he says 'hot.' If I say 'I like,' he says he doesn't like."

Aurora knew her son well. I'd forgotten until that moment what Pietro had told me when we first talked on the phone. "James, my mother and her carpenter built a *mezzanine* in the garage for *wwoofers*. I think you will like it. It is really quite nice." Those were his exact words. No mention of blowing things up. Just a compliment for his mom on the work she had done to create more living space. But in front of his mom, he said he wanted a couple of bombs to take care of the problems she had created.

I slept well that first night in Aurora's loft. Headroom may have been lacking, but in exchange I got well-insulated walls and a warm bed, two features missing from the amenities list of the camper I had slept in my first week in Italy. At breakfast Aurora served me Earl Grey tea, my second favorite behind Lady Grey, along with bread and plum jam, also a favorite, and asked about my knees as though for the first time. I assured her yet again that I liked the loft—that I had slept well and was looking forward to picking olives.

"Did you use a net to catch the olives at the other farm?" she asked.

I told her that we did, and that I didn't much care for the brambles that were forever getting stuck in it.

"You may like it here. I pick only by hand and only into a basket." She handed me a traditional hand-crafted basket that had yet to have even one olive dropped into it—still clearly marked with a price of 35,00 euros.

I loved the craftsmanship, the feel and look of the basket. It was a work of art. Picking olives into the basket was simple and direct. My fingers caressed the olives. I felt the increasing weight on my stomach as the basket filled. We worked together in the same tree, picking Aurora's first olives of the year. The morning was beautiful, peaceful, and calming. Pietro wasn't there. He was taking Joshua to school.

"How long has the farm been in your family?" I asked.

"I bought this farm in 1981 or '82 maybe. It was in awful condition." My hope for a family farm with centuries of tradition vanished.

"Were you a farmer—was your dad a farmer?"

"No, no, I am—I was a professor. My husband had died and I wanted to have my own place. I wanted to live on the land and grow my own food. I wanted to pick olives."

"But who taught you to farm, how to take care of the place?" I asked.

"I learned a little here, a little there. The neighbors were good to me. They took pity on a widow." Aurora thought about it and laughed. "Good thing they did, too." I knew without a doubt that I wanted to work on her farm. I liked her sense of humor—her sense of self.

"I'll bet you fell in love with the place the first time you saw it," I said, thinking back to the first time I saw my farm in the unglaciated hills of southwest Wisconsin—land I hoped someday to farm with my son Christopher and his family.

"No, no, no. I don't think so. The house did not even have a roof. The whole place was in terrible condition." She started to say something, hesitated, then laughed again, putting her hand to her mouth as though she were embarrassed. "Have you read *Under the Tuscan Sun?*"

I nodded.

"It was like that. James, you will not believe, but my real estate agent showed me that house, Bramasole, before Frances Mayes bought it. But I did not like it. I did not like its position. It would, like she wrote, always be looking for *sole*. I wanted sun, as much sun as I could get. I didn't want to be in the shade of a mountain, praying for sun all day long."

She sighed, got lost in thought for a moment, and then said, "Oh, *Baa booo.*"

When she began talking again she said, "She and I are very much alike, Frances Mayes and myself."

I didn't ask if she knew her. I just said, "Ah," hoping she would keep talking. I loved hearing her tell about her life. We had eaten three meals together, and at every meal the conversation rivaled the food. Aurora went on to tell me that she and Frances Mayes were about the same age, of similar stature, both were professors of literature, and each had paid a fortune to local craftsmen to bring back to life an ancient, much-neglected farmhouse.

"Oh what a difference it would have made if only I had bought that house. Maybe she would have bought a house someplace else and driven the real estate prices sky high there instead of here or maybe, with God's help, I would have written a book about restoring Bramasole and I would now be rich."

I only smiled. From what I had learned of her, I didn't think she wanted to be rich. She had already convinced me that she liked hard work and loved the look of a just-pruned olive tree.

We continued picking. My basket was now even more beautiful, filled as it was with plump, luscious olives. Aurora picked into a plastic, multicolored shopping bag that hung from an old brown belt. She was wearing dark blue rubber boots and a faded cotton sweatshirt covered by a loose-fitting wool vest. She looked totally comfortable but not very stylish, color-coordinated, or traditional. She began talking again. "I should write a book and tell the story of my life, my pain, my joys. The only problem is that I do not like to...how do you say...I do not like to..." she trailed off, frustrated that she could not think of the word in English.

"To rewrite—to edit," I said.

"Yes, James. That is it. I want to write once and be done with it. So I will probably never be a writer. I am too impatient."

She was not impatient as a farmer, however. She was very careful with her olives. The first *cassetti*, large plastic containers as Americans would call them, she filled only half full so the tender olives on the bottom would not be crushed under the weight of those on top. She told me not to fill the *cassetti* to the top until the day her olives were scheduled at the *frantoio* to make her precious olive oil.

Aurora was teaching me to respect the olives and to respect the process of making olive oil. She deeply loved the tradition of growing her own olives, of caring for her own trees. Even though she was not raised as a farmer, she thought like a farmer—a farmer with agrarian sensibilities. I liked the way she thought. I liked the way she picked. I especially liked that we talked while we worked. What we were doing, and the way we were doing it, was just as it was done when the northwestern walls of Cortona, on the shady side of her valley, were built centuries ago.

Aurora looked at the land with the eyes of a stranger,
with fresh eyes, having lived in Tuscany only thirty years.

Chapter Two

Wisdom begins in wonder.
SOCRATES

Learning Italiano

Connubial—that's what Aurora called it.

The sun had been at work drying the dew-wet olives for two hours by the time Aurora and I began climbing the ancient terraces of the Etruscans. Aurora was carrying *una cassetta, un coltello, e un cestino*. I was carrying the same—a large plastic container for carrying and storing the olives, a foldable pruning saw, and the handcrafted willow basket that fastened around my waist with a knotted length of sisal baling twine. By the time we began picking, the sun had finished its job. The olives, although still cool, were dry—dry enough to be picked, dry enough to be stored.

The sun, following its daylong arc from the slopes of L'Alta Sant'Egidio to the fog-layered hills of Montepulciano, was also doing a good job of painting one beautiful picture after another on the rugged but domesticated hillsides surrounding us. Throughout the day I had been moved to comment on the beauty of the land as the sun worked its way around the sparkling blue sky, highlighting first a tower, then an ancient house, and after that, a field lined with trees. Each time I said, *"Bella, bella,"* Aurora would tell me another story of the land and its people.

Late in the afternoon, when the glorious beauty the sun was creating was reaching its climax, Aurora glanced up at the exact moment the big orange ball settled with perfect precision onto the rim of the distant hills. Every vineyard, olive grove, and stone wall in the valley glowed with a transforming halo. She considered the mystical panorama for a moment, then uttered the single word, *"Connubial,"* and went back to picking olives.

But I didn't recognize the word as *connubial*. I thought she was using a single Italian word, even more perfectly suited than the sweet sound of *bellissimo*, to describe the wondrous beauty that lay before us. Upon seeing the sky light up, Aurora had chosen, I was assuming, to utter the word at the exact moment of perfection as a point of emphasis in my Italian lesson for the day. She and the radiant sky had my full attention. This word, which I presumed described ultimate beauty and transcendent sublimity, was definitely going to make my list of favorite Italian words. I had, by then, seen enough of the country that Dante called *il Bel Paese* (the beautiful country) to know that Italy contained sufficient natural wonders to make such a word eminently useful.

Aurora, who in her former life had been a teacher, was helping me learn *italiano*. Each day as we picked olives, our conversations were a combination of English and Italian. Just as with all the other words Aurora had taught me, I repeated this word over and over to myself. Aurora's delightful accent had completely disguised the word *connubial* to my ear.

The sun, now resting for a brief moment on the horizon before continuing its journey, was drawing my eyes to walls and farmyards and fields scattered throughout the valley that I had not noticed in the full, undirected light of day. The light, reflecting off haloed clouds lying just above our heads, was painting everything in a heavenly glow. Aurora looked up and noticed I was still transfixed by the sun's transforming rays.

"God and man are married here," she continued. "Nowhere will you find a more perfect collaboration between the beauty of God's creation and the handiwork of man." And then she said again with emphasis, "Connubial."

This time I understood. She was using an English word, with Latin and Italian roots, that captured the essence of Tuscany. With a poet's delicate mastery of metaphor, Aurora opened my eyes to a truth never before expressed so succinctly.

"I think I see this land more clearly than my neighbors do," Aurora added.

I nodded in agreement, wishing I could have overheard the conversations with her neighbors that led her to that conclusion. She certainly was helping me see the land clearly. Aurora was helping me see not only this land, but Tuscany, Italy, and all of farming more clearly. The land had the look of wisdom and antiquity, and so did Aurora's gaze as she considered *la campagna*, the countryside. How fitting that the word for "countryside" in Italian resonates with the sound of "companion" in English.

Aurora looked at the land with the eyes of a stranger, with fresh eyes, having lived in Tuscany only thirty years. I began thinking of all the stories she had told me about her valley, especially of the old farmers who showed up at her door now and then to tell her with pride that they once worked this land—land that she was now caring for with the humble and subtle sensibilities of a thankful steward.

I too was thankful, thankful for Aurora's vision and for people like E.M. Forster, who made me wonder about Italy. He was the first writer I read who clearly expressed the view that Italy and Italians are in some mysterious way, unique: "Love and understand the Italians, for the people are more marvelous than the land." He was not the first person, the first writer to be smitten with Italy, nor will he be the last. The list is long of writers who have fallen in love with Italy and Italians: Mark Twain, D.H. Lawrence, Henry James. Goethe, having sojourned in Italy from 1786 to 1788, remarked: "Italians consider themselves the finest people in the world, an opinion which, thanks to certain excellent qualities they undeniably possess, they can hold with impunity." Goethe was also impressed with the land. Of the countryside surrounding Cortona he wrote: "...no field or clod of earth is kept better than here, and everything is clean..."

But Italy had been through a lot in the last century—Mussolini, Hitler, and World War II—and now the euro and the Common Market. Could it be possible that Italy and its people had retained the qualities that led Forster to proclaim them special? I was convinced that only by living, working, and eating with Italians would I have any hope of finding out if the Italy that Goethe and Forster discovered and loved had endured. And if it had endured, I hoped that by immersing myself in the dailiness of Italian life, I could figure out why Forster should foster such folly that one country, one land—even one singularly blessed with the unique, recognizable shape of a boot—should be granted the special capability of making people who are marvelous.

I had yet to find a reason to quibble with Forster. At first his fascination with Italians seemed a little over the top, but on reflection, *marvelous* did seem to be a good word to describe them. On that morning Aurora had given me a new way of looking at the world, but she didn't solve the mystery. I had not yet comprehended why Italians should be more marvelous than other people. But that they were, seemed no longer in doubt.

The country was full of marvels that I was glimpsing through the eyes of an Italian who had lived long enough with the land to begin to know it. Aurora showed me on that chilly autumn afternoon as the sun was setting over the luxuriant Val di Chiana what I would not have had eyes to see had I not spent the whole day with her quietly picking olives from trees that had been alive since the Renaissance. And once she had opened my eyes to marvels such as five-hundred-year-old trees, and Etruscan terraces that were old when Jesus walked the earth, I could not imagine a better, more fitting description of the Tuscan countryside than *connubial*—a marriage of God's creativity and man's thankful stewardship.

I had arrived in Italy ten days earlier, without the poetic purity of Aurora's vision, but with enough knowledge of Tuscany's charms to be predisposed to like it. But it was not love I was seeking. I wanted understanding. I wanted to know why this land, why these people, have such a hold on writers and romantics, on people who are chafing from a world that now seems so ill-fitting—*tutto maledetto.*

I had been reading about Italy for much of my life, and had studied it intensely for a year in preparation for my voyage. I sought to understand the Italian character by reading Luigi Barzini, Giovanni Boccaccio, and Alberto Moravia. Knowing that I didn't have time for more than one region, I chose Tuscany—the land of the Etruscans and the land of the Renaissance—the region that gave birth to Italian, the language now spoken by all of Italy. If a book had been written about Tuscany, I tracked it down and read it. I studied the picture books, the travel guides, the pull-up-stakes-and-move-to-Tuscany books, but still I was not prepared for the feeling of being in Tuscany.

The first few days I was enchanted, as most tourists are, by the beauty of the countryside. But the more grapes and olives I picked, the less I felt like a tourist, and the more I felt that Tuscany, that Italy, would eventually reveal some of its secrets. I tried to look at everything with fresh eyes, to experience it anew so that I might see it clearly and get at the *why* of this land and these people. I began comparing, hoping that by not skipping over the obvious, I would notice the hidden. The streets were narrower, steeper, the cars smaller. After only a few days in Italy, the MINI Cooper morphed into a rather large car and the Cinquecento—the Fiat 500—took its place as the quintessential small car.

I continued the comparisons, always asking why, trying to get at the heart of Italy, wanting to know why life felt so different. The houses were smaller, looking as if they had grown right out of the soil, and would be around for a long time. I found few suburbs in Tuscany. As I biked I was either in a town or among farms. The land was productive—food growing right to the edge of cities. I rarely saw huge lawns, except in public parks.

I noticed all these things, the why of which seemed to reside in a different attitude about preservation, but might be attributable merely to the fact that Italy had been around a lot longer and had less room to expand. But I didn't feel these observations held the answer to my question. I was searching for something, but I didn't know what. I was just certain that I had not uncovered it in the books I had read. I was looking for something that made Italy unique.

I noted the distinctive qualities of every town I biked into: the architecture; the vitality of the town centers; the stores, which tended to be small and clustered; the people, who were walking rather than driving; the way the streets followed the terrain rather than the tyranny of a grid. No one would likely mistake America for Tuscany. But I had to start somewhere.

Something beyond the hilltop towns, the vineyards, the cathedrals, and the olive groves was escaping my conscious attention that would help me begin to understand the *why* of Italy. I was biking around Tuscany with the same sense of anticipation I have when I walk into my house and sense that my wife has moved a piece of furniture, or bought something new, but I can't figure out what she has changed.

Late in the afternoon of my first Sunday in Tuscany, the light was fading and pockets of cool air were cascading down the hill. I was only a kilometer or two from the ancient fortified town of Montefollonico, but still biking through dense woods. I heard people talking, but saw no one. *"Se sara asciutto abbastanza per nove, potremo iniziare a raccoglierle."* They were talking about olives, wondering whether it would be dry enough by nine in the morning to start picking. Just everyday talk, but to my ear, with the long rays of sunlight streaming through the trees, their *italiano*, overflowing with energy and inflections, sounded like poetry.

The sound of my front tire slicing through a pile of crisp, dry leaves covered the voices and sharpened the chill of the evening air. I looked down to watch the tire sweep through the gentle curve, following the tire's hypnotic movement through the swirling, earthy colors until the leaves disappeared. The tires rolled silently again and the sound of the voices returned, drawing my eyes through the trees to three people walking up the road. The warm, soft shafts of evening light painted a scene of timeless rural beauty. They were walking, not with a purposeful gait, but with the ambling cadence of friends engrossed in conversation. I followed along, mesmerized by their shimmering silhouettes in front of a sky glowing pink, red, and blue—thrilled by the simple pleasure of it all. How little that happy moment was costing them. Even though the road was quite steep, they seemed to consider their walk not a hardship, but a joy. I was pleased that I was beginning to understand Italian well enough that I caught that they had spent the afternoon with their neighbors—eating, laughing, and drinking wine from their own vines—and they had been at it for quite some time.

Even though I was by now only a few meters behind them, they had not realized they were no longer by themselves in the woods. To avoid startling them, I softly cleared my throat. As they were turning their heads toward me, I called out *"Buonasera."* Their age stunned me. They were in their seventies, but they were walking as if they were fifty.

As they, in lyrical unison, sang out *"Buonasera,"* a chill surged up my spine. What I had been sensing but not seeing was right there in front of me—*old people.* Tuscany was *full* of old, hard-working, story-telling, life-loving people. The images of all the old people I had biked past in the last week flooded my memory—old people still full of life—still walking up and down the roads of Tuscany sharing life with their neighbors. The camaraderie of these three old people, I was convinced, was revealing the *what* of Italy that would lead me to the *why.*

Instantly my thoughts about old people changed. I had always dreaded getting old, but these people and the others I had seen all over Tuscany rewrote the story. Old age suddenly looked good. It was as though an earthquake of perception had swung my compass from "North" to "True North." I didn't want to get old all of a sudden, but I no longer feared old age. The question at that moment was not whether I had the wealth, but whether I would have the health to be old. My last years should have the vibrancy of these three people. Some might feel they were poor and to be pitied, but to me they looked blessed, sharing the good of their lives, and the food they had grown with their neighbors.

My concept of stewardship expanded to the very bodies we inhabit. The *giftedness* of life, of our bodies and our minds, in that instant of truly seeing these three vibrant people, left an imprint that has not faded. And in seeing the giftedness of life, I became acutely aware of the Giver of the gift, and thus my *responsibility* for thankfulness.

If a friend gives you a bottle of wine, you feel a desire—a need—to thank him, especially if it is wine from his own vineyard. How, I wondered in that moment of discovery, of revelation, *questa bella scoperta*, had I spent so much of my life oblivious of my responsibility to be thankful for the gift of life itself, as well as my responsibility to take good care of that life, that body, and that mind I had been given. Twenty years ago Wendell Berry posed the question with his provocatively entitled book *What Are People For?* The joy of those three people on the road to Montefollonico showed me as good an answer as any I could imagine.

As I continued to think about why this vision was impacting me so profoundly, I realized that I was seeing a lot more old people in Italy than I do when I bike around America. I love my country, I love our freedoms and our inclination to innovate, but at that moment I wondered whether we take our freedoms for granted and abuse the gifts we have been given. To see as many elderly people in the United States, I would have to be visiting nursing homes and hospitals. Rarely in America do I see old people walking along the streets, working in the fields, or gathering in the town centers, or leaning on their back fences talking to their neighbors. Our supposedly easy lives have spawned an ugly old age. American life, especially for the elderly, struck me at that moment as soft, segregated, and detached—old people spending their *golden years* watching life instead of living life and giving life to their friends and neighbors.

I was sensing that life in Italy is harmonious. Old, young, middle-aged, rich, poor, all living together—no ghettos of conformity. Italians still live in communities, and old people are venerated.

Overwhelmed by the revelation, I biked the last, very steep pitch to the heart of Montefollonico. Not one car did I meet, but I rode by lots of animated people. Two teen-age boys were kicking a soccer ball back and forth across the road as they walked up the hill. One saw me coming, held the ball with his foot, and watched me pass. "*Bella bicicletta,*" he sang out.

The other smiled, gave me a thumbs up, and said, "Way to go," in clipped English before switching back to flowing Italian, "*molto forte.*"

I wasn't however feeling particularly strong at that moment, too winded to do more than smile and say, "*Grazie.*"

A woman in her sixties carrying canvas bags full of vegetables, turned and smiled when she heard me thank the boys. I returned her smile. Farther up the hill, just below the city walls, two old men were walking arm in arm. (It's a delightful Italian custom that put a smile on my face every time I saw it and made the world seem less threatening, less competitive.) So comfortable were these two with each other, it was easy to imagine they first began walking together up that hill seventy-some years ago when they were schoolboys. I slowed down and followed them, thrilled to be able to listen to their good-natured ribbing of each other while I cooled down from the long climb. They made me wonder what it would be like if my childhood friend and I were still walking arm in arm to town. What stories would we be telling and retelling?

The two men led me to a small park by the main gate to ancient Montefollonico, where they joined a group of men their age near an ornate fountain. Four younger men, in their forties and fifties, were gathered on the patio of a *taverna*. They were laughing, telling jokes, and toasting each other. Life looked good. I couldn't say for sure that these people were happy—that they would overlook their worries and admit to good fortune, but they sure had the look of people who recognized what was good about their lives.

The men in the *piazza* were making me feel good too. They were vibrant, healthy, and productive—and they looked like they knew how to enjoy one another. One hundred years after E.M. Forster fell under the spell of Italians, I too was succumbing. If I would have joined in a conversation with the two men walking arm in arm and quoted Forster's thoughts about Italians, they would have written me off as a picnic basket several sandwiches short of a full lunch—a naïve American. Italians are suspicious of those who see their lives as noble or special. They know that Italians have struggled for years, even centuries, and many of them are what the world calls poor. As a country they are deeply in debt. Tourists may think Italians are living the good life, but Italians don't see it that way. Even at a table overflowing with laughter and good times, they wonder about a life of things and free-flowing money.

Listening to the easy-going banter in that *piazza* made me realize I wanted to work for old people. I had been in Tuscany for a week and had managed to find work on one farm, but the fit didn't feel right. Inspired by the people of Montefollonico, I decided it was time to step out in faith, to find farmers whose roots ran deep.

The decision of a young man from London to shorten his stay from two weeks to less than twenty-four hours and return to his first farm, confirmed my suspicion that it was time to look elsewhere. While we were picking olives the day after my Montefollonico epiphany, he told me he had felt just like family at his previous farm. Emboldened by the young lad's tales—and his departure—I decided to thank my hosts and tell them I'd be moving on, despite feeling slightly impetuous for leaving with no certainty of finding another farm.

The sky was dark when I woke up the next morning. But by the time I finished packing my trailer, rosy fingers of light were gracing the eastern horizon. As I pushed my bike from the caravan that had been my chilly home, I felt adventurous but slightly foolish, like a VFR pilot flying above a cloud cover with no certainty of finding a place to land before the tanks run dry. But the picture my English friend painted of his days as a Tuscan olive picker contrasted greatly with mine, and gave me the courage to seek my own picture-postcard-perfect farm complete with seven-course meals, friendly animated conversation, and free-flowing wine in a vine-covered arbor.

I planned to bicycle to Pienza, find an Internet point, compile a list of farms, and keep calling until I found one needing a worker straight away—as my young English friend was fond of saying. Biking the steep hill to Pienza was the easiest thing I did all that day. But it didn't feel like it at the time as I struggled up the winding road at less than five miles an hour. Despite the cool air of the morning, I peeled off three layers on the climb to the level streets enclosed behind the city walls.

I rode to the center of town, parked my bike, put the layers back on, then pulled out my laptop to search for an Internet connection. But none worked. The library was not yet open, neither was the tourist office, so I went in search of an Internet café and discovered a Hollywood-type crew

These two fine-looking actors struck up an engaging pose when I asked if I might take their photo. The working title was I Prefer Heaven, but I've not yet found a movie released by that name. The streets of Pienza were perfect for the Renaissance film. Were it not for the crew it would have been easy to imagine that I had done some time traveling that morning. I especially enjoyed watching the antics of the street urchins. I'd love to see how the scene played out on the big screen—and whether the two actors who posed for me had a speaking part.

from Rome filming a few scenes of the movie *I Prefer Heaven*. The setting was Renaissance Tuscany. The costumes were extremely believable. The cobblestone streets, the draft animals, the street urchins, and the market vendors made me feel like I had traveled back five hundred years by biking five kilometers.

When the doors of the café opened, I and a significant number of those who had been watching the transformation of Pienza surged inside—some to eat, some to surf. I paid five euros and began searching for a farm. Looking though the descriptions took most of what was left of the morning. I came up with six farms that appeared to be owned by older farmers. A good portion of the afternoon was gone by the time I called the last farm on my list. I was beginning to fear that I would have to give up on the idea of working for older Tuscans. But that sixth call connected me to Aurora and Pietro. That was the good part. The bad part, or so I thought at the time, was that Pietro said I couldn't make it to their place by dark.

My attention shifted to finding a place to sleep for the night. Pienza was my first choice, but the town was booked solid with cast and crew from the movie company. Decision-making is a very important part of travel, especially when you are living on the edge—traveling by bike, and trying at the same time to spend very little money. With much uncertainty about where I would spend the night, I strapped my computer inside my backpack, topped off my water bottles, and coasted out of town. Leaving a Tuscan hilltop town was always a thrill. Invariably it meant a high-speed descent, but Pienza gave me an extra shot of adrenalin. Just before the road hit the bottom of the valley, while I was coasting around a curve at sixty-some kilometers an hour, the dreaded *throp, throp, throp* of a blowout jerked me out of the ecstasy of my teary-eyed descent.

Every fiber of my body snapped to attention. I quickly prayed that I could slow the bike without locking the wheels, going down, and smashing my face into the rocks and boulders lining the road. Or worse—and more likely since I was on an inside curve—sliding across the asphalt into the path of the huge truck coming at me.

Dear Lord, help me ...

Chapter Three

There are only two ways to live your life.
One is as though nothing is a miracle.
The other is as though everything is a miracle.
ALBERT EINSTEIN

The Mysteries of Montefollonico

Thank God, it's the rear tire. No place to pull off. Too fast anyway. The image of sliding into the front wheels of the truck wouldn't let go of me. *Still going too fast, but speed is better than locking the brakes.* The front of the truck flashed by and my eyes locked on the wheels of the trailer. The right wheels were off the pavement. The left wheels were almost at the edge. *Don't go down.* The image of sliding into the rear wheels froze in my mind—just as the wheels flashed past me. *Thank you, Lord.*

The driver must have recognized I was in trouble and moved over as far to the right as he could. The truck's vortex swirled up a huge cloud of thick, yellow dust. No longer paralyzed with the fear of slamming into the truck, I squeezed harder on the brakes, the bike slowed, and I pulled off the highway onto a gravel shoulder. My front wheel slid, jackknifing the bike—I had to throw my foot out to avoid sprawling on the ground. I looked down at the still-whistling tire that almost put me under the truck just as the dust cloud rolled over me. A car whizzed by within feet of me, rocking me with a blast of air. I doubt the driver would have seen me through the cloud even if he'd been looking—he was probably looking in his mirrors to see what would happen to the truck. I'm sure he thought the driver fell asleep, ran off the road, and almost killed himself.

Life is like that. We're certain of our view of reality, unaware of all that we haven't seen, that we don't understand. The driver of that car will never know how close he came to a tragedy that would have haunted him the rest of his life.

The person who almost got killed was me, not the truck driver. Had the driver of the car shot into that dust cloud five seconds earlier, he would have discovered, to his horror, a man on a bicycle materializing out of that yellow dust. Half a second later I would have bounced like a rag doll off the hood and windshield of his car. That two-second clip, running in slow motion, would have played out in his mind forever, always accompanied by a gut-tightening, eye-closing thud as his car plowed into my body.

This was my first flat with the Bike Friday and I discovered that getting a tire off a twenty-inch rim is not easy. One of my tire tools snapped as I tried to force the too small, too stiff tire off the rim. I fought with that tire for forty-five minutes, and nothing worked. All my life I've been changing bike tires and had never had this much trouble. Of course I'd never changed a tire this small before.

I quit trying for a while, took a drink, wiped the sweat off my forehead, and considered my options. None looked good if that tire didn't come off the rim. Walking back to Pienza pushing my bike on the highway was out of the question. I had to get that tire fixed. I took a deep breath, remembered my close call, and thanked God that I didn't have bigger problems. The pause in my efforts seemed to give me renewed resolve—or maybe just a better technique—and within five minutes the tire finally slipped off the wheel. I pulled the tube out, slapped a patch on it, and within fifteen minutes the wheel was back on the bike, the trailer was hooked up, and I was ready to roll. I thanked God again and concluded by asking Him to nudge me along the right path toward a place to stay for the night.

I had chosen this route, not because it was the shortest, but because I was familiar with quite a few miles of it. I had ridden it on Sunday going the opposite direction as I swung through Montefollonico to check out a farm I had first learned about before coming to Italy. I knew the owner was out of town, but I had wanted to bike past her farm. You can tell a lot just by looking at a farm. I might decide I didn't want to work there—or maybe I'd decide to jump through hoops for the chance.

For some reason the GPS was able to get me close, but not able to take me to the farm. While I was checking my map, hoping that I might find it the old fashioned way, a woman on her evening walk happened by, and offered to help. She not only knew where the farm was, but confirmed that the owner was indeed out of town. She offered to lead me to the lane that would put me on a path to her neighbor's farm so that I could program the location into my GPS.

The farm had looked promising, so going through Montefollonico on the chance that the farm owner had returned from vacation seemed worth a few extra miles. But when the tire blew, I considered bypassing it. The flat had cost me a full hour of daylight. The best I could hope for was to get to Montefollonico about sunset, but my alternatives, now that I was behind schedule, didn't look good either, so I stuck with my decision. As the road snaked higher and my moving average dropped lower, getting there before dark began to look ever more doubtful.

The climb to the old town was slow and painful. I looked down into the valley, second-guessing myself, wondering whether I should have stayed low and traveled faster and farther. As I struggled up the slope I prayed that God would give me a sign that I would find a place to sleep. At that very second church bells began to peal in Montefollonico. I knew it might only be a *coincidence*, but I smiled and thanked God nevertheless. I felt better thinking that the pealing of those bells at that very moment was a sign of God's grace. The alternative—the view that I held until I almost died in a horrific car crash thirty years ago—was not nearly so appealing. Until that day I had held the materialistic view that God plays no part in our lives—that life is but a string of coincidences.

Life is enough of a mystery to take a bit of comfort when such things happen, especially when it's almost dark and you have no idea where you're going to spend the night. Fifteen minutes later another mystery strolled my way. I was close enough to the walls of Montefollonico, with just enough light in the sky to see that people were gathering on the same street where only two days earlier I had seen the two old men walking arm in arm.

As I got closer I realized the gathering was a farmers market. When I was close enough to see people as individuals, my eyes landed on a woman who was walking toward the market from a side street. We each got to the same stall, a vegetable stand, at exactly the same moment. And we each recognized the other at exactly the same moment. I knew only one person in all of Montefollonico, yet two days later she—the woman who had been kind enough to lead me to the farm that my GPS couldn't find—arrived at the farmers market at precisely the same time I did.

Another coincidence perhaps, but I said *Thank you, Lord* nevertheless. I didn't yet know how thankful I was about to become. We talked for a while. She told me of the popularity of the market, how much it had grown in recent years. I thanked her again for her thoughtfulness. I asked her if her friend, the owner of the farm, had returned. She hadn't seen her, but offered to call her. She suggested that I follow her to the *taverna*. I suggested that she finish her shopping first.

She began filling her bags with vegetables. While waiting, I watched the other shoppers. The setting, against the background of the towering city wall, looked ancient and impressive, but in its essence, it looked just like farmers markets back home—producer and customer coming together to feed local people. And just like back home, people were talking as much as they were buying. Small markets build communities in Tuscany, in Colorado, in Wisconsin, wherever people gather to do it the old fashioned way.

My new friend, Mrs. M (I could neither pronounce her name nor hazard a guess as to how to spell it), returned with two bags full of vegetables and led me to the tavern. She went inside to call and left me outside with my bike—defenseless against an onslaught of *italiano*.

"Why is your bike so funny-looking?" I heard someone behind me ask. I turned and saw two men studying my bike. The taller of the two looked at me and asked, "Why are the wheels so small?"

Piccolo? I didn't have any problem understanding the question, but the answer was going to test my Italian. "This is my airplane *bicicletta*—it folds up and fits in this suitcase—and I flew to Italy with it." That's what I tried to tell my inquisitive friends, but in *italiano*, it wasn't quite so straightforward. I had to use gestures for *fits* and *folds*. I could see they hadn't understood me, or believed me, so I pantomimed removing the saddle and handlebars, folding the bike, and stuffing it all into the trailer.

"*Si, valigia,*" the shorter one said.

The taller and bolder of the two asked, "Are you spending the night in Montefollonico?"

Albergo I remembered, so I had no problem asking if the town had a hotel. They told me that rooms were available but that they were extremely expensive—that I wouldn't want one. I asked how much and gulped at the answer. I wasn't sure how they knew that I didn't want to pay almost two hundred dollars a night for a place to sleep, but they had correctly discerned that I was traveling *a prezzo stracciato*—on the cheap.

The next leap in the conversation I understood even less clearly. I had been thinking, reminded by the pealing bells, that if I found no other place to sleep, maybe I could sleep in a church. I had done that about fifty years ago when I took my first cross-country bike trip, and was exposed to grace, but did not yet know enough about it to recognize it, or even know it had a name.

Somehow, without me mentioning a church, these two new friends started asking passersby if they had seen the local *padre*. A young boy happened by who knew exactly where the priest was and when he would be returning. The boy, Volario, the men informed me, lived next to the church, and worked a few hours each week for the parish.

Mrs. M came out of the pub and joined us. She was disappointed to tell me that she had been unable to contact her friend. When she heard that these men were looking for the priest, her demeanor picked up. She asked Volario a couple of things I didn't understand, and then disappeared inside the pub again.

I had been in town for about an hour, and for all but a very few of those minutes, these Tuscan strangers had been working on finding a stranger among them a place to sleep for the night. The two men asked where I planned to eat. I shrugged. They told me that near the church I would find a grocery store, but that I really should consider eating at _____, and they said something I didn't understand. Seeing my confused look, they both gestured, leaving little doubt that I was to cross the street to eat. I saw only a door, no signs of a *trattoria*, but my curious friend kissed his fingers to tell me all I needed to know—that nowhere would I find better food.

My two friends kept talking, telling me more than I could take in. My mind kept returning to the thought of the time and energy these people were investing in me. And now Mrs. M was offering to walk with me to the church. I told her that I could find it, but she insisted. The time she was investing made me feel a part of the town—not at all like a tourist, more like I was visiting a friend's hometown. I said goodbye to the two men and walked with Mrs. M through the old gate and into the heart of the town. Not one moving car did we encounter on the narrow cobblestone streets as we walked the four or five blocks to the church. We saw only three cars, and they were parked tight against the buildings. Mrs. M waved to the clerks as we walked past the grocery store. They waved back and sang out, "*Buonasera.*"

A few meters past the grocery store, the first car I had seen in motion since we entered the walled part of the village pulled past us and stopped. A young boy hopped out. He ran ahead and threw open two small doors. When he turned toward the car I recognized him—it was Volario. The driver pulled the car into an opening that looked much too small to hold a car, but somehow it fit, and the man was still able, miraculously it seemed, to get out of the car. He closed the cupboard-like doors, securing the car inside, and walked over to join us. Volario introduced his father and the church cat, which by now had also joined us. We talked for a few moments about the friendliness of Montefollonico, then Volario and his dad excused themselves and went into their home.

Mrs. M pointed to the church steps where the cat had been sleeping and asked me to wait there. She looked at her watch and then apologized for being unable to wait to introduce me to the priest. I thanked her for her hospitality. She shrugged and raised her eyebrows. She was telling me with that wonderful Italian gesture that she was happy to have been able to serve. And with a *"Ciao,"* she turned and headed back toward the city gate, back down the hill to her home, carrying her two bags of vegetables.

I thanked God again for His grace and sat down to pet the cat. The view from the church steps looked like it deserved a picnic, so I walked to the store for some vegetables, a few slices of meat, cheese, and bread. But I found a lot more that looked tasty. As I looked around the store, I eavesdropped on the conversations between customers and clerks. Grocery stores reveal the pulse of the town, and this little community seemed to be in good health, but it did have a taste for *la dolce*. I took note of the desserts the locals were buying and bought a few in celebration of my good fortune—the *coincidences* that led me to this town, this church, this grocery store. I paid for the food, gathered the bags, and walked back to the church. The cat greeted me even more warmly than before. I now had milk.

I pulled a small jar of honey from my backpack. It added weight, but it was part of my emergency kit, as important as Band-Aids, disinfectant, and gauze. I spread honey on the bread, added some peanut butter and jam, then dined while waiting for the priest. Across the street from the church, I noticed flowers flowing from a vase on either side of a doorway. The bricks of the wall looked like they had been in place for centuries, but the door, while not appearing at all modern, nevertheless looked as if it was cleaned and polished daily. The town, and this street, glowed with pride and stewardship.

I looked up and down the street. Nothing was uniform. But the personality of the inhabitants was shining through. None of the homes had yards, or if they did they were very small, and behind walls, in courtyards. The window coverings, the door knockers, and the hinges all spoke of loving attention to detail. The flowers, which each home lovingly displayed, spoke of the villagers' connection to the land.

Lost in thought, I didn't hear or see the priest walk up. "I have just the place for you, but I must warn you I do not have a bed in the class room." I wondered how he had so quickly determined that I was a person who meant to do neither him nor his church any harm. He directed me to the side of the church, which happened to be where I had posed my bike two days earlier to frame a shot of the surrounding countryside.

While I maneuvered my bike and trailer up the side steps, the gentle priest entered the church though the huge main doors. Just as I reached the side doors, the priest pushed them open from the inside. Although not as impressive as the main doors, they were beautifully crafted. He held them open and gestured that I should wheel my bike and trailer inside.

He noticed my grocery bag and asked what I had to eat. I showed him the food I had bought at the store, as well as the food I was carrying. He looked it over, then solemnly pronounced, "*Non frutta,*" which happened to be about the only thing I didn't have. And with that he left the room, giving me no indication where he was going. I never found out whether he had a stash in a nearby room or whether he had run to the *alimentari* next door, but three or four minutes later he came back with two huge pears.

We were in a classroom, what I would call a Sunday School room. But it looked like no other classroom I had ever seen before. The room was dominated by a huge fireplace. Art from children of all ages hung on the walls. The priest spoke very little English, but speaking slowly in

Italian he told me the history of the town and its many festivals, and the history of the church. I tried to imagine the stories these walls held.

I wanted to tell him how touched I was by his hospitality, but my Italian wasn't up to it. He knew I was grateful, but I couldn't express how deeply I saw his kindness as a manifestation of God's grace. I tried to express the mystery of it all in the thank you note I left for him the following morning, but I'm not sure my written Italian was any more capable of the task. Telling a priest that you feel he has been an instrument of God's grace shouldn't be that hard, but then again, God's profound mysteries don't translate easily to words, no matter who you're sharing them with.

The grace of the hospitality that I was shown in Montefollonico can, of course, be explained away as nothing but coincidence. But the word *coincidence* is without meaning, useful only for pointing out the weirdness of life. We use the word to express bafflement when things happen simultaneously or in sequence that are hard to account for in a world of time and chance. But because I had asked God for a bit of encouragement, I took the events of the evening to mean something profoundly different from mere happenstance. A string of *buona fortuna* had just come my way, and a bit of thanking seemed in order, so I expressed it to the priest and to God.

What happened to me in Montefollonico would not convince a skeptic of God's grace, but on the ride into town I had been thinking that I might have to throw my sleeping bag under a bridge so *grace* seemed more appropriate than any other word I knew. I didn't want to call it *coincidence* or cite the numerical probability of the one person I knew in town showing up at the market at the very same instant I did. I simply wanted to say *Thank you Lord*. The materialist I was thirty years ago would have balked at the suggestion that God had anything to do with my good fortune, but that guy didn't survive the crash on that snow-covered road.

As I biked away from the church and into the warmth of the morning sun, I was feeling euphoric. The road carrying me from Montefollonico was the same road where I had seen the two old men walking arm in arm, and where Mrs. M had strangely appeared. I followed the road until it turned and led me back to where I had seen the two boys kicking the soccer ball back and forth across the road. Then I followed it out of town and into the woods, where two days before I had received the epiphany of living well and thankfully into old age. God's grace at that moment seemed as real to me—if not more so—than the bike I was riding and the GPS that indicated an arrival on Sodo Street in Camucia at "0934."

I turned my attention from my mystical journey to my physical journey. For the first hour or so, the GPS's ETA (estimated time of arrival) slowly decreased. But each time I stopped for a photo of the fog burning away to reveal a farmhouse, or a village on a hill, the ETA would climb back up. On a long, steady climb I glanced in my rearview mirror and saw a bicycle far down the road gaining on me. I held him off until the end of the climb, then slowed down to catch my breath. I planned to talk with him on the descent. He caught and drafted me, but never pulled alongside. I called out, "*Buongiorno*" over my shoulder, hoping that a "Good day" sent his way would encourage him to ride next to me. He replied with a phrase that I couldn't figure out. But the clipped cadence of his response revealed that he too was hurting.

While waiting for him to recover in my slipstream and pull up next to me, I scrolled through the readouts on my GPS and discovered that in total I had cut almost ten minutes off my ETA—plenty of time to slow my pace and talk to the man. I turned around to look back, but he was no longer there. I looked farther back. He was off to the side of the road hoisting his beautiful Colnago onto the top of his car, his morning ride completed. I regretted racing him to the top. I wished instead that I would have let him catch me when I first saw him and then picked up my pace to talk with him. But instead I was watching my ETA. I vowed to not let that happen again. This is one of the dangers of technology. We lose sight of the important things and begin looking at the trivial. All I learned from focusing on the GPS was that I had a few more minutes of time. I wished I would have used them talking to a fellow lover of fast bicycles.

A few kilometers down the road I heard his car shifting down, as he slowed to make sure that it was safe to pass. He then zipped around me, his engine fully revved, his gorgeous Italian racing bike gleaming in the sunlight atop his sleek red Audi. We exchanged hearty waves, but that was it. I was disgusted. *If I'm going to learn the why of Italy, I'm going to have to take my eyes off that blasted GPS.* I stopped, shut the thing off, and pulled out a paper map. Who knows what I might have learned from that man?

I might have been able to ask him if my observation about Tuscan drivers was accurate. He seemed to confirm, with the way that he quickly passed me, that Tuscans, at least when they are behind the wheel of an automobile, like speed. But—and this is an important distinction—they don't seem to be in a hurry.

If it was safe to pass, drivers would zip by me in their small cars. But if the curves were too tight on the road ahead, or the cypresses lining the road were too close together to see clearly whether a car was coming, drivers would gear down and follow at my speed—a speed that on Tuscan hills, pulling the load I was pulling, was at times very slow.

The hilltop town of Valiano and the mountain on which it is perched had been the focus of my attention for ten or fifteen kilometers. I had been checking the map every few minutes, trying to figure out a way around what appeared to be an excruciatingly long and steep climb. But nothing looked promising. Getting from here to there didn't seem possible without going through Valiano. Ahead of me, I saw a couple of policemen at the intersection of a road that seemed to be my last hope. I pulled off the road, grabbed my map, and asked in my best fractured Italian, "Any way to avoid climb?" while pointing at the map. "No, no. You must go over. You must go through Valiano," one of the cops quickly responded in Italian, then English, as he drew an ever-widening and tortuously crooked circle on my map with his finger. And then we talked about bikes, travel, and the ways of Italian drivers for as long as it would have taken me to bypass Valiano. In Tuscany, it can be argued that the best use of time is for talking and sharing of lives, not for bypassing towns like Valiano.

When at last we finished talking, it was up and over. Nearing the top I began to hear the deep vibrations of a truck approaching. I couldn't see it in my mirrors, but I could tell by the heavy roar coming from the switchbacks below that the truck was huge. I looked for a place to pull off, but the road had not a hint of a shoulder. I had no choice but to keep pedaling and hope I could reach a straight stretch of road before the truck caught up to me.

At nine kilometers an hour though, you don't cover much ground. Around every corner lay another corner. I was stuck in a section of turns and switchbacks. I bumped my cadence up as high as I could push it in my lowest gear. Sweat was pouring down my face, but still the driver caught up with me right at the beginning of a big, sweeping curve. With not a hint of impatience in his driving or his demeanor, he deftly shifted the transmission into his "granny gear" and lumbered up the hill behind me. We must have been quite a sight to oncoming drivers. An old man on a weird-looking bike pulling a suitcase on wheels, followed by a huge eighteen-wheeler. Both inching up the hill. Both in granny gears.

My mind was fully focused on how much I was delaying the driver. I must have glanced at him in my mirrors fifteen times as we met car after car with never a large enough break for him to be able to pass. Not once did he show a hint of annoyance. After what seemed like forever at my maximum heart rate, we had a clear view of the road ahead. I took one last look in my mirror. He still seemed unconcerned. As he pulled alongside I gave a weakened wave of appreciation for his patience. He waved back with a slight toot of his horn. And that was that—or so I thought.

I eventually got to the top—to a statue in the town park honoring the bravery of Signor Valiano, where I paused for a moment to recover. I put my windbreaker on, took a swig of water, and coasted out of town. On the downhill side of Valiano, the farm fields were larger and the road somewhat straighter. In a distant field, I saw a man filling a grain drill. By the time I got to him, he was pulling a *panino* out of his insulated cooler as he made himself comfortable sitting on the grain box above the press wheels. The sight of him relaxing reminded me that I also had a sandwich in my pack, so I pulled off the road, hoping to be able to strike up a conversation. I was curious about what he was planting. When I tried to go beyond asking the size of his farm and his choice of crops, and on to what changes he had seen in the markets for his products since Italy joined the Common Market, I discovered that my Italian wasn't up to the nuances of agricultural policy.

His English was nonexistent so we turned to exchanging pleasantries about family and travels. As he was closing his cooler, I was startled by a loud blast of a truck's horn. I turned to the road, expecting to see a friend of the farmer driving by. I was shocked to see the truck that had inched up the hill behind me. The driver was leaning out of the cab, smiling and waving, his arm extended high over the cab.

"Friend of yours?" the farmer asked.

"I guess, you might say. We lumbered up the hill together into Valiano this morning," I said, or something as close to it as I could get in my tortured Italian. I was reminded again of E. M. Forster. These indeed are marvelous people, even more marvelous than this beautiful field in which I was enjoying lunch in the sun, waving to a man who, instead of giving me the finger for slowing him down, was waving to me like I was an old friend.

These tradition-bound Tuscans, with deep roots of hospitality, do indeed have a few things they can teach me. The truck driver could have allowed himself to be annoyed by my presence on *his* road when he was making deliveries, but instead, just by his attitude, he made a friend and a statement. A wave and the blast of an air horn colored my impression of all of Tuscany and the Tuscan people—indeed, all of Italy. The evidence was mounting that Italians are a friendly bunch of people, but was I really any closer to solving the mystery? Why are these people the way they are? What is the common thread?

I would have liked to have been able to share with my farmer friend some of what I was feeling—how impressed I was with the character of his countrymen. He probably would have thought I was making too much of one truck driver's wave on one morning, so I said nothing but *"Grazie"* and *"Ciao"* as I thanked him for sharing a bit of his morning with me. If I had been fluent in Italian, I would have tried to make the case that it wasn't just one wave on one morning from one truck driver. A whole town, or at least everyone with whom I had come in contact in Montefollonico, had worked together to find me a place to sleep the night before, and who knows how many people, the previous afternoon, had walked past my backpack in the park where I had absentmindedly left it unattended while I searched the list of WWOOFing farms. No, this was more than coincidence, more than random acts of kindness, but exactly *why* such things happen in Italy, I did not know. To ascribe it to tradition is about the same as labeling as *instinct* attributes of animal behavior about which little is understood. The question of why remains unanswered. How can salmon return to the waters where they were spawned? How do honeybees communicate to other worker bees the location of nectar? Why are the traditions of Italy what they are?

On my first evening in Tuscany, I learned that my host did not hold tradition in high esteem. I discovered also that my host was not born a farmer. I asked him who became his mentor, his teacher of farming wisdom. I used a variety of words, both Italian and English, to get across what I was asking, but he couldn't comprehend what I was getting at. I had been hoping that he would launch into a heart-warming story of an elderly neighbor who took him under his wing and began passing on a lifetime of accumulated wisdom and stewardship that he had picked up from his father's lifetime of accumulated wisdom and stewardship, that he had picked up from *his* father *ad infinitum*.

Eventually my host understood what I was asking. With a touch of exasperation, tinged with pride, he told me a very different story. Nobody taught him how to farm. He had taught himself. He seemed disdainful of anything his neighbors might know about the land and farming. It was this attitude that convinced me to set out in search of a farm like Aurora's, where neighbors might take pity on a widow who was thankful to be learning from others. And that is what I found at Aurora's farm, plus a lot of what I had not even known I was seeking.

My first farm wasn't a good fit, but the location was beautiful. It was on a hilltop, and because of a few moist days, I and another wwoofer, a man from Switzerland, who also happened to be traveling about Tuscany by bike, found time to explore the region. I fell in love with the hilltop setting of Pienza surrounded by wide open vistas of wheat fields, vineyards, and olive groves. The stories told by a young English lad of free-flowing wine, seven-course meals and Italian hospitality at his previous farm convinced me it was time to find a farm with a greater sense of tradition. This beautiful scene greeted me the morning I climbed into Pienza to find an Internet connection to begin my nervous search for a new farm.

This is the house I was looking at while waiting for the priest to arrive. I was struck by the pride of ownership—the flowers and the beautifully finished doors. I wanted to know these people—I imagined they were as warm and inviting as the front of their house. The whole town exuded a warmth that was personified by the priest. He immediately invited me to wheel my bike and trailer into the church through a side door that led to a Sunday School room. And that's where he invited me to throw down my sleeping bag and spend the night. He also made sure I had plenty to eat.

The wheat farmer in me liked the wide open vistas on the downhill side of Valiano. I had not expected such large fields in Tuscany. I stopped to eat my sandwich with a farmer who was taking a break after filling his grain drill with seed. This photo was taken on October 27, and were I still farming I would have been doing the same thing a few weeks earlier in Nebraska. I enjoyed talking with the farmer, but our conversation exposed the limits of my italiano—I couldn't find the words to discuss farming except in the most basic way. He knew absolutely no English. That was not the situation at Aurora's. Pietro had lived in Australia, and Aurora had a poet's command of the English language. She was also a very good teacher of italiano.

The basket Aurora presented me was a beautiful work of craftsmanship that looked even better the more olives I plopped into it. From the moment I first saw her farm I knew I was going to like picking olives in her valley. But when she handed me a brand new basket and told me she didn't much like knocking the olives off the trees into nets I knew I had found a kindred spirit. I also liked that I could look out toward the walls of Cortona and see other farmers picking olives on the hillside. I immediately felt part of a community.

Chapter Four

The greatest fine art of the future
will be the making of a comfortable living
on a small piece of land.
ABRAHAM LINCOLN

Whose Farm Is It?

Each day on Aurora's farm was unique. On my second day a woman hopped out of Pietro's car and immediately joined Aurora and me in the olive grove. She was wearing a heavy woolen military jacket, black boots, and her dark blonde hair in long, thick braids. Aurora introduced her by telling me that two years ago Annamarja had come to help for two weeks and ended up staying a whole year. "Maybe you too will stay for a year, James," Annamarja said.

"I don't think so," Aurora said. "Pietro, I fear, will drive you both away."

"Pietro, I fear," Annamarja countered, "will drive you away as well, Aurora."

Annamarja was also a *wwoofer*, and like many people who volunteer to help farmers, she dreamed of someday having her own farm. Anna Maria (American pronunciation and spelling) was in her late forties, maybe early fifties, strong in both body and spirit. "Remember last year, how cold and wet it was," Annamarja said.

"You're right, Annamarja. We should pick the good olives in case it's too wet again this year." We were among poor trees with small olives. Our baskets were not filling very quickly. And so we left the weak trees for the end of the harvest and climbed to a terrace with big, plump olives, and that is where we picked until the sun drifted below the horizon, telling stories and getting to know each other.

Our meal that evening took on an added level of intensity. Pietro and Annamarja fought with each other like a married couple with deep-seated, unresolved hostilities who had been battling with each other for years. Pietro called her "Tito." She called him, in her deep, guttural voice, "Da Big Boss." The big shocker to me was to learn at the end of the evening that when Pietro had picked Annamarja up at the train station earlier that afternoon, they were meeting for the first time. Their dinner battle was but one more example of the willingness of Italians to express themselves forcefully with loved ones and acquaintances, even strangers.

I didn't know whether Annamarja and Pietro had squabbled during the drive from the train station to the farm. I knew only that Pietro hadn't joined us in the olive grove. Their hostile engagement at dinner may have been a repeat performance, but thanks to Pietro's wit, the evening was not uncomfortable; it was entertaining, even educational, as they pressed their points about Fascism and Communism and the challenges facing Italy and the European Union.

My third morning at Aurora's cloistered sanctuary began calmly, in stark contrast to the previous night's flareup. Pietro had taken Joshua to school, giving us an hour or so of peaceful picking. A little after ten I noticed Pietro climbing toward us with a basket in his hand. When he was a couple of terraces below us, he shouted, "Have you finished picking all the trees in the row you're working on?"

Thinking that Pietro would be proud of his mother's foresight, I yelled down to him that we had skipped over the trees with small olives. Too late I realized that if either Aurora or Annamarja had been within a boot's reach of my shins, they would have kicked them.

"Go back and pick them," Pietro ordered. "I want a system—I want to know that every tree has been picked as we work our way up the hill."

I'm not sure why Aurora wouldn't have heard Pietro, but if she did, she said nothing. Annamarja also said nothing as she climbed down from her ladder. She was going, or so I thought, to pick the passed-over olives. I quit picking plump olives and walked back to the trees we had skipped. The contrast with the olives in my basket was stunning. "It will take the rest of the morning to fill a basket, and all day to fill a *cassetta*," I grumbled, but Pietro was not close enough to hear me. He was two terraces above, filling his basket with fat, juicy olives.

Quite a few minutes of picking in silence passed before I realized that Annamarja had not joined me, but had walked up three, possibly four terraces higher on the hill and was picking olives about as far away from Pietro as she could get. She was as far to my right as she could go and still be on Aurora's farm, and Pietro was just as far to my left. I doubted they could see each other. I could barely see either of them. Aurora I could not see at all. Each of us was picking in a separate tree. The joyous mood of the day had moved to a nearby olive grove. I couldn't see Aurora's neighbors, but I could hear their light-hearted banter. I wished I could have understood them better so I could get my mind off the funk that had descended on our olive grove.

All day long we picked that way, each in our own closed-off world. Not until Tuscany's big, yellow sun was about to turn orange, were we once again picking near each other. Pietro had gone to pick up Joshua from school to take him to his tennis lesson. Aurora and Annamarja were speaking Italian. They seemed to be talking about a light-weight structure covered with animal skins or canvas—what I knew to be a yurt. I joined the conversation and told them about spending part of a Sawtooth Mountain winter in one while making *Mountain Time*, a backcountry ski film. Annamarja surprised me by telling me she intended to spend a big part of a Tuscan winter in one. Aurora and Annamarja were returning to a conversation from the previous year, discussing the olive grove I had noticed the day I arrived—the one that had not been pruned for decades. Aurora was offering to let Annamarja live on the land if she would bring the neglected trees back to life. The yurt would be her home until she could build something more permanent. I now understood why talk of yurts came up only after Pietro had left for the day.

I had noted in my journal that even though Annamarja had stayed a year the first time, I didn't think she would last a week this time. The first time she was here, Pietro had been in Australia. This time he was here telling Annamarja and Aurora that almost everything they did was wrong. Their disagreements didn't end with politics, but extended to cooking, farming, and stewardship. They disagreed, as far as I could see, about everything.

As we made our way down the hill in the fading light, carrying our *cassetti* heavy with olives, I was thinking of dinner, and not just because I was hungry or because of my love for Tuscan meals. No, on this night the attraction would be more than food. The stage had been set for some interesting theatrics, and although it might get embarrassing, I was looking forward to seeing this story play out.

As much as I liked Pietro, his energy, his smile, and his wit, my sentiments often were not with him. He was too harsh on people, his mom of course and relative strangers as well. And as Annamarja repeatedly pointed out, Pietro did not think like a farmer. He wanted to impose his system, his need for a businesslike order, onto the very natural process of growing olives.

Aurora had found over the years—or she had picked up the wisdom from neighbors—that it was good to skip trees that for whatever reason weren't producing well in a given year. Aurora's rationale made a lot of sense to the farmer in me. But it assaulted Pietro's sense of efficiency and order. Who could say that one was definitely wrong and the other definitely right? But that's the wondrous thing about farming. I'm forever learning that working with nature is sufficiently complex that it is impossible to ever say you have it figured out. Farming is a natural act of love based on the rhythms of the year. Each day a farmer learns more about his land, his trees, the crops, the weather, the averages. Farming requires a humility that seemed absent in Pietro. He didn't have the manner of someone willing to let nature teach him how to farm. Farmers need to be humble generalists in talent, temperament, and crops, not proud specialists. Otherwise the land suffers.

I expected conflict at dinner that night, but Pietro surprised me once again. Whether he had previous plans or just chose not to eat with us, I never found out. Without him there, the conversation turned again to Aurora's childhood, and the war briefly, but she focused on her years in boarding school. The memory of those traumatic eight years clouded her countenance as we talked. She got smaller. Her eyes dimmed. She told me she felt abandoned by her father, whom she loved, and betrayed by her mother, whom she hated. Her mother she saw as the consummate hypocrite, using the Catholic Church when it served her purposes, thumbing her nose at the Church when it didn't.

She hated her loss of freedom at boarding school. She vowed she would let her child have all the freedom he wanted. She denied Pietro nothing. Her husband warned her many times over the years she was going to ruin Pietro—giving him so much freedom.

"Oh, *Babbo*! I fear now that he may have been right. What have I done? I desperately wanted freedom when I was a child, so I gave it to my son. Maybe too much."

The next morning the olive grove was peaceful again. Pietro had taken Joshua, who was suffering from a sore throat, to see the doctor. The sky was deep blue, the air clear and cool, the sun warm. I was picking, and had been for much of the morning, in the same very old, heavily laden tree. Aurora was picking nearby in an equally productive tree. Annamarja had already filled one *cassetta* and had gone up the hill to smoke and to see if she could find mushrooms, some *porcini funghi per il nostro pranzo*.

I had been thinking about what Aurora had said the night before about her childhood, her deep desire for freedom, and how she had raised Pietro. I too wondered if there was a connection—if she had given Pietro too much freedom, and whether all that freedom was now imprisoning both of them.

At that moment Pietro drove into the yard. As he got out of the car he saw me high above him on the terrace.

"*Come va*, James?" he yelled out.

"*Va bene.* It's going very well, Pietro. This old tree is full of big fat olives—by far the best yet."

"Oh yes, James, I know that tree. I have worked hard to keep my mother away from it. So, it's no wonder the olives are big. My job here is to keep her black magic away from the good trees. As you can see, with that tree, I've been very successful. You must remember, James, she has killed two husbands—my father and another. She kills everything she touches."

It was vintage Pietro, but far from the truth. This tree was producing well because Aurora had taken good care of it. Olive trees thrive with judicious pruning and a bit of manure. From what I could see as we worked our way around the olive grove, both Annamarja and Aurora had learned well the art of pruning olive trees. And as for the fate of Aurora's husbands, I doubted that was true either, literally or figuratively.

But Pietro's comment underscored what Aurora had said about him: "He's a good boy. He just has a bad habit of saying bad things about his mother." To which I might add, since I was still thinking about it minutes later, very surprising things as well. I shouldn't have laughed when he said it, and Pietro shouldn't be called a boy. He was after all, I had learned the night before, forty years old. But the comment caught Aurora by surprise and made her laugh too—and if she wanted to call Pietro her boy, I realized as well that my wife and I occasionally still speak of our oldest child as our boy even though he is in his middle thirties. We don't easily let go of our children, especially when we are mulling over whether we have done a good job of raising them.

Making full use of a comedian's sense of timing, Pietro had turned and disappeared into the house. Aurora began talking of her hopes for the farm, not just for the next generation, but for future generations as well—for Joshua's and beyond. "I admire how connected Tuscan farmers feel to the land, how strongly they value tradition. I don't think Pietro has that regard at all. He is, I am afraid, stupid. He won't listen to anyone but himself," Aurora concluded.

I grabbed one handle of a *cassetta*. Aurora grabbed the other. As we Mutt-and-Jeff-ed it to the storage shed, I tried to put a happy face on the situation. But I was beginning to worry about Aurora. Hearing Aurora speak of her son as stupid surprised me. She had not before said anything harsh about Pietro.

When we stepped into the house for lunch, I was surprised that it was waiting for us. Pietro was hard to put in a box. He had prepared pasta and Annamarja had fried up some wild mushrooms—mushrooms that Pietro refused to eat.

"I know about poison mushrooms, James. You eat first. If they do not kill you, I will eat."

I returned Pietro's smile and began eating them. Pietro paused to watch me. The mushrooms were delicious. I complimented Annamarja, and asked if there were more. She filled the serving dish. I offered them first to Pietro.

"No moooshroooms for me," Pietro said.

Pietro's mocking of Annamarja's Slovenian accent quieted the room. The silence hurt my ears. Remembering that Pietro had not eaten with us the night before, I asked if he had been out looking for a place to live. He hesitated as if thinking about what to say, then glanced toward his mother.

"No, I was not out looking for a house. I have already found one."

I was surprised. Neither Aurora nor Annamarja had said anything about Pietro finding a place to live. He looked around the room. Only then did I notice his wry smile. His eyes settled on his mother. Once again Aurora was holding her head in her hands.

"Oh, *Babbo*. Oh, *Baa booo*. What is to become of me? Where will an old woman go?"

I liked the idea of leaving behind evidence of having been on Aurora's farm, of rebuilding what most likely were Etruscan walls, but I didn't like the thought of Pietro making fun of me.

Chapter Five

Not what we have,
but what we enjoy,
constitutes our abundance.
EPICURUS

Pietro's Etruscan Wall

"Do you like?" Pietro asked with respect.

Pietro had noticed me studying an icon of Mary and the Christ child as we were getting ready to sit down to eat lunch a few days later. My mood was subdued. I had promised to stay until Aurora had produced her first batch of olive oil. The next day at ten, after a week of picking, we were on the schedule at the *frantoio* to press our olives. I wasn't looking forward to leaving. Despite the occasional disagreements between Aurora and Pietro, and between Pietro and Annamarja, I enjoyed being on Aurora's farm. In exchange for a few days of picking olives, I had become part of a Tuscan family.

Pietro was right. I had been admiring the icon. It evoked feelings of ancient serenity, as though it had been hanging on that wall long before Aurora bought the farm. I turned slowly from the icon to Pietro as I sat down and reverently said, "Yes, I do."

"Then make me an offer," Pietro deadpanned. He had me again. Pietro the irreverent rock.

"It's not for sale," Aurora shouted from the kitchen.

Pietro frowned. "I'd rather not have it looking at me every time I sit down to eat. James should take it with him back to America."

What I was assuming had been an offer from Aurora to help her son had become in Pietro's mind a transfer of ownership and management of the farm. He had taken over much of the house and would be taking over yet another room when his Australian wife arrived in a couple of months. And now Pietro was needling his mother again—offering to sell what Aurora most valued and taking a subtle swipe at her religion. What Aurora had seen as a trial period, Pietro saw as a done deal.

That worried Aurora. She didn't feel Pietro was deserving. To her, transferring ownership of a farm was much more than a legal transaction. The farm would go to Pietro if she were to die, but until that day she felt she had obligations to the land. "I have been here on this farm for almost thirty years, but I'm still viewed as a newcomer, a bit of an outsider," Aurora told me later that day while we were picking olives.

"Does that bother you?" I asked.

"No, no, James, it does not. I have not been here long enough to prove myself. Tuscans feel very attached to their land, their homes, their communities, their traditions," Aurora answered. She was making me realize that Tuscans view a family's permanence not in years, but in generations.

I looked across the valley to a farm that had a look of long-standing vibrancy. "How many years has that family been farming in this valley?" I asked. The olive groves and the vineyards were perfectly cared for and arranged on the hills with an eye for artistic design as though the farm were as carefully planned as a bouquet of flowers, and just as beautiful.

Aurora followed my gaze. "Oh, they're newcomers just like me. Maybe forty years. They rent the land from the church. They are perfectly happy there. They say they would not change a thing." Aurora turned and looked straight at me. "James, the road to Cortona goes right through their farm. You must go see Cortona, and you must see their farm."

Each morning I had looked across the valley to see them spread their nets under the trees to catch the olives. I had listened to their stories and their laughter echoing against the hills. Farming is not lonely in Tuscany. I remember days as a boy in Nebraska when I carried my lunch to the fields—I would see no one for twelve hours straight. I would hear nothing except the drone of the big diesel engine—no voices, no bird calls, no wind—nothing but the incessant, mechanical roar of the tractor from dawn to dark.

"Have any of the neighboring families been here a hundred years?" I asked.

"Only one. The push to get farmers to head up north to the factories in the sixties was quite successful. Hardly anyone was left on the land around here. The *mezzadria* came to an end then."

"Mezza-what?" I asked.

"Oh, I am sorry," Aurora said. "That is what our system of farming was called until it was outlawed in the early 1960s. If you owned land, you kept fifty percent of the income from the land. The tenants got half, the owners got half. *Mezza* means half."

Aurora went on to explain, "The system worked well. It is hard to believe now, but whole families—extended families—could live on half the income from farms of forty-some hectares. Now those same acres, I guess it would be about one hundred, cannot support even one family. But the government decided the system should be outlawed so the farmers could own the land. But I think the real reason was to force, maybe I should say entice, the farmers into the city for factory jobs. Italy needed good workers, and the best place to find those workers was on the farms."

"But wasn't the idea that farmers should own the land rather than sharecrop it?" I asked. "That sounds like a good idea."

"Sounds good, but it wasn't. When people in power want something, they always try to make it sound good, James," Aurora said. I could see that she was looking way back, to the plight of *contadini*, of farmers, and further back to the war as well—to Mussolini and the Fascists. The story that Aurora told of the flight of Italy's farmers to the city sounded very much like the exodus of American farmers to the city and to the factory jobs awaiting them there. The political climate was different in the United States. Most farmers owned their land, or at least the mortgage, but the results were the same. *The Unsettling of America* was what Wendell Berry called it. As a young man I participated in it. I fled, but it was not until years later when I read what Mr. Berry had written about what I had done, that I understood that it was not a good thing for so many people to leave the land.

At the time I accepted the loss of farmers as an inevitable consequence of progress. Today I don't see it that way, and neither does Aurora. Propaganda was used. Stories of the good life that awaited them in the city convinced many farmers to leave the land. For some the dream of an easier life came true. But for many the price proved to be too high— they felt alienated and dislocated. Especially hard hit were the farming communities those families left behind. Cheap transportation and a nine-to-five job in the city proved to be too much competition for the small towns of America.

I told Aurora the story of my hometown, Hayes Center, Nebraska—of how the loss of Wednesday night shopping was the first indication our town was in trouble. Television also changed our tight-knit community. I remember the excitement when a distant television station erected a satellite tower ten miles north of our town. The year was 1956. Suddenly families stayed home for entertainment, rather than driving to town to shop and be with their friends and neighbors. They quit going to the White Theater, which my best friend's parents operated along with their restaurant. We could now watch *Gunsmoke* on Saturday night; we no longer needed John Wayne on the big screen. First, one grocery store quit staying open on Saturday night, then one of the hardware stores, and then my mother's cousin, Bob the butcher, decided it wasn't worth it to stay open late. Within a few years not one store was open on Saturday night, not even the pool hall. When Ross and Sarah closed the movie theater, Saturday night became as quiet as Monday night in my little hometown.

Aurora told me of the changes that had come to Italy. I told her more stories of my childhood. But there is a difference in Tuscany. The loss of farmers was not as complete as it was in America. Small communities still thrive throughout Tuscany.

The farm across the valley showed the difference. Farming in Tuscany still requires people. Machines cannot pick the grapes or the olives. But in much of America, especially the heartland, huge tractors and combines have replaced people. It takes people to make communities. Big tractors kill communities; they transform farmers into economic slaves of debt and boredom. That may seem a harsh judgment, but I am old enough to have seen the way it used to be. And throughout my life I have had the opportunity to talk to farmers who have not only seen it, but have lived it.

While Aurora and I picked olives, I told her about an older farmer I had interviewed for a film I made about family farming. He had lived through the transition from horse and man power to tractor power. I told her how he had begun his story by leaning way back in his chair. "I remember the salesman telling my dad he wouldn't have to work such long hours. That he could keep city hours if he'd just buy this shiny new tractor. And do you know what my dad discovered after he bought that tractor? That his neighbor had bought one too. And that man's neighbor as well. Before long they all had big, shiny new tractors."

I told Aurora about the old farmer taking off his hat and scratching his head to punctuate what he was going to say next. "You know what else my dad discovered, when he looked back at that day a few years later?" The farmer paused again. "He never again had the free time he had when he farmed with his horses and that supposedly too-small tractor. In fact, he and his neighbors found out they had to buy something the salesman hadn't mentioned. They found out they had to buy lights for the darn things because there weren't enough hours in the day to make enough money to pay the banker. And then they had to buy more land. And to top it all off, they discovered that along with not having any time, they didn't have any neighbors either."

Aurora smiled, recognizing the truth of the story. I told her about the old farmer pulling out black-and-white photographs from the thirties and forties to show me the gatherings at his farm—neighbors sharing labor for harvesting and haying—and a photo of his father taking a nap after lunch. He got nostalgic as he remembered his father sleeping under the shade tree in the yard, even wistful. "I never get to take naps. I farm more acres than my dad, but I don't make any more money. I know I have lots less time for things like ball games and fishing. My dad even had time to play town league baseball. No one has time for that anymore. We're in the fields, locked up in our air-conditioned cabs, twelve to fourteen hours a day—and during harvest even longer."

Aurora was shaking her head in agreement as I finished the story. She too wants to see people on farms. She has confronted the question, *what is the appropriate level of technology?* The answer is not the same everywhere. Even on adjoining farms the answer is not the same. The land, and the people farming the land, must answer the question.

I didn't ask the question. I got out of farming when I was thirty years old. Wendell Berry published *The Unsettling of America* about the same time my neighbors gathered at my place to buy my farm equipment. Berry saw the damage that was being done as the farmland of America was being "un-settled." I didn't become aware of his prescient book until ten years later. It took another twenty years for me to return to farming. Thank God for prophets like Wendell Berry who helped us see the consequences of stripping the land of people.

Aurora wants to continue picking olives the old fashioned way. She questions the price and cost of progress. The thought of losing more community saddens her. She wants to be tied to the land and her neighbors, and not to machines or speed. Pietro seems to me to be like the farmer's father, contemplating the purchase of a shiny new tractor. The man wanted the extra speed with which he could travel through the fields with bigger equipment. He was not focused on the costs associated with that speed—costs that must be paid for by the land and the community—costs that land and communities can no longer afford.

Ultimately the battles for the control of farming come down to individual stories playing out all over America, Tuscany, and the world. Eventually Aurora's businessman son will inherit her farm, but until then she would like to maintain traditional practices. Her hope is that before she dies, some of the accumulated wisdom of the ages will rub off on her son. But he does not want to wait. He is certain he can, because of his education and training in the business world and college, do a much better job of farming than his mother and her ignorant, uneducated neighbors.

The battle between Pietro and his mother symbolizes the conflict between farming as business and farming as stewardship—between farming for money and farming for living. Farming is organic, life-affirming. It does not translate easily or well to the language or the methodologies of the businessman. Farming is a unique enterprise. And as Aurora said about the landscape, farming is connubial—a marriage between man and God to produce food and fiber. Or, if you prefer, a marriage between man and nature. But whether you believe in God or not, the consequences of believing that farming is a survival-of-the-fittest enterprise are becoming painfully apparent. The past half-century has demonstrated that a philosophy of competition results in death. Farming is stewardship. Nothing else works—not for long anyway, and certainly not forever. When farming is overwhelmed by the businessman, the farm becomes a factory. The consequence of that kind of thinking is disastrous. Aurora and I had discovered that despite coming from very different backgrounds, we agreed that farms and farmland need stewards who love the land; otherwise the land dies.

Discussions about land dominated the conversation much of the morning in the olive grove. At lunch, while we waited out a rain shower, the conversation again turned to farming. Pietro talked, Annamarja and Aurora offered the occasional counterpoint, and I listened. My sentiments, for many reasons, were mostly in line with Aurora's. Pietro was looking at the land abstractly, as a means to the end of making money. Annamarja jumped into the conversation and railed against Pietro for his disregard of tradition and for his socialist leanings.

Pietro didn't take the bait. Instead of responding directly to Annamarja, he looked at me and said, "James, do you accept farm subsidies?"

Dangerous ground this, discussing politics in a heated setting. I wanted to stay on the sidelines and just listen, but Pietro, who had just been accused of being a Socialist, hadn't asked me how I *feel* about subsidies, he had asked whether I *accept* subsidies.

"No, I don't. I haven't signed up for any government programs," I told him.

Pietro pounced. "Aha! Would you believe my mother accepts subsidies? She doesn't realize they aren't helping small farmers, they're controlling farmers."

It felt strange to be agreeing with Pietro. I added, "Subsidies are wolves in sheep's clothing. We've got a lot of programs like that. They hand out money telling us it will help people, but what they're really doing is making people dependent." My words shocked me. I was surprised I spoke out so forcefully. Listening to Annamarja and Pietro go at each other swept away my tendency toward political correctness.

"Are you against single mothers?" Pietro asked me.

"What do you mean?" I was stalling. Aurora was already feeling the heat from me siding with Pietro about subsidies. Most likely Pietro was asking me if I agreed with giving extra benefits to unmarried women who have babies. If I had the math right in a story from a couple of nights ago, Aurora didn't get married until Pietro was five years old. I wanted to answer honestly but was afraid the words might hurt Aurora, even though I doubted very much that Italy gave extra money to single mothers back then.

"You know what I mean, James. Should the government be taking the place of deadbeat fathers?"

"Oh, *Babbo*, Oh, *Baa booo.*" Aurora's head was in her hands once more.

My stomach knotted as I felt Aurora's pain. But which pain was she feeling? Was it the pain of rearing a child alone for so many years? Was it the pain of a son sounding ungrateful for her sacrifices? Was it the pain that Pietro would be so blunt at the dinner table?

Pietro was showing his hand, alluding to the social engineering programs that are bankrupting governments all over Europe. Feel-good government aid is hard to be against, but the time may be coming when bureaucrats won't have to see the errors of their ways—that by paying money for kids born out of wedlock, they are encouraging the bastardization of America, of Italy. So I took the coward's way out, "We may not have to be for or against it, Pietro. We're all going to be broke soon. Neither farmers nor unmarried mothers will be getting money from the government."

That's what I said to Pietro and to Aurora, but I was thinking that giving extra money to single mothers discourages marriages, pure and simple. If we as a society dangle the carrot, should we be surprised that so many women take it?

"You're right, James. We're all going broke trying to be good guys," Pietro said looking at his mom. "But Italy is not as screwed up as England and Sweden. Twenty percent of families in Sweden are headed by a single parent. In Britain the rate is nine percent. Here, the rate is just one-half of a percent. Guess which countries in the European Union pay the most money to unwed mothers?"

"Sweden and England, maybe?" I volunteered. I had not expected to be agreeing with Pietro about so many things in one afternoon.

"The divorce rate in Sweden and England is over forty percent. In Italy it is eight percent," Pietro added.

Pietro's statistics reminded me of an article I read while waiting for my plane in Philadelphia. "I just read that forty percent of the babies born in the United States are to unwed mothers. And it keeps getting worse every year." I didn't add, because it might have hurt Aurora's feelings, *These payments that we are told are good for children are instead destroying kids, communities, and society.* I said none of that because Aurora might think I was talking about her and Pietro. As I thought about what

I was *not* saying, I realized that what I was considering tact, or political correctness, could also be called cowardice.

I did get up the courage to say that a similar thing goes on in farming. "The government gives away money, and that money buys votes." I wanted to say *No wonder our farms and families are in such bad shape*, but I couldn't do it. What I said was, "Pietro, I don't think the sun is going to come out and dry the olives. Let's go rebuild your wall—the one you told me you've been saving for a *wwoofer* with a strong back and a weak mind."

"Really, James? You want to work on that wall?" Pietro was looking straight at me. He was cautious, thinking I was about to jerk his chain, just like he jerks mine.

Aurora reached out her hand. "No, no, James, you don't have to do that. Go rest. The sun will come out soon and we will go pick olives. You'll break your back—those stones are heavy." But Pietro was already heading toward the door.

"Follow me, James. We will go get the shovels and a pickaxe."

"Do you have a tamping bar?" I asked, but Pietro was gone. I pushed back my chair and smiled at Aurora. "Don't worry, Aurora, I'll take it easy."

We walked to the same shed where we'd been storing the *cassetti*, half full of olives. Pietro reached in and pulled out two shovels and a pick and handed them to me. He grabbed a tamping bar and a stiff-bristled broom. We followed the well-worn path to the olive grove. A section of the terrace about twelve meters long just behind the house had given way. The stones were scattered about. Some were almost completely covered with dirt, others were tipped at odd angles. We began digging, working our way down to where we hoped to build a strong foundation of stones.

"Have you ever built a wall before, James?" I wasn't sure how to answer the question. Pietro tended toward perfectionism. I was hoping he would take the lead and I'd supply muscle power and determination and learn a bit about the ancient craft of dry-stone walling. We have stones on our farm and our land is also blessed with pines and hardwoods. I studied architecture and construction in college, but I didn't pursue them professionally. However, my high school dream of someday building my own home has never left me. I was hoping that working with Pietro would be another opportunity to pick up valuable skills to help me get closer to my dream.

In the weeks before coming to Tuscany I had skimmed through a few books about building with stones, but I didn't want to come off as knowing more than I did. Pietro could be very demanding. I had not forgotten his insistence that we follow his procedure, not Aurora's, for picking olives. I fully intended to build this wall just the way Pietro wanted it. But I didn't want to seem uninterested either, so I said, "I've read a couple of books."

"Then you know more than me." And with that Pietro put down his shovel and walked away. He had me again. Stunned, I watched him leave.

When he reached the tool shed, he noticed that I was watching him. As he grabbed a weed whacker, he yelled out, "Just make sure you build it straight enough to last at least one hundred years." With a flair he yanked the starting rope and destroyed a perfectly peaceful day. I returned to digging, smiling and shaking my head as I thought about Pietro's wily, Tom Sawyer-like qualities.

Pietro surprised me, giving up so quickly on the wall. I suspected he was just not comfortable with manual labor. He preferred to let a machine, to the extent possible, do the work. I have never understood the preference to be tied to the noise of an internal combustion engine. Just the day before I had told Pietro I used a scythe to control weeds on my farm. He said he didn't know that anyone except the Amish still used scythes. I told him—with a smile on my face—that I bought my farm just so I could get away from the noise of all my neighbors in the suburbs who use weed whackers and leaf blowers on Sunday.

As I sorted the stones according to size and shape, I began wondering why Pietro preferred noise to the peaceful work of building with stones. Aurora must have been right. "If I say up, Pietro says down." So maybe it's no wonder that Pietro preferred the whine of a weed whacker.

The high-pitched wail assaulted my good mood. In what I thought would be peaceful Tuscany, I was listening to the shrill shriek of the suburbs. I dug through the dirt to foundation level. Down on my hands and knees, I sighted along the intact portion of the wall and determined where to position the first course. The noise of Pietro's machine was bothering me. I kept hoping he would either get tired, move far away, or at least go to the other side of the house—or better yet, give up on weed whacking and take over the decision-making. Which stones to start with? What goes where? I was having trouble getting started. I was feeling the weight of making choices that would remain on this land for years, if not generations, and I wanted to share the burden. The terraced walls had been around for centuries, and except for this one spot, they were in good shape.

I liked the idea of leaving behind evidence of having been on Aurora's farm—of rebuilding what most likely were Etruscan walls, but I didn't like the thought of Pietro making fun of me. *"Is this how you build walls in Wee-scon-sin?"* or something abundantly more witty. I hoped to avoid the embarrassment of a stinging rebuke from his sharp mind. He was getting inside my head just as he had gotten inside Aurora's. Just as I began wrestling the largest stone in the pile, he shut off the weed whacker. I looked at him and silently mouthed, "Thank you, thank you, thank you."

Whether he read my lips, I don't know. But he was watching me wrestle the large cornerstone that would, I hoped, forever define the pathway to the olive grove above. Once I had it in place, Pietro turned and put the weed whacker in the shed and then quickly pulled out a lawnmower. He jerked the rope and was immediately swallowed up in a cloud of dust; the blade was set way too low. The engine was not quite as high pitched as the weed whacker, but still unpleasant to my ear, especially the sharp thwacking sound of twigs ricocheting around the yard.

I tried to shut out the noise by focusing on choosing stones, looking for the largest and most squared off to tie into the cornerstone and run in a straight line to the old wall. Even though these stones would be covered by dirt, it was important to set a good foundation if the wall was going to survive freezing-and-thawing cycles for the next few centuries.

That afternoon I promised myself to someday build at least part of my house out of stones. I was totally absorbed in the wall, playing a hard-fought game of chess, as I figured out my moves far down the line, making sure each stone lying about was used in the best place possible. My shirt was soaked with sweat even though the temperature was only sixty-five degrees Fahrenheit. I wasn't, as I assured Aurora I would, taking it easy.

Every once in a while I was brought out of my super-concentrated state by the sound of the mower as Pietro shoved it into the too-tall grass, killing the engine. He would restart it, kill it a few seconds later, then start it again. After a half hour of that, he moved to the other side of the house. In the relative silence, I lost track of time. I became absorbed in the rhythm of my movements—a dance that was not interrupted until Pietro returned to my side of the house to attack the overgrown grass again. And just as before he killed the engine every few feet. When he got tired of that, which was definitely not soon enough for me, he pushed the mower down the hill and stopped a half-dozen feet from me. Once he saw that I had quit moving stones and was looking at him, he killed the engine with a flourish. "Now that I am finished annoying you, I will go in."

He didn't wait for me to respond. Just as well. I couldn't have come up with anything half so perceptively sharp-witted.

When I began the project, I thought it might take a few evenings to complete. Now, as I studied the remaining stones, and the wall, I was envisioning placing the capstone before Aurora called me to dinner.

I wasn't rushing, but I had developed a rhythm. I would place two stones, then walk away far enough that I could sight down the original wall to the cornerstone to judge the placement of the latest stones. Not only did that walk ensure that the wall was straight, but walking upright relieved the tightness that was beginning to set in from the bending, kneeling, and lifting.

Besides, it was satisfying just to look at my work. Whenever I build something in my wood shop, several days pass before I tire of looking at it. Something about the creative process inspires a person to enjoy just looking at what he has built. Apparently, it has been like that since God created time. One of the most oft-repeated phrases in Genesis is "And God saw that it was good." I love to imagine God stepping back to look at His creations, especially the last time when He looked "and saw all that He had made, and it was very good."

I didn't have that much confidence, to call what I had built "very good," even though I was enjoying looking at the wall, which I continued to do every fifteen minutes or so. Two hours later Pietro walked up and said, "Let me see what you have done, James." I had just placed the last stone and was filling in dirt behind the wall. His tone sounded ominous. I thought he was going to tell me to forget it, which I would gladly have done. I was tired, and I was going to be more tired by the time I backfilled the dirt.

Pietro stared at the wall. I stared at him. His face showed no expression. He turned to look at me. I held his gaze and said nothing. He neither smiled nor frowned; only his eyes moved. He said nothing. Not knowing what he was thinking made me uncomfortable, but I remained silent. He looked back at the wall. My mind raced. *What the heck is he thinking? He has to see that my whole shirt is soaked in sweat. Is he trying to come up with the right words? Is he trying to be gentle with me? He knows I've been working hard for a long time.* I expected him be either sarcastic or witty, but not silent. He stepped back and took another look at the wall, yet still he said nothing, holding a perfect poker face.

I wanted to ask, "Do you like?" Just as he asked me when he saw me staring at the icon of Mary and Baby Jesus. I was trying to think of something clever to say, to catch him off guard, to do what he always does to me. He continued looking at the wall. I was convinced that he was trying to choose his words very carefully. I was sure, given how much time he had taken, that when he finally did say something, it would be funny. Criticism is easier to take if it's witty.

Finally he broke the silence. While still looking at the wall he quietly asked, "Must you leave tomorrow?"

I was flabbergasted.

"*Bravissimo,* James. This is pretty good. This is very good." He turned to me and smiled. "Why, James, why do you have to leave tomorrow?"

I let out the breath I had been holding and smiled, still not sure what to say. "If you will stay, James, I will prepare you a *Tuscanissimo* meal. It will be the best food you have ever eaten." Pietro spoke with the calm assurance of a chef who delights in pleasing his guests.

"The farm where you are planning to go—Valter's—Annamarja stayed there only five days. Here she stayed a year. What does that tell you? Why would you want to leave here? I will convince you that you should stay."

For once I had the upper hand. It was my turn to play poker with Pietro. In my mind I said, *Perhaps one more day.* But to Pietro I said, "Valter is expecting me."

I loved the change of roles. Pietro was genuinely moved by what I had built. He looked again at the wall, stepped to the side, and studied it for a long time head-on. Then he looked back at me, a mischievous smile of recognition crossing his face. "You've built walls before, James. You've done more than read a few books. You devil, James."

Pietro wanted me to confess. But there wasn't much to confess. Rocks don't grow in southwestern Nebraska. Sand yes, but no rocks. My farm in Wisconsin has rocks, and I've placed a few of them on top of each other to divert water on hillsides, but the rock walls I've built have been in my dreams—my plans for my own Tuscan-like home some day.

"So, you have other walls you want to build, Pietro?"

"James, if you stay, there is no end to the things we can get done around here. We will celebrate tomorrow. We will eat *bruschetta*, the best you've ever eaten, made with our fresh olive oil—with the olives you and I have picked."

He looked at me and smiled. "You do realize Valter is German, don't you?"

I returned his smile.

"Did you come all this way to Tuscany to eat German food?"

I toasted Pietro and our good fortune. We took a sip of superb wine from nearby Montepulciano, from a vineyard I had biked past on my first day in Tuscany. "Grab your camera, James. You need to get a picture of us in front of this oven so you can take it back to America to show your wife what good care we take of you."

Chapter Six

One of the very nicest things about life is the way
we must regularly stop whatever it is
we are doing and devote our attention to eating.
LUCIANO PAVAROTTI

A *Tuscanissimo Feast*

I awoke early the next morning, still basking in the glow of Pietro's praise, still debating whether to call Valter and tell him that Pietro and Aurora wanted me to stay longer. But I didn't make that call. Instead I went for a walk. No one was awake yet, and we weren't scheduled at the *frantoio* until ten.

As I walked past the front of Aurora's house and looked across the valley, the sun's rays were just clearing the mountain, highlighting the towers and walls of Cortona, but our hillside was still in shadow. Just beyond the *bagno esterno* that Pietro threatened to blow up, the gentle path deteriorated into an overgrown trail clinging to a sidehill before dropping quickly down to the level of the creek. I crossed the stream on a small wooden bridge. It wasn't rustic or quaint, just flimsy. I grabbed the two-by-four railings to take weight off my feet as I tiptoed on the water-logged boards.

Pietro had warned me the going would be rough, but he hadn't mentioned that it was so rough I might get lost. My hunch was to follow the stream. But the trail seemed to be going nowhere, so I recrossed the stream on some rocks, then followed what looked like a path jutting sharply upward through low-hanging branches. The distance seemed much longer than the kilometer Pietro told me to expect, but at last the trail broke out onto a tree-lined road. I grabbed a few rocks and erected a small cairn to mark the spot where I'd need to duck into the underbrush to follow the trail back to Aurora's.

Walking on the road was easy, the grades more gradual—no more wondering whether I was on the right track. Within a kilometer the road broke out of the trees and led me through the pasture just below the farmhouse belonging to Aurora's neighbors who rent from the church— the forty-year "newcomers." The fields were fenced with a combination of stone walls, wooden poles, and woven wire following the contours of the land. The road ran along the house, so close that the edge of the road was the side of the house. Before walking into the tunnel created by overhanging trees on one side and the house on the other, I turned and looked back across the valley at Aurora's farm, now bathed in sunshine. I saw nothing moving; even the yap-all-night-dogs were now sleeping.

Walking within feet of the neighbors' house, I felt as if I was invading their privacy. But I didn't hear them; I heard only birds singing and bells on sheep, and farther away the tolling of the bells of their landlord, Santa Maria Nuova, a sixteenth-century church. On the other side of the house I found olive groves, small fields, tractors, plows, and disks. The barnyard and pastures were nurturing a lively mix of draft horses, sheep, goats, donkeys, geese, chickens, and roosters.

I liked the feeling of approaching Cortona on foot, of sensing the pulse of the town from the sounds of the morning—the awakening roosters and braying donkeys—as I made my way up the ancient cobblestoned, tree-lined Via Santa Maria Nuova. The town was not yet fully awake. I looked up at a clock tower and noted the time. Despite the difficulties of the trail, it had taken less than an hour to get to the northwestern gate—the Porta Colonia—and its massive and beautifully carved wooden doors.

By the time I got to the center of town, the Piazza della Repubblica, which appeared to have about a dozen streets converging on it at all angles, schoolchildren were gathering, people were on their way to work, and shopkeepers were flinging open their doors. I liked the bustle of it; however I felt like a voyeur. Aurora didn't send me to buy bread or vegetables. She sent me to town just to look. For the first time since arriving in Italy, I felt like a tourist. I didn't like it. I felt displaced. But I kept walking. The museum had not yet opened its doors. Just as well. I would rather share the experience with someone, maybe with my son who's studying to be an artist.

I had no where to go, so I walked and looked. I began thinking about olives, about the work we had done, and the work we had yet to do. I wondered whether Aurora still found it exciting, that first taste of *olio d'oliva nuovo* each year. Looking in shop windows held no interest for me. I was thinking of the *frantoio* and of helping Aurora load the heavy *cassetti* into her car.

Even though I had been been up and down most of Cortona's downtown streets, it was still too early to walk directly back to Aurora's, so I sought higher ground, taking a circuitous route to the farm. The natural flow of people was along Via Nazionale. I joined in. After a few blocks I noticed that all the adults had turned into the shops or other doors along the way or had slowed their pace, leaving me the lone adult surrounded by a group of school children—an energetic, but not boisterous bunch. I was surprised by how many of them were overweight, almost fat. Maybe my idolization of the Tuscan diet was unwarranted, or maybe the younger generation was not eating the Tuscan diet, not living the Tuscan life.

The street dropped the children off at school, then led me to Santa Domenico, a beautiful church surrounded by gardens and lawns, and beyond it, a wide, level thoroughfare capable of handling the movement of thousands of people, but at the moment reserved only for me and two street sweepers with long, flowing brooms. Via Le Giardini Pubblici was well-named. What once was a major thoroughfare was now a long public garden suited more to repose than travel.

The garden was on the southeastern side of Cortona, on the side where Aurora could not find all the sun she wanted. I tried to envision the location of the farm she chose not to buy, looking for a house tucked in a mountain shadow. I wished that Aurora was with me, sharing the history of the land and the people. I walked all the way around Cortona, coming back into the city through what most likely was an Etruscan gate that led me to the stunningly beautiful Santuario Santa Margherita, perched high on the hill.

My research had alerted me to the treasures residing in the churches of Italy, but still I was not fully prepared for the experience—*stunning* was the word I used just about every time I walked into a church in Tuscany. By time I got to Santa Margherita, which was about two weeks into my journey, I was expecting to be transfixed when I walked through its doors. I was not disappointed. Every church in Tuscany must have magnificent paintings inside, maybe every church in Italy. The size and beauty of the paintings was overwhelming. Even in the churches of the smallest towns in Tuscany the art was glorious. Rural and small town parishioners must have felt the same call to praise God in paintings as did the faithful living in cities.

The builders of Santa Margherita also chose to praise God with the location of the church. The site was so high on the hill that many of the streets leading back to the Piazza della Repubblica were cut with steps. But despite the beauty of Cortona and its churches, and the charm of its streets, I preferred the feeling of being in Tuscany for a reason—of helping to bring in the harvest. I liked dressing like a *contadino,* but walking those ancient streets I looked like a tourist—a camera bag strapped around my midsection. I would have preferred to be wearing the olive basket, a long-sleeve shirt, and a floppy straw hat to ward off the sun and the sharp branches. Helping pick the fruit of the tree helped me feel some of the aches and pains, and yes, the tedium of bringing olive oil to the table. A little sweat on the brow was required, some tired muscles in the shoulders, arms, and back—maybe even a little too much Tuscan sun. It may be a good life, but it is not necessarily an easy life. Not many of the good lives are easy lives. But in experiencing the pains of the Tuscans I gained a greater appreciation for the joys of the Tuscans.

I wanted to be working.

Nevertheless, I took a few photos, just to prove to Aurora and to my family that I tried to be a tourist. But my heart wasn't in it. I arrived back at Aurora's just as she was walking up the hill to the storage shed to load the olives.

Packing three hundred kilos of olives into a tiny Fiat was like going into battle against a real-time 3-D Tetris puzzle. Many years of accomplishing the feat had taught Aurora just how they needed to be arranged, and just how much weight the overmatched springs of her car could handle and still clear the boulders in her road.

We arrived at Paolo's for the olive pressing with the load perched precariously in the folded-down back seat, accompanied by the sound of Aurora's little car groaning under its load. The place was buzzing with activity. I was reminded of the grain elevators back in Nebraska that I first visited with my father during wheat harvest. Once a year we would gather with our crop, just as these farmers were doing. Paolo, the owner of the *frantoio*, was the star. And he was playing the part well. A sense of joy pervaded the place, the farmers reaching out and placing a hand on Paolo's shoulder to emphasize the good feeling of once again being in his company. They wanted Paolo to treat their olives well, to get them into the press as soon as possible, and to keep them segregated from their neighbors' *inferiore* olives. Paolo accepted their greetings with good-natured aplomb. I was witnessing a celebration—a dance of the harvest. Paolo was moving gracefully from hopper to press to flowing olive oil and then back to each newly arriving customer to assure him that he would take good care of his olives.

Aurora was moving gracefully in the dance as well. She told me that when she first began bringing her olives to Paolo she was, for a few years, the only woman. She then turned and directed my attention to an attractive middle-aged woman working out of the back of a large step van. The woman was dumping her overflowing *cassetti* into the hopper that funneled the fresh olives onto the conveyor belt where they were washed. Aurora also told me that in the early days the process involved only pressure from heavy grinding wheels to extract the oil. Now heat and mechanical pressure were being used and the noise was oppressive, almost painful. I was glad Aurora's olives were not in line behind the large load in the hopper. As much as I was enjoying this climactic event of the year's olive harvest, I didn't want to subject my hearing to the roar of the room longer than necessary. While waiting I took a few photos of the *frantoio*, making sure to include Aurora. This was the first time I'd been able to get her to stand still for a photo. She had nothing to do but wait and watch her olives go through the massive green machines that reminded me of Hoover Dam turbines.

My eyes turned again to Paolo. I loved watching him move from machine to machine like a ballet dancer. He had honed his moves over years of practice, each time placing his feet perfectly, moving with no wasted motion or energy. His pace quickened. He motioned to Aurora. She grabbed her *fustino* and they met at the far end of the tangle of steel, hoses and pipes. Paolo removed the *fustino's* lid, positioned the spigot, and the precious bright green oil began flowing. The color surprised me. It was radiant. Aurora motioned me to come closer. I moved in and she offered me a taste. The oil was pungent and full of subtle flavors. Never before had I tasted fresh olive oil. Within a few minutes the stainless steel container was full. Aurora spun the lid on and we each grabbed a handle. Paolo leaned toward us to tell us it contained forty-seven kilograms of oil—over one hundred pounds. The Fiat groaned again under the concentrated weight as we placed the *fustino* in the open hatchback.

I thought of all the work that had gone into making this oil. No wonder olive oil was precious. No wonder farmers were irritated by cheap prices and inferior oils that weakened the market. I vowed at that moment to buy as much food at local markets as I could and whenever possible to put that money directly into the hands of farmers. What better use could be made of the money that came my way, than to use it to buy food that sustained me, and at the same time sustained farmers and the communities they lived in. It was a good circle, and I, with the taste of fresh olive oil still dancing in my mouth, vowed that I was going to remain within that very close family of food growers and makers. At the center of that circle now sat the *fustino*, surrounded by a week's worth of memories for me and a year's worth for Aurora. If ever again I heard people complain about the price of olive oil, I'd have a story to tell them.

On the drive home from the *frantoio* Aurora was quiet, and so was I—an after-harvest letdown. I felt it as a kid after wheat harvest, and I was feeling that sweet sorrow again. Pietro had promised me the best *bruschetta* I'd ever tasted in my life and a *Tuscanissimo* meal, but the prospect of leaving was making me sad—a mood that was not broken until Aurora stopped by the *frutta e verdura negozio*, the fruit and vegetable shop, doing as she has always done—staying in the circle. We picked up some black cabbage and potatoes. I liked the easy familiarity of the place, the light banter, the way the food was piled in bulk. Huge pallets of apples were scattered about the store, not packaged, looking as though they had been delivered on the back of a farm wagon pulled by draft horses. No one was in a rush. People were talking and making jokes while they waited and looked. When you go to the market in Tuscany you get more than food—you get the news of your neighbors, your community.

Our next stop was Aurora's bakery, another nondescript storefront where the main attraction was food and conversation, not convenience. It would not have bothered me if the line had been even longer. I was enjoying the interactions of shoppers and shopkeepers, always a good chance to learn *una piccolo italiano*. But we were in and out quickly by Tuscan standards; Aurora needed only bread for Pietro's *bruschetta*.

"You know, James, Annamarja stayed at Valter's only five days and here at my mother's farm, she stayed a year."

Pietro was repeating what he had said last night, playing the part of the good host, acting as though he had taken over the farm and it was now his responsibility to show me a good time on what might be my last night. He was fanning the flames in the outdoor wood-fired oven, a dome-shaped classic that he was very proud of. He told me of his plans to rebuild the house and enlarge the kitchen and that this oven would be its centerpiece. "The meat that comes out of this oven is always cooked to perfection, and the breads too. And the pizzas, they're to die for. You can find no one who can build such an oven anymore. The talent has been lost."

Just when I thought Pietro was all business and technology, he surprised me yet again, expressing deep admiration for craftsmen and the knowledge that was being lost to modernization—Pietro the thankful steward, a keeper of Tuscan ovens. He continued , "If this oven needs repaired, I am going to have to figure out how to do it myself. This oven cannot be duplicated. My aunt's oven needed work, but she could find no one to repair it and it collapsed. What a pity."

I toasted Pietro and our good fortune. We took a sip of superb wine from nearby Montepulciano, from a vineyard I had biked past on my first day in Tuscany. "Grab your camera, James. You need to get a picture of us in front of this oven so you can take it back to America to show your wife what good care we take of you."

If I had known how it would affect Pietro, I would have rebuilt the wall the first day I arrived. He was now a gracious host. And I was "one of the good guys" on his *uwoofer* list, as he told his mother. I was surprised that Pietro attached so much importance to rebuilding a wall. That wall must have been a test, and I had passed. But with Pietro, the fear of the other shoe dropping was always present.

Pietro prepared Tuscan sausage, pork ribs, potatoes, and black cabbage, *cavolo nero*. As he promised, his *Tuscanissimo cena* was the best food I had eaten in Tuscany. I paced myself so I could enjoy every course. I was, as Aurora said, *un buona forchetta quello sera*, a hearty eater (a good fork) that evening. If Pietro would cook like this each evening, and especially if each night he would be such an engaging person, I would repair walls for him all day long. We did not leave the table until midnight—talking about everything and nothing—and enjoying every minute of it. Pietro told a long, complicated story about his MBA thesis that I hoped I'd get to hear again, a story that convinced me Pietro is a many-sided enigma. I fell asleep that night under the influence of good food and good wine while trying to make sense of an Iliad-inspired MBA thesis.

The yapping dogs awoke me in the middle of the night out of a dream and into the conviction that yes, even though Pietro had treated me to the best *bruschetta* I had ever eaten, I still needed to keep my commitment to be at Valter's a few hours later that morning. Rain was forecast, but still I hoped to bike to Ristonchia. In deference to Aurora's wishes, I didn't pull my fifty-five-pound fully-loaded trailer up the hill to Valter's place. In deference to Pietro's *Tuscanissimo* meal, I promised to come back to pick more olives. Pietro was kind enough to keep my trailer and my stuff—as collateral.

Pietro was right. The last five kilometers climbed straight into the sky. Ristonchia is an ancient hilltop town, just a collection of buildings all joined, looking like a fortified castle—so small that I mistook the whole town for a farm and began cycling past it, until I realized there were no more buildings to come.

I turned around and pulled under an archway to park my bike out of the drizzle. Somewhere within this collection of buildings must be Valter's place. I stuck my head into what looked like a woodworking shop and yelled, "*Guten Morgen*, Valter."

From the dark interior I heard a voice: "You vill not find Valter in here." Out of the black materialized a man with wood shavings dropping off his shoulders. "Follow me, I vill show you Valter's place." He led me under a low arch, around a corner, and into a courtyard. He pointed up the hill toward an open door.

"*Aperto porta?*" I asked.

He responded, "*Si,*" and turned back toward his shop.

"*Guten Morgen*, Valter," I yelled again when I got to the doorway.

"Enter," a voice boomed at me.

I made my way up a narrow, dark labyrinth of a staircase that dropped me out into a room that made me feel I had stepped back in time a thousand years. The huge mantle over the fireplace was charcoal colored, scorched a deeper shade of black with every fire lit in it over the centuries. I walked through the darkened room, which, when my eyes adjusted, I discovered was a kitchen, and found in the adjoining room Valter and a young couple seated around a large table, drinking coffee.

Valter would have had no trouble playing Santa Claus. He had the build and the face and a hearty laugh to boot. The couple had been coming to Valter's for almost a dozen years to help him with his olive harvest. Before I had time to slip out of my rain jacket, we were joined by two other workers who also spoke German. I felt out of place. The language reverted to their mother tongue. I found it easier to follow than Italian; I could tell where one word ended and another began. But I didn't come to Tuscany to learn to speak German. Pietro's voice rang strong and clear in my ears as I sipped the lukewarm, almost tasteless tea and bit into the stale bread—*come back when you get tired of Valter's German food.*

I heard Pietro mocking me again when we got to the olive grove. Valter thrust a yellow plastic hand into mine with which to strip the olive branches and said, "I don't know how you picked olives at Aurora's, but here we do it quickly, efficiently." It pained me to observe the efficiency with which Valter and his workers picked olives. The efficiency that Valter worshipped resulted in olives being squashed under his boots as he walked around the tree with a noisy electrical shaker on a pole, his eyes fixed on the branches. Valter was a good, kindhearted man, very giving of his time, as I was later to learn, but at that moment I wanted to jump on my bike and pedal as fast as I could back to Aurora's where the olive, not productivity, was on a pedestal.

Despite Valter's insistence upon efficiency, I noted that the six of us picked only one hundred kilos of olives. I compared that to the sixty-five kilos Aurora, Annamarja and I had picked a few mornings before. We had used no tractor. We had no batteries, no electrical cords to untangle and move, no nets to reposition, and no mechanical shaker. We just had trees, olives, a couple of ladders, baskets to unload into hand-carried *cassetti*, and no squished olives. Efficiency is abstract, olives are concrete. Valter's way may be efficient, but Aurora's way was pleasing.

The question was not whether Valter honored the land. Annamarja praised Valter's husbandry, and I saw examples of it in the manure surrounding the trees, but the abstract quality of efficiency seemed, at least on that morning, to be the final arbiter of the decisions that Valter was making. Like many farmers today, Valter seemed tied to the mechanical solution. And even if, on another day, it could be demonstrated that his way did result in more olives in the *cassetti* than Aurora's way of picking, I would not choose Valter's way. The tractors, the gas, the batteries, the electrical shakers, and the nets all cost money and must be maintained. Those expenses must be factored in. Every farmer will choose what importance to give to those considerations, but I feel it is a huge mistake to think that high tech is always better just because more ground is covered, and more trees are stripped. Being tied to the noise of a machine does not automatically make you a better farmer, and rarely does it make you a better steward.

The whole complicated picture must be looked at. Focusing on quantity compromises quality and leads to cheap prices. That leaves the alert farmer asking if he is better off for all his mechanization. The important question is not how much money we bring in, but how we use the money that comes our way.

While we were eating, rain began falling again. The pace of lunch slowed. The conversation turned to agritourism. I learned that Valter made some money from farming, but more came from guests. He took pride in his repeat customers; one family had been coming every year for fifteen years. Now even the children were coming as adults. Photographs of that family covered the walls.

I asked Valter about his home. "This house is six hundred years old, but the foundation is even older. It is Etruscan and is maybe two thousand years old. And I hope it will be lived in a thousand years from now," he told me, reminding me that stewardship is not limited to land.

Valter's centuries-old house made me want all the more to build with stone. The feeling of permanence, protection, and continuity was comforting and transforming. If I had walked out and seen knights in armor on the streets of Ristonchia, I would have been only mildly surprised. The ceiling was made of beams spaced about every four feet and purlins between spaced at one foot. The doorway to the dining room was an arch. A huge fireplace dominated one wall of the kitchen. The steps were massive stones three feet by ten inches and three inches thick that revealed, despite their hardness, cupped patterns of wear, leaving little doubt they had been trod on for centuries.

Rectangular red tiles four inches by twelve inches covered the floor. The walls were plastered and appeared to be about two feet thick. I wanted my home to have such a feeling of permanence—I wanted five or six generations of my family to live in the home I built. Valter's woodstove heated the water as well. His house seemed efficient. Except for his farming equipment, I imagined that he had few expenses.

"Can a farmer can make a living from the land?" I asked.

He quickly responded, "Ninety percent of my income comes from tourists and ten percent from farming."

"But how much time do you spend farming—about half?"

"No, no," Valter countered, "I spend only thirty percent of my time with tourists. Seventy percent of my time I spend farming."

"You're kidding," I said.

"No, I'm not. And most of that money comes from subsidies," he admitted.

"How did things get so bad?" I asked.

"Foreign money coming into Tuscany and buying up all the land," Valter explained. "Who can afford to farm now?"

He gave me no indication he saw the irony—whether his foreign money could be part of the problem.

"It's also all the subsidized grain being dumped on the world market, especially from America. Who can grow wheat, who can grow corn that cheap? You can't. It's a mess," Valter concluded.

He picked up his plate and bowl and walked to the kitchen. I followed and washed the dishes while he put the leftovers away. Valter and I were in full agreement about the evils of subsidizing agriculture and the unintended consequences of making farmers slaves of big government and big corporations. I was beginning to think after talking with Aurora and Pietro, and now Valter, that these consequences are not unintended, after all. These conversations reminded me of the demise that was predicted for my Amish neighbors because they refuse to be sucked into the glories of modern agriculture—big tractors and big subsidies. They refuse both, yet their farms prosper and so does their land. People who are not slaves to consumerism and free money are hard to control.

After spending a lonely night and morning out in the poorly insulated shed, which I dubbed *Capra Casa* because of the goats at my front door, I decided it was best to tell Valter what was on my mind—that I had come to Tuscany to speak Italian and to live with a truly Tuscan family. I was thankful that rain had descended yet again on Ristonchia. We would not be rushing out to the olive grove. I was the only worker who joined Valter for breakfast—that made it easier to find the nerve to tell Valter of my quandary, of my desire to work on a multigenerational farm of Tuscans.

"I can help you with that," he said. "I am the regional coordinator of WWOOF." And with that Valter sat down at a table that looked to be hundreds of years old and uncovered a twenty-first-century computer— the ultimate anachronism in his Etruscan castle. He spent the next hour compiling a list of farms. As he worked, I wondered whether he was aware of my embarrassment. I had expected a couple of recommendations from memory and then for him to send me on my way. But instead of exhibiting German efficiency, Valter displayed the slower-paced concern and hospitality of his adopted country—caring for the gift that had come his way.

As we said goodbye, Valter handed me a list of Italian families who spoke little English and farmed using traditional methods. He sent me on my way with his blessing and told me I was welcome to come back anytime. He even said he would come to Wisconsin and help me farm. And I hope he does.

I left *Capra Casa* cleaner than I found it and hoped that would contribute to Valter feeling that ours had been a good exchange. I said goodbye to the friendly goats that reminded me of my farm and the rooster with half a crow that got me up long before first light. Valter and I had uncovered points of disagreement about farming, but he had dismantled the edifice of political correctness that says you either have to leave things unsaid or agree with someone about everything to hold that person in high esteem.

I wheeled my bike through a shed, past Valter's old articulated tractor, down a steep path, and onto the road. The sun broke out from behind a cloud as I jumped onto my bike, and its warmth followed me all the way back to Aurora's. Coincidence or confirmation, who can say. But on that long, downhill coast to Castiglion Fiorentino, I chose the thankful route.

Annamarja came running to greet me as I wheeled my bike into the farmyard. I felt like the prodigal son returning even though I'd been gone only slightly more than twenty-four hours. She hugged me, then asked, "Why back so soon, James?"

"I miss you and Pietro. I miss your squabbles," I said as I parked my bike.

"I am glad you are back. We do not fight so much when you are here," said Annamarja.

I smiled at that thought, of the fights and bickering, and clever retorts I'd missed.

Aurora joined us. "Welcome back, James. Did you enjoy Valter's?"

"Not so much. I miss speaking—I miss trying to speak Italian." I corrected myself. "I prefer your quiet farm." I told her about the rooster just outside my window that stretched out his neck time after time in the predawn light, but could muster only an emasculated "Cock-a...," the "doodle-doo" missing from his repertoire for the first sixty or so cries of the day. Aurora smiled, but it was a weary smile. In the one day I'd been gone she had lost her zip. She was coughing. She looked exhausted, fearful.

I told Aurora and Annamarja how Valter picked, but I didn't mention what Valter had said when he handed me the yellow plastic hand. I did, however, mention all the cables, nets, shakers, and batteries before I realized that none of this was news to Annamarja—or to Aurora either, I guessed.

Aurora sighed. "We all have our own ways." She then muttered, "Oh, *Babbo*," under her breath, and I realized that her mind had switched from thinking about Valter to worrying about Pietro.

We sat down to a small lunch. I was happy to again hear Aurora and Annamarja speaking Italian, and English when I couldn't keep up. After we'd been at the table for an hour, Pietro walked in. "Aha! Eating at three in the afternoon, while the neighbors, even my asshole neighbor, who has been here a hundred years, yet never gets his work done on time, is picking olives. But here we sit, doing nothing."

Maybe I was too hasty—maybe I should have given German food more time to grow on me.

Pietro had returned to his former self, no longer playing the part of the perfect host. No wonder Aurora looked tired.

I told Pietro about *Capra Casa*, of choosing to freeze rather than breathe the petrol fumes of the portable heater. But only the story of the testosterone-deficient rooster with half a "cock-a-doodle-doo" brought a smile to his face. "And what did Valter feed you?" Pietro asked as his smile turned to a mischievous grin.

"Potatoes and some vegetable Valter told me was good for my digestion."

"That had to be celery. Was it bitter?"

"Yeah, bitter and tasteless at the same time. It was not *Tuscanissimo*."

"So James, you came back. In only one day you got tired of German food."

I gave Pietro an Italian shrug and said, "*Ma*," an all-purpose utterance that conveys whatever the situation calls for, depending on what your hands and face are saying.

"I told you so. Good thing it rained yesterday. You did not miss so much work." Pietro sent an Italian shrug back at me.

Pietro le spiritoso.

In one day I had also grown to miss Pietro's lively wit. I should have found a way to tell him.

The stonework in Ristonchia was fascinating, some of it dating back to the time of Jesus, Valter told me with pride. His house had a sense of veneration that was undeniable. He was pleased to be able to tell the history of his home. The thick granite steps cupped with the wear of repeated footsteps over the centuries backed up Valter's stories. The flower boxes spoke of the villagers' pride of place and their connection to the land. Flower boxes are found everywhere in Tuscany. Each time I saw one I thought again of Aurora's use of the word, connubial—God and man getting together to create beauty. Not everything in Ristonchia was ancient, but it all had the look of belonging even if it was built in 1964. I loved the touch of the drinking cup waiting patiently for the next thirsty soul to come along.

Chapter Seven

Lord, make me an instrument of your peace,
Where there is hatred, let me sow love;
Where there is injury, pardon;
Where there is error, truth;
Where there is doubt, faith;
Where there is despair, hope;
Where there is darkness, light;
Where there is sadness, joy.
O Divine Master,
Grant that I may not seek
to be consoled as to console,
to be understood as to understand,
to be loved as to love.
For it is in Giving that we Receive
It is in Pardoning that we are Pardoned,
And it is in Dying that we are Born to Eternal Life.

SAINT FRANCIS OF ASSISI

Saint Francis himself could hardly have been more suited to the site, to the monastery, and to the message of loving compassion for all of creation. Only the addition of a few chickadees fluttering about this humble monk's shoulders could have made the scene more complete.

In the Footsteps of Saint Francis

The next day started off misty and beautiful—not a good morning for picking olives, but a good day for recharging the soul. Aurora joined me for Earl Grey tea, toast, and plum jam. Our words flowed with the pace of a wet morning. The sun had to do its work before we could do ours. After we talked about Valter and his farm, and Annamarja and her dreams, and Pietro and his plans, she told me she had not slept well, that she had awakened even before the sun, thinking about all the olives she had on her trees and all the olives she didn't have in her shed, and that she wanted me to stay another week.

Each farmer I had contacted on Valter's list had all the help he needed. Every family sounded interesting—either because of the setting of the farm, the nearness to a village, the animals they kept, or the traditions they maintained—but I was thankful none of them needed me. I happily committed to another week. I would have committed to two weeks if Aurora had asked.

By the time the sun and the breezes had finished their work only Annamarja and I were around to go to the olive grove. Pietro was sick, and Aurora had driven to Camucia for medicine. Annamarja and I were talking about other farms we had known. Sunlight was streaming through the trees and we were treating the olives well. Annamarja was teaching me *italiano*—speaking even slower than usual to make it easier for me. We were picking *vicino, vicino,* closely together in the same tree.

Annamarja and I were choosing our branches carefully; some of the olives were still moist from the morning mist. Pietro would have been annoyed that we weren't picking faster, but the olives would not let us. We had to find branches that had received the first rays of sun. In an hour or so, they would all be dry, but not now.

"James, I must tell you. You wasted your money on Rosetta Stone. The best way to learn to speak Italian is to watch television. Every night I watched *Who Wants to Be a Millionaire Italian Style.* You hear the question. You see the question. We watch tonight."

"How long did it take you?" I asked.

"About three months," she said. "*Me la cavo*—good enough I get by."

Annamarja did not go off for a smoke or to pick *porcini* mushrooms. She was telling me of her traditions. "You know James, in Slovenia, we have a saying, all the work you do on Sunday will be undone on Monday."

I switched to English so I could tell her of things in America. "We have a similar saying. My father always said that if we worked on Sunday, we would have breakdowns. Something would cause us to lose more time than we gained. So we might as well take it easy on Sunday."

Annamarja said, "Yah, that is true."

"The only time I ever saw him break that rule was during wheat harvest. He always allowed the custom combiners to cut wheat on Sunday."

"Did they have, what you call it—break ... downs?" Annamarja asked.

"Always, always. Yet always they worked on Sundays," I said. "When I was real young I wondered why Dad didn't tell the harvesters about working on Sunday. When I got older I just figured Dad thought it was none of his business whether they worked on Sunday."

"If his land, then his business." Annamarja's world was missing most shades of gray. No wonder she and Pietro clashed.

"Do Aurora and Pietro go to church?" I asked.

"Pietro, never. Aurora, almost never." Annamarja grabbed the short ladder, propped it against a low branch, and climbed into the tree. She quit talking. My mind stayed on Aurora, on what we had been talking about last night.

"My mother had no use for the church," Aurora said. "She was a Catholic only when she thought she could use one of their rules to condemn someone. And that someone? Usually me. We did not get along."

"Did you get along with your dad?" I asked. Her face brightened the moment she heard the word, *babbo.*

"Oh yes, I adored my dad. He was wonderful to me." Aurora smiled at the memory. She reached for the wine bottle, filled my glass, then poured more for herself. I returned her smile. I was expecting her to tell me more about her father.

"Are you a Christian, James?"

"Yes, yes I am," I said.

Aurora prodded. "Are you Roman Catholic?"

"No, I'm not. I love the traditions, I love the music, I very much liked Pope John Paul II, but I'm not Roman Catholic."

"What sort of a Christian are you?" Her bluntness caught me off guard. While I was trying to figure out how to answer the question, she jumped back in: "Are you like George *Booosh*? Are you like him?"

I sensed trouble. Aurora was putting politics and religion together. *I follow the radical Jesus.* I tried it out for a nanosecond, and decided against it. It turned out to be a good decision. In that moment, Aurora contorted her face into a frown and added, "I don't like his Christianity, I don't like George *Booosh's* Christianity."

For all I knew, my Christianity might look to Aurora like President Bush's Christianity. What can anyone know of another person's relationship with God, or with Christ, or what another person thinks of yours? I suspected she knew more about George Bush's politics than about his faith in that radical God/Man Jesus, and possibly confused the two. But in any case, I was afraid of a deep theological discussion or a venture into politics. I enjoyed being with Aurora too much to risk offending her. I shouldn't have been such a coward, but I decided not to tell her how weak, almost nonexistent my faith once was and how strong it is now—how a car crash changed everything.

Whether from cowardice or a genuine interest in Aurora, I couldn't say, but I wanted to understand the pain Aurora went through as a child. Loving her father, and hating her mother. So I said, "I am simply a Christian, a follower of Jesus the Christ." Though even as I was saying it, I knew that only those whose world has been transformed by the life-changing reality of the Messiah, would understand the inclusion of *the* before the title of "Christ." Thirty years ago I would not have understood such an answer.

Referring to myself by the naked name of *Christian*, without the covering garment of a denomination, did not satisfy Aurora's curiosity, or increase her understanding, but she allowed me to steer the conversation back to her. She told me her father became a devout believer when he was twenty-six, but that her mother never did in the eighty-nine years of her life. As she was saying the words *devout believer* I wondered whether she was thinking of her dad as a devout believer of Jesus or of the Roman Catholic Church, but I didn't ask. Such questions require a commitment to precise language and religious thought that I was not prepared to wrestle with—nor did I, at the moment, think Aurora was either.

"She was as selfish the day she died as the day she was born." Aurora was echoing a story that Pietro had told about his grandmother during the many hours we spent at the table following *la Tuscanissimo cena*.

"James," Pietro began, "I must tell you about my mother's mother. But first I must ask you if you have ever been to a funeral." He paused and looked into my eyes.

I nodded my head. "Yes, I've been to a few," I said guardedly, wondering how Pietro was going to get me this time.

"Then think back. Did you ever hear anyone, during any of those funerals, say anything bad about the person? Even if the departed was the worst scoundrel in town, something good will be said about him." Pietro looked to me for assent: "*Correto?*"

I nodded again, this time more emphatically: "*Essattamente.*"

"James, you would not believe. At the funeral of my grandmother, there was not one person who had anything good to say about her—not in her eulogy, not at the funeral, not at the graveside. Nothing good." I looked at Aurora. She wasn't protesting the picture Pietro was painting of her mother as the worst of the worst, despised by everyone.

"So James, if you should ever hear anyone say Aurora is like her mom, you will know this person is just flattering my mother." Pietro turned from looking at me and looked toward his mother.

"Compared to my mother—my grandmother was a saint."

A delayed downbeat and a Rodney Dangerfield rim shot later, the mischievous jab registered. I smiled despite the joke's cruelty. I was embarrassed, but surprisingly, Aurora wasn't protesting. She was thinking instead of her mother.

"My mother was beautiful. She was beautiful her whole life. But she was selfish her whole life. Even as she lay dying she was like a child, thinking about how she looked. I don't think she even noticed we were there; she only wanted to know if someone could bring her a mirror," Aurora confided, as though she agreed with the portrait Pietro had painted of her mother.

"Your dad was a devout believer all those years, but your mother not at all?" I asked.

"I don't think so. She never believed in anyone but herself." Aurora sighed, stood up, and reached for my plate. I handed it to her. The weight of the memory registered on Aurora's face. And her face weighed on my heart. Most of Aurora's stories, no matter where they started, came back around to her hatred of her mother. But when it came to faith, Aurora seemed closer to her mother's lack of belief than to her father's certainty. Aurora placed the last of the plates on the stack in front of her. She paused and then asked with no energy, "How can you believe?" The emphasis was on the word *can*, not *you*. She picked up the plates and turned toward the kitchen. She wasn't wondering how *I* could believe, she was wondering how *anyone* could believe.

She returned to the table, but I didn't offer an answer. I left the question hanging over us. I didn't think the question could be answered in a way that would convince her. My answer, the only answer I knew to give, the only answer she might pay attention to, was to live my life as though I believed. People have reasons for faith, but people rarely reason their way to faith.

Faith is a deep and great mystery. To tell her that I have faith in Jesus would not convince her that she too must have faith, that she must believe. She also may not understand the distinction I make between faith in Jesus and faith in the Church. As Aurora put it, "My mother had no use for the Church."

We were talking about an unseen world, a world not entered by reason, the very quality for which Aurora praised Buddhists. She had told me a few days earlier of her younger days, of a retreat she had attended with forty or fifty people to learn how to meditate. She came away from the experience preferring Buddhism because, as she said, "It is more rational than *our* religion," which made me think that Aurora viewed Roman Catholicism as a state religion one is born into. At that time she had not yet asked if I was a Christian, so "our" must have referred to Italians.

If she did believe that, she was missing, it seemed to me, the one great truth that makes Christianity different from every other approach to God. One is not born a Christian. One becomes a Christian only by accepting the very *unreasonable* claim of Jesus—that He is a unique emissary from another world with the capability to forgive sin—the only one with such power. His is not a message of being good, but of recognizing our sinfulness and the need for forgiveness.

To admit such a need is not an easy thing to do, especially for the *good* person. It took a car crash that almost killed me to get me to do it. I couldn't expect a few words from me to change Aurora's mind. For the good, educated, successful person, such an admission is almost impossible.

Aurora continued, "I do not like certainty. I like the search."

I was glad I had just listened. I had been thinking about what she doesn't like—the certainty of Christ—certainty that is impossible to see without the kind of help Peter received two thousand years ago when the Holy Spirit made it possible for him to recognize who Jesus is.

"I agree. The search is the thing. Without the search you will not find faith," I said, but felt like a hypocrite because I wasn't searching when I was given the conviction that Jesus transcends religion. Instead of telling her of my journey, I said, "I have three favorite words regarding faith: *enthusiasm, mystery,* and *paradox.*"

"Good words, yes," agreed Aurora.

I don't know whether it was working together in the olive groves, or the slow pace of the meals, or the wine we drank, but we often would not get up from the table for hours, even though we had a TV set within a few feet of us. It was as though we had jumped back into a world before television when people talked and told stories, and so on this night I told Aurora about my favorite words.

"A few years ago, I happened to look up the word *enthusiasm* and I noticed that *theos,* which is *God* in Greek, is the heart of the word *enthusiasm.* That really struck a chord with me."

"Yes, it is similar in Italian, *Dio,*" noted Aurora, ever the professor.

"I've always been very enthusiastic, very passionate, blessed with more energy than my wife knows what to do with. I can't account for it—I just have it. Seeing the word *God* in the middle of *enthusiasm* said to me that at one time, when the word was first being used, everyone must have recognized that our passions were a gift from God. *"Inspired-by-God-isms,"* I said.

Aurora rocked her head ever so slightly up and down as though she was pondering the possible implications. I continued, "*Mystery* and *paradox* I like because much of what Jesus says is inexplicable, counter-intuitive, beyond the reach of reason. Jesus sees two worlds, and we see only one. But He points toward the other, hence the *mystery* and *paradox,* and His enigmatic sayings like, *The first shall be last and the last shall be first* and *You must lose your life to gain it.*"

I knew I was treading dangerous waters mentioning Jesus to Aurora. Most people are comfortable talking about God, but not Jesus. He's confrontational, not inclusive enough, many feel, even though His message excludes no one. God seems generic. Jesus does not. Jesus calls for a response. He offers a gift, but an ultimatum is attached. Jesus speaks as one who has ultimate authority, and that scares people.

"I do not think so much. I have only one credo. *Do no harm to anyone,*" Aurora said.

"I like that," I said.

"I learned it at a very young age. I was only four. The pain of watching my mother and father fight taught me that," Aurora sighed. "I have tried to live my life to harm no one, but I do not know if I have succeeded. Look what I have done to my son."

"Our best intentions don't always turn out as we had hoped," I said while thinking that on another day, maybe Aurora and I could talk more about Jesus. But immediately I remembered what Jesus said about not coming to bring peace, but to bring division: "Do you think I came to smooth things over and make everything nice? Not so. I've come to disrupt and confront! From now on, when you find five in a house, it will be three against two, and two against three; father against son, and son against father." I began to feel less like a wise diplomat and more like a sniveling coward as my mind replayed our conversation. Aurora had brought up a subject of great importance and I had found only enough courage to tell her about my three favorite words.

"James, *lei mi mano l'coltello.*" Annamarja jerked me out of my thoughts with no warning, no clearing of her throat. I turned toward her voice. She was on a ladder in the tree next to me and wanted me to hand her the pruning saw, which for some reason is called a knife in Italian. I looked, but didn't see it. "*L'coltello dietro tuo cassetti,*" Annamarja told me and pointed, just in case the Italian didn't register, toward the tree where we had left our *cassetti* when we began picking three hours before.

As I reached down to pick it up, I heard the strong voice of Aurora far below us, near the house, "James and Ann-naaa Maa-reee-aaa—*pranzo.*" When Aurora called us, she always drew out the sound of Annamarja's name and changed the rhythm so that her invitation to lunch sounded like the words of a lovely Italian song.

"*Un momento,*" I shouted and turned to yell up the hill to Annamarja, but she had already climbed down the ladder and was emptying her basket into the *cassetta* that we would carry together to the shed. She had told me of another Slovenian saying that she was forever demonstrating,

"Never walk anywhere on a farm without carrying something." We did not walk to lunch empty-handed on that day or any other.

While we were eating the *tortellini* Aurora prepared for Annamarja and me, Pietro walked into the kitchen, lifted the lid on the saucepan, took a deep breath, then complained "the olives are not amassing quickly enough in the storage shed." He then ticked off the days: "Tuesday, Wednesday, Thursday, Friday. What do we have to show for all those days?" he asked.

Apparently he had forgotten that on Tuesday we went to the *frantoio*. Wednesday I was at Valter's, and it rained beginning at noon. Thursday we picked after I returned. And mist delayed our start this morning—Annamarja and I were able to fill only one *cassetta* and a part of another. "Tomorrow," I said, "Weather Underground is forecasting a good day for picking."

"Sounds subversive," said Pietro as he headed back to bed, coughing.

Pietro was showing signs of fretting for fretting's sake. He was trying to work against what nature was giving us. "Urgency is not present when heat is not present," Aurora said just loud enough to be heard only by me and Annamarja.

"Da Big Boss is always in a hurry," Annamarja said in a voice loud enough to be heard by Pietro even though he had disappeared up the stairs. We could still hear him coughing.

"When it turns hot we will pick the olives. The olives are fine right where they are on the trees until then," Aurora told us and maybe herself as well. She may have been thinking about worrying too, but Pietro reminded her of the ugliness of worry.

Pietro wasn't living in the moment; instead he was letting his god of abstractions dictate to him what should be happening. Rain was delaying us. Give thanks for the rain and enjoy it. We could be in a drought. Short-sighted thought is the danger that comes when you are not willing to trust grace—not willing to let the game come to you and you to it.

Aurora, the steward, was looking at the whole picture. She was thinking of the olives, the weather, and the need to work with what came our way. Aurora was trusting. Pietro was whining. Worries like Pietro's lead to thoughts of spending money for mechanical shakers so that olives could be picked faster when the sun shines. Seeking a mechanical advantage is legitimate, but short-sighted if you forget that with mechanization comes a torrent of extra costs, costs that have a way of always escalating. They just keep coming once you determine you are going to try to overpower nature. Aurora chose to work with nature. No wonder I loved being on her farm—the philosophical battle between the factory farmer and the thankful steward was playing out before my eyes.

Friday afternoon we picked *piano, piano, piano*—slowly, slowly, slowly. But we enjoyed, enjoyed, enjoyed. Aurora had joined us. We picked less than two *cassetti*. We worked at most four hours. The mood was relaxed. While I was climbing the ladder into an overgrown tree to cut one of the branches shooting straight up, I involuntarily let out a short, but audible toot. Aurora tried to hold back, but the harder she tried not to laugh, the harder she laughed. Before long she was doubled over. Her giggles reminded me of my mom in her later years when she would get to laughing at her own elephant jokes: "Why did the elephant wear pink shoes?"

Mom would start laughing even before she blurted out, "Because her polka-dot shoes were dirty." Aurora was convulsing just like my mom, bent over, holding her tummy. Between gulps for air, she began telling me about a prim and proper English *wwoofer* who had tried to put on airs. But one day, climbing in the branches, doing much as I was doing, she let go of a big one. At first she tried to pretend it had not been a fart, but with that *inganno piccolo*—that bit of deception—Aurora began laughing so hard that the principled and proper lady saw the humor of her gaffe and began laughing too, so hard that she lost her balance and fell off the ladder, onto the soft, dug-up dirt of the *cinghiale's* snout, where she lay laughing hysterically. The memory of her flailing about on her back was too much for Aurora. Before long her laughter had turned to tears.

We shared no moments like these at Valter's. For starters, no one would have been able to hear a fart. And smelling a fart is not nearly so funny as hearing a fart. You can't tell a story when the noise from the mechanical hands are shaking up your brain as much as the olives. To my mind the sight of Aurora laughing had a value that must be considered when choosing how to manage a farm.

Valter, had I told him of my love for stories, might have countered that Aurora does not have to make her living from farming. And I would have said to Valter that he was not making his living from farming either—only ten percent of it, he had said—and that percentage might be higher if he had fewer expenses. Aurora is not earning her living from farming, only some of it, but she is living well. Her decision to turn her back on the consumer society is a big part of thankful stewardship—living well is the best revenge. A lot of people could afford Aurora's approach to farming if they were willing to re-evaluate their life—to use a different yardstick to measure it.

"Pietro will be horrified with our production. He will say, NO FOOD," mocked Aurora as we carried our two *cassetti* and good memories to the storage shed. But like every other night, we ate, and we ate well. Aurora and I didn't get up from the table for five hours. Just before midnight Annamarja joined us. She had been in the kitchen making preserves while Aurora and I talked. Annamarja told me of her dream to have a farm modeled on the practices of Louis Bromfield's Malabar Farm in Pleasant Valley, Ohio. She was thrilled to discover that I knew of Louis Bromfield—that I had read his books, and that even though he has been dead over fifty years, it was still possible to visit his farm.

I told her that Pleasant Valley was only a few hundred miles from my own Rock Ridge Farm and that we must go visit it when she comes to America. Annamarja was dreaming that night and was excited that Aurora may help her realize her dream, a dream for which she was prepared to fight. Throughout the evening while Aurora and I talked, Annamarja and Pietro butted heads, discussing Fascism, Communism, and Nazism, as well as farming, in antagonistic volleys as Pietro walked in and out of the room. He would make a point, withdraw, and then lob another attack into the kitchen where Annamarja was pinned down making jam. The battle line was Pietro's opposition to allowing Annamarja to live on Aurora's land.

"Do not worry, Annamarja. Pietro does not understand people. He does not understand farming, cooperation, or giving. He does not even understand *wwoofing*," Aurora told Annamarja when she brought some jam for us to sample.

"Why you making jam, Annamarja?" I asked in the best Italian I could muster.

"To prove to Pietro I can make money," Annamarja said with a touch of defiance. "Here, try it. You will like it."

I spread a spoonful on a piece of bread and took a bite. "Ah, very good," I said. "You will make money. People will buy this."

"I think you are right. But James, I will not stay here if Da Big Boss does not leave," Annamarja said to me, in a whisper, so that neither Aurora or Pietro heard her as she put the lid on the jar. "Put in your backpack, James. It is yours." Annamarja returned to the kitchen and began washing the big pan she had used to boil the jam. Pietro had apparently grown tired of arguing with Annamarja—he walked past her, saying nothing, and joined us. He was no longer coughing and seemed to be feeling much better. He sat in his usual chair, the one facing the icon of Mary and the Christ child.

"You know *Life Is Beautiful*, James?" he asked.

"Yes, yes, I do Pietro, I know that *life is beautiful*," I said with pointed emphasis, even though I knew he was referring to Benigni's movie, because he had, for the past three hours, been making life anything but beautiful for Annamarja.

"No, I mean the movie *Life Is Beautiful*. Roberto Benigni, the star and director, is Tuscan, born not far from here in Castiglion Fiorentino. You biked through there on the way to Valter's. Arezzo, where the movie takes place, is just north of there. Benigni, Dante, Michelangelo, all Tuscans," Pietro told me. "And Saint Francis, he is almost Tuscan."

"Why do you say Saint Francis is almost Tuscan?" I asked.

"We would like to claim him, but he was born about thirty kilometers away, in Assisi, in Umbria, but that is as close as Florence, and Firenze is, of course, in Tuscany. Saint Francis spent much time in Cortona. He may have even walked across this farm, when he and his followers were building Le Celle. Who can say that he did not?"

"Le Celle? What is Le Celle?" I asked.

"Oh, James, before you leave our farm, you must visit Le Celle. There is not a more spiritual place in all of Tuscany. You must go. You cannot leave Tuscany without visiting Le Celle. You know of Saint Francis of Assisi?"

"Yes, yes, I do. I know some of his story. *Lord make me an instrument of your peace...*" I trailed off.

"Then you must go and learn more. You will not be sorry. The next time you wake up and find dew on the olives, you must walk to Le Celle. Just follow the road above the farm until you see a splotch of red paint on a tree. Follow that trail of paint and you will be walking in the footsteps of Saint Francis," Pietro assured me.

For this suggestion alone, I was convinced I would never forget Pietro—*Pietro l'enigma.* Even if I, like Annamarja, stayed a year with Aurora, I would not understand Pietro. I was coming to that realization even before I visited Le Celle—before I learned so much about Saint Francis, and maybe by extension, a little about Pietro. Pietro was harsh one moment, gentle and thoughtful the next. I went to sleep that night praying that one day soon I'd wake up to find dew again on the olives.

At the end of Federico Fellini's dream-like masterpiece *La Dolce Vita*, an angel, represented by a pure young girl, beckons to the protagonist, Marcello. She is offering him the grace of a good life—1. The innocent child offers to show him how to begin truly living. He considers her a moment, before turning and walking back to his indolent and self-destructive ways. We, as a society, and each of us individually, are each day, each moment, faced with that same offer of grace. Artists like Fellini see that. Most of the rest of us do not.

The beckoning angel represents nature, natural forces, and God's grace, *grazia di Dio,* that will show us how to live, how to take care of ourselves and creation, if we will only accept the invitation and be *co-creators* of that sweet life. At the end of the movie the young girl waves as Marcello walks away. She does not scorn him, she just continues innocently waving. The lingering gesture tells us that she will still be there if Marcello changes his mind. Fellini, in that one scene, perfectly encapsulates the message of the grace of Jesus. His limitless love ever beckoning us.

But Marcello doesn't see the girl. He can't see her. She is part of a world that he refuses to think about—a world that takes more than eyes to see—a realm accessible only by a faculty that he considers in his hubris to be a weakness. He continues walking up the beach, away from the young girl, and disappears in the distance.

The girl then turns slowly toward the camera and looks at us and offers to us the same grace if we will only accept it. She continuously turns to us and says, *will you accept the gifts I have been giving you and am giving you, or will you in your pride and your insistence on living only in the seen world, try to do it your way? Your choice. I offer you the good life lived by trusting grace or the greedy life that you fashion by yourself.*

Saint Francis is the patron saint of the choice before us. He was born into a family of wealth and influence in Assisi. But he wanted more. He saw more. The immaterial world became real to young Francesco. In a dream, he received the message that he was to rebuild God's church. He renounced his possessions and those of his family, and devoted himself first to rebuilding a physical church. Then, having completed that task, he devoted himself to rebuilding the church of believers.

That this part of the world should give birth to Saint Francis now seems natural. This humble man became an icon of stewardship, of caring for all of God's creation. He was the perfect embodiment of the words of Jesus—that we should care for the *least of these.* These few words inspired Saint Francis to seek to meet the needs of everyone he met.

But I was surprised that it was Pietro, the irascible Pietro, who insisted that I must hike to Le Celle, just as Saint Francis began doing so many years ago, before the monastery existed. I didn't have to wait long for dew. The very next morning the valley was layered with fog, so I followed Pietro's advice and hiked up the terraces and hacked through the brush until I found a track climbing higher up the mountain.

I followed it for a couple of kilometers before finding my first splotch of red paint on a tree that led me off the road and onto a well-worn foot path. I followed it through the woods for two or three kilometers, moving from one red splotch to another, until I came upon a stone wall materializing out of the deep forest. I followed the curved wall as it grew into a massive structure fashioned of stone towering above me. The effect was stunning, rising as it did with no warning in the middle of the woods. Neither the beauty of the site, nor the architecture was I prepared for. Pietro had told me it was special, but this was Machu Picchu-like in its spiritual splendor, of its marriage of spectacular site and man's command of stone construction, and in the incomprehensibility of its being in such a remote site, with no warning in the dense woods that it was coming.

As I followed the trail to Le Celle, a sense of discovery carried me back to the early thirteenth century and the time of Saint Francis. I saw nothing along the trail that spoke of my century. Although not nearly as strenuous or time consuming, the feeling was similar to the thrill of arriving at Machu Picchu in Peru, if you hike for three days over fourteen-thousand-foot passes between twenty-thousand-foot mountain peaks to get to the site, just as the Incans did five hundred years ago, and do not arrive by train or bus. Technology often robs us of an intimate relationship with God and creation. The feeling of being in Machu Picchu at sunrise, at that mystical moment, was possible only because our film crew, with the help of porters, hiked to that hidden mountaintop city rather than choosing to arrive from below through what is now the front gate, where hordes of tourists arrive each morning, four hours after the sun first bathes the sacred city in glorious light. We had no choice but to hike to Machu Picchu, because we wanted to film the rays of the sun striking Intihuatana, the Hitching Post of the Sun, at dawn on the shortest day of the year.

The comparison turned out to be similar for Le Celle—not because of a desire to catch a mystical once-a-year moment, but just because Pietro insisted that such a place as Le Celle can be truly experienced only by hiking to it. And he was right. A road will carry you from Cortona to Le Celle, but I was glad that Pietro insisted that I hike on the ancient trail.

"*Buon giornata,*" the gentle monk said to me with a wave and a soft smile. I had not before heard the expression. But then I had never before been talking to a monk like this. The valediction was dignified, warm, and respectful. He was wrapped in an unadorned piece of brown cloth, a fold of it covering his head. I was reminded of the biblical term, *sackcloth*. He was old. He was stooped. But above all he was serene. We had been talking about the beautiful garden on the terrace below us. I had asked, in Italian, if it took a lot of work to keep it so beautiful. With a wave of his hand, he said, "No. Very little for me. God does most of the work." To emphasize his point he pointed skyward to God and the clouds. "*Piove*," he concluded.

"Ah, yes, rain. Life-giving rain," I said.

He was carrying two white plastic buckets, each containing a few pounds of *grano* for his chickens. His features were chiseled into sharp points; Hollywood could not have cast a more fitting monk. Saint Francis himself could hardly have been more suited to the site, to the monastery, and to the message of loving compassion for all of creation. Only the addition of a few chickadees fluttering about this humble monk's shoulders could have made the scene more complete.

He shuffled off and pulled on a string, releasing a handle that allowed the door to the chicken coop to open. The latch was an ingenious piece of engineering the likes of which I had never seen before—a three-foot length of rope threaded through a foot-long pipe. The weight of the pipe kept the door open while the monk went about his chores. And when he had finished, that same pipe became the lock that ensured that a fox or other bandit would not be able to harm the monastery's chickens. The wood upon which the pipe rested was carved in a deep, graceful arc of sufficient depth that it told a story of a locking mechanism that had been in use for centuries.

A sense of veneration hung in the air like the mist from the cascading water that flowed through the granite canyon over which *le celle*, the cells, had been built where monks lived, and had been living since the days of Saint Francis more than seven centuries ago. Being in this place, on this softly lit morning, with this benevolent monk who made me feel his peace with God and this world, was even more spiritual, more memorable than Pietro had promised it would be.

I felt suspended in a timeless adventure. This meek monk walking across the bridge spanning the waterway appeared to me a contemporary of Saint Francis in every sense of the word until my eyes landed again upon the plastic pails in his hands. Those swinging white buckets pulled me back to the radical message that Saint Francis carries for us today—*that whatever you do for the least of these you do for me.* That message of Jesus will, most likely, be radical no matter in what age it is carried.

I recalled the radical reason I had come to Le Celle. The supposedly irreverent Pietro, the man Annamarja accused of hating religion and hating God, had told me I would not find a more spiritual place in all of Tuscany. Because of Pietro I had met a self-effacing soul who was this morning clothed as a monk—and in the next life, who knows. This gave me great hope, not just for Pietro, but for all of us.

When I got back to Aurora's, Pietro asked me about my *una scampagnata,* my walk in the countryside, *la campagna.* To help him understand how appreciative I was, I began by telling him of Machu Picchu, and how much the sublimity of Le Celle reminded me of that hidden Incan city. As I told Pietro of feeling God's presence in settings like that, I glanced at his eyes and got the impression that despite his repudiation of the Church, Pietro already knew of feeling God's presence in Le Celle. Maybe Pietro was pulling everybody's leg. His argument may not be so much with God, as it is with religion—with man's sometimes misguided attempts to confine God—and not so much with God's offering that made His presence known to man.

The good news of Jesus, the Gospel, is embodied in the life of Saint Francis. He lived the life that Jesus offers everyone. "Come to me all you who are weary and heavy laden" or as Eugene Peterson's *The Message* renders the words of Jesus in Matthew, "Are you tired? Worn out? Burned out on religion? Come to me. Get away with me and you will recover your life. I'll show you how to take a real rest. Walk with me and work with me—watch how I do it. Learn the unforced rhythms of grace. I won't lay anything heavy or ill-fitting on you. Keep company with me and you'll learn to live freely and lightly."

"Learn the unforced rhythms of grace…" Grace is, I think, the central message of God through Jesus, the message of how we can live in this life if we will accept God's grace—his unmerited divine assistance. My walk in *la campagna* to a most sacred spot, at the urging of a person who supposedly hates the Church, is but another supreme example of "the unforced rhythms of grace so freely given."

That certainly seems to be the story of Francesco, the insolent, carousing young man who was born neither saint nor Christian. Francesco, by his own admission, was not a Christian and definitely not a saint. He was a bawdy womanizer and rabble-rouser—an indolent man who heard God's challenge and accepted it.

Months later, when I saw the movie *The Flowers of Saint Francis* by Italian filmmaker Roberto Rossellini, Pietro's gift of understanding came to mind. At the beginning of the film, one of the young men following Saint Francis confronts him: "Why does the world follow you? You are neither handsome, nor great, nor noble. Why, Francesco, does the world follow you?"

Francesco looks straight at him and answers, "Because God saw among sinners no one more vile than me, so that men would see that every virtue and good comes from Him. Glory be to God forever."

"And that's why I follow you too, Francesco," the questioning disciple responds.

Pietro told me that if I am serious about wanting to understand Italians, I must study and learn to appreciate Dante's *Divine Comedy*. Most Italians, Pietro told me, have not only read the *Inferno, Purgatory*, and *Paradiso*, but they also have many lines committed to memory. He proudly informed me that each summer Roberto Benigni presents *The Divine Comedy* from memory in live performances in *piazzas* throughout Tuscany.

Pietro then handed me a DVD of one of the performances. I suggested that we watch it. He said I had to learn Italian first.

Pietro the clue-giving enigmatic rock.

Pietro told me that I could not leave Tuscany until I had seen the monastery that Saint Francis founded. And so, on a foggy morning when there was too much dew on the olives, I began climbing the terraces above Aurora's house, looking for red paint on trees that would tell me I had found the trail. I wandered down the wrong path a couple of times but finally I knew I was headed toward Le Celle when I found myself walking through the forest next to a massive wall. The feeling of rounding that last bend and seeing the unexpected grandeur of the monastery reminded me of arriving at Machu Picchu in Peru after having trekked through the Andes.

The only thing that could have made Le Celle more memorable would have been a rainshower up valley that would have sent water cascading down the granite gorge over which the monastery was built seven hundred years ago. For almost an hour I wandered around the walkways and bridges and and saw no one. But I did see evidence of loving care—and an architectural integrity to the site. I wondered if this gorge and this monastery were the inspiration for Frank Lloyd Wright's Fallingwater House that I had drawn many times as a young architecture student. Mostly though, my thoughts were peaceful. I wondered what Saint Francis felt the first time he saw this beautiful spot and how long it took him to decide he was going to build a hermitage on this spectacular site.

The morning I visited Le Celle was among the most memorable I enjoyed in Italy. Even though Pietro had told me it was special, I had not expected to be overwhelmed. It reminded me of the morning I spent at Machu Picchu in Peru. I had walked to Machu Picchu and I walked to Le Celle and I had come through, what is today, the back entrance to both sites—the way of the pilgrim. I had seen no one that morning—it was just me and the birds, the chickadees, as it was in the days of Saint Francis. The monk was the first person I saw that day, in fact, he was the only person I saw that morning until I returned to Aurora's farm and told Pietro about the experience. In classic Pietro fashion he said, "What did I tell you James? Did I not tell you it was the most spiritual place in all of Tuscany?"

The prayer life at Le Celle was everywhere in evidence. This beautiful sign, which I translated as "Please enter in silence" I could not bring myself to obey. I felt my presence would be an intrusion. Whether I would have found anyone inside I do not know. I had seen no one since arriving at Le Celle. It was just me and the birds and the beauty of the morning in one of the most spectacular, yet peaceful settings I have ever seen.

Chapter Eight

Be joyful always, pray continually,
give thanks in all circumstances...
SAINT PAUL

Romita Ramblings

Aurora convinced me to take the train part of the way to my next farm. She wasn't comfortable with the idea of me biking one hundred twenty kilometers on a day when rain was forecast. Aurora assured me that Romita, which was near Lorenzo's farm, could not be more than thirty or forty kilometers from Florence.

We got to the station early, located the automatic ticket machine, and that's where we stayed. Inserting and reinserting coins. Reading and rereading the instructions flashing on the screen. Nothing worked. Every time we put money in, it popped right back out. We tried every coin I had in my pocket. Still no ticket. Aurora grabbed a handful of coins from her purse and began stuffing them one by one into the machine. She was still inserting coins when we heard the train pull into the station. I grabbed my bags.

"No, James," Aurora said, deeply serious, "You must have a ticket."

A warning from the guidebooks popped into my mind. It is a high crime in Italy to get on the train without getting your ticket time-stamped just before departure. And being a stupid tourist is no defense. The guidebooks made no mention of what would happen if you tried to board without a ticket. Apparently, no one has ever been fool enough to try that in Italy.

I looked for another machine but found none, except for the time-stamper. I couldn't believe the train wasn't putting me out of my misery by pulling out of the station. I was getting desperate. I paused, took a long, deep breath, grabbed a fresh coin, and reread the instructions for the umpteenth time. Then I did something I should have done ten minutes earlier. I prayed.

The funny thing is, I can't remember what I prayed. *Dear God, please make this machine work...*or did I pray, *Your choice, Lord, am I supposed stay and help Aurora...*or did I pray simply, *Your will be done, Lord.* I know it wasn't a long prayer; Aurora and I were both close to panic, having passed frustration a long time ago.

Whether Aurora thought to pray, I don't know. I also don't know if we did anything differently. I know I read the instructions one more time before inserting the coin. This time the machine did what we thought we wanted it to do. It kicked out a ticket. I grabbed it, validated it, and reached for my duffel bag. But it was gone.

I looked around and saw that Aurora was gone too—my fifty-pound bag weaving wildly behind her. Despite being sick with congestion in her lungs, she was running with my bag, and on her short legs, surprisingly fast. I yelled at her to leave it. Whether she heard me over the noise of the plastic roller wheels on concrete, I don't know. She disappeared down a corridor with my duffel bag skidding cartoon-like around the corner.

Please let the train be on the near track I prayed, but it wasn't. Aurora was halfway down the flight of stairs leading to the tunnel by the time I caught sight of her. I yelled again, "Please, Aurora, leave it for me." She was shuffling down the steps with the suitcase cradled in her arms, like she was carrying an overweight grandchild. Her shoulders were rising and falling with each gasp for air. I feared she was going to have a heart attack. She got to the bottom of the stairs, set the bag down, and began dragging it again. She disappeared from sight. When I got to the bottom of the stairs, I looked down the tunnel expecting to see Aurora, but she had already disappeared up the stairs. I was struck by how weird and lonely my duffel bag looked sprawled at an odd angle two steps up from the bottom of the stairs, as though it had grown weary of being carried, and refused to go any farther.

By the time I got to it, Aurora was almost at the top of the stairs— almost back to track level—yelling back over her shoulder.

"Don't worry, James, I will hold the train." She bounded over the top step and disappeared again.

I reached down to pick up the bag with my free hand. A beautiful young girl, a woman in her twenties, flashed by me. She halted in mid-stride and backed down the steps toward the bag. "*Scusie,* may I help you?" she said as she reached for one handle and motioned for me to take the other one.

I was shocked. Had I become so old that I looked frail and overwhelmed? It had never occurred to me that a girl would offer to help me. By one thoughtful act, this young woman shattered my self-esteem, turning me into an old man with a few kind words.

I refused her gracious gesture much too quickly, and to make things more embarrassing, I refused the offer in English. I should have at least said *No, grazie* if I couldn't find the grace to accept her kindness: *Molto gentile da parte sua.*

The hike to the top of the stairs would certainly have been easier, and more interesting—learning a little of her story, maybe even talking with her during the ride to Firenze. She may have wanted to practice her English, and I certainly could have used the work on my Italian. I felt foolish on every level. She was gorgeous—*la belladonna*—the kind of beauty Italy is famous for—the kind I had been smitten by at eleven years of age.

That's how she appeared to me. How did I appear to her? Had I crossed that dreaded barrier to tottering old age? I didn't feel that way. I was wearing a fully stuffed backpack, reaching for an even heavier duffel with one hand, and had a huge overweight Samsonite in the other. I felt strong.

But still I feared I might have to start running up the stairs carrying my load of over one hundred twenty-five pounds. However, no whistles blew during the long trip back up to ground level. I kept replaying in my mind the image of the girl bending down to offer to help me. I knew I was making too much of it, but better to think of her than my heart rate. It was beating like I was in a bunch sprint straining for the finish line. I got to the top of the stairs and stopped to check my recovery rate like I do at the end of a bike race, to see if my heart rate will drop fifty beats per minute in the next sixty seconds. I looked up and saw Aurora "holding" the train, and forgot all about my heart. I rearranged my bags into a caravan and wheeled them one-handed the final fifty meters to where Aurora was frantically waiting, half on the train, half off. Neither she nor I need have worried. The train was in the station a full five minutes after I boarded, apparently waiting for the posted departure time.

Aurora and I had time to talk—time for her to thank me for picking olives and building walls and time for me to thank her for the good times, the good food. "You must stop, James. You say more and I will begin not to believe you. Pietro makes everything difficult. I don't know what I will do. How you can say you had a good time? Pietro is impossible."

I wanted to reassure Aurora, and thank her, so I tried once again to tell her I had enjoyed myself, but she said, "James, I cannot believe you.

Stop. You are just trying to be nice. I don't know what I will do with Pietro. He will drive everyone away."

"I will come and help you again, Aurora," I said and felt my throat tighten. I didn't want to be going. But she needed the loft. A friend was arriving later that day who wanted to help her pick olives. Annamarja had offered to give up her room, but it seemed like a good time for me to go. Aurora had given me as a gift the basket she had handed to me on my first day.

"So you will remember the good times," she told me.

"I will, and I'll be back," I told her, but her eyes didn't light up. She looked tired, even defeated.

"Who knows what will happen to me. I am an old woman," Aurora sighed. She didn't say, "Oh, *Baa booo.*" I wished she had. I'd grown to love the sound of her voice when she sighed those words.

"Maybe you will write that book. *Arrivederci*, Aurora. *Ciao.*"

She smiled and rocked her head slowly back and forth. "*Ciao*, James. Be careful."

As I watched her walk away, I noticed her shoulders were sagging. I wished I had called her Dawn instead. Her father named her Aurora, because she was born not long after Mussolini was executed. Fascism was collapsing, and the war was ending. He hoped a new day was coming, a new light for Italy—the dawning of good things.

But for Aurora her name meant humiliation. She hated it when she was a child. Kids laughed when they heard her name. None of her friends were called Aurora. She didn't even know anyone named Aurora. But she especially hated it because she couldn't pronounce the letter *r*. Eventually, she learned to pronounce it, but for a long time, her name was one of the scars of her childhood. Only in adulthood did she come to appreciate the benefits of having a unique name.

If I had called out her name in English, she might have heard it as a word rather than a name. She would have thought of her father's hopes for a new day, and his hopes for her. She might have realized that she too was coming to a new day. And instead of worrying about what would happen because of Pietro, she might have decided to embrace the grace that would accompany the dawning of her new life.

As the train pulled from the station, I looked at the rounded hills and realized that the day had just dawned as well—another gray day that would further depress Aurora. She felt that each day it rained meant more sniping. Pietro's mistreatment of his mother made me uncomfortable, but I found it impossible not to like him. Aurora thought I was leaving because of Pietro, but I was just trusting grace. *Io fiducia grazia.* It felt right that I should go.

It also felt right to travel by train. No rain yet, but the skies were threatening. The countryside was beautiful—lots of fields and pastures dotted with sheep and goats on rolling hills, and plenty of tunnels. The bike ride would have been slow, and most likely wet. And as an added bonus for riding the train, I'd get to see Florence.

I didn't doubt that I should go, but still I was feeling the pain of leaving. Life had grown into a comfortable routine at Aurora's. I never knew what to expect from Pietro, but I had begun to cherish the rhythms of the day, especially the beginnings and the endings—reading, eating, talking, and just absorbing the light—that mystical orange life-giving light that played upon the hills. I fell asleep hoping that the light would be just as beautiful at Lorenzo's, and woke up in the outskirts of Florence. My first impression was that the city looked old, respectfully old—the kind of city that promises to enchant.

My second impression, when I arrived in the heart of the city, was that it was crowded. Despite the hordes of people inside the station, I found an empty sidewalk outside and began putting my bike together. The voice of a young man, very close, startled me. I thought he had asked, "What do you think you are doing?" I looked up while trying to process the Italian, wondering if I was breaking some kind of law. He asked again, this time gesturing toward my bike, and I realized he was asking not about me, but about my bike.

My heart began beating again and I started explaining my Bike Friday to him—that only moments before it had been in my suitcase. He told me he was planning to travel next summer by train and bike. He wanted me to compare my bike to a fold-up with which I was not familiar. I apologized. He asked where I was going. When I told him I was riding to Romita, he let out a whistling sound as he turned to go and warned, "You, my friend, have steep hills ahead of you. You will be tired and hungry tonight."

With his whistle ringing in my ears, I decided to forgo yet again being a tourist. I entered Lorenzo's address into the GPS, choosing to let an electronic circuit be my tour guide. It did OK. I saw what I most wanted to see, Brunelleschi's dome, as the GPS led me in what seemed like a circle around the train station. On the second pass, it directed me out of town and over a bridge with an unobstructed view of the Ponte Vecchio and the Arno River.

The traffic was heavy and fast-paced, and though I never felt I was in danger, I was glad when the GPS pulled me off what seemed to be a major thoroughfare out of the city and sent me up a very steep street that led to high ground and a stunning panorama. I was reminded of the expansive views of Florence in the films *Room with a View* and *Where Angels Fear to Tread*.

While I was catching my breath at the top of the hill and taking a picture of this *most beautiful of Renaissance cities*, as all the guidebooks attest, an older man dressed in black biking tights maneuvered a gorgeous red Colnago on its rear wheel out of a nearby house. I hurried back to my bike, hoping I would be able to ride along and chat with him. But the road was so steep I dared not even try to keep up. He shot down the hill and disappeared from sight in seconds.

The route the GPS chose was a favorite of the local bike club. Brightly clad riders would appear in my rearview mirrors and within minutes pass me. Each time I tried hard to keep up, enjoying the camaraderie of riding in a group, but with each rise in the road I would fall quickly off the back.

While biking comfortably along, checking the rearview mirrors for approaching bikers, I passed by a cemetery of astounding beauty—row after row of simple white crosses and a few Stars of David—paying homage to the remains of thousands of American men who died liberating Italy.

What a different world it was then! If I could travel in time, it would be to Italy before World War II. I carry a soft spot in my heart for the camaraderie of the villagers in Italy during the war—the closeness of the people in films like Roberto Rossellini's *Paisan*.

While lost in these thoughts and the mesmerizing beauty of the rows of white crosses flashing by, two bikes whizzed by within inches of me, redlining my heart rate. The fault was not so much theirs, as mine. I had not been concentrating on riding a straight line. I tried to draft them, but I couldn't, even though they were riding along, casually talking.

I resumed a comfortable pace. My heart rate settled back to one hundred thirty-five beats a minute. I kept an eye on my mirrors. Within a few minutes a group of six appeared. I glanced ahead and saw a slight downhill. *Perfect—should be able to draft them.* When riding downhill extra weight is an advantage, at least on the open road, where abrupt stops aren't likely. I picked up my cadence and added eight kilometers per hour to my pace. When the first rider reached me I started pulling even harder. By the time the sixth rider got to me I'd almost doubled my speed. I dropped in line and felt another surge of speed—exhilarating.

Riding with these guys made me think of my training rides back home and the pace we would maintain—a pace that would have covered the distance to Lorenzo's place in less than two hours if I was on my Orbea road bike, Spain's equivalent of Italy's Colnago, and not pulling a trailer and wearing a backpack. But on this day, because I could stay with these *pelotons* only until the next rise in the road, I'd be riding for over six hours.

The GPS took me on the shortest route, and delivered me to an empty apartment. Nearby, I found an olive grove. Lots of men were scattered about the grove, but not one of them was named Lorenzo, nor did any of the men know of a Lorenzo. Perplexed, I asked for the owner of the farm. He had heard of Lorenzo. He thought for a moment, made a quick phone call, then sent me on down the road. I'm thankful the road remained on top of the ridge. But again, I didn't find Lorenzo, or his farm. And again I inquired of a farmer in an olive grove. This time I found out I'd ridden two kilometers too far.

By the time I finally found it and discovered that I'd be living alone on the farm, I was regretting my decision to come to Lorenzo's. I thought back to the morning's panic at the train station. I still couldn't recall exactly what I had prayed. I was beginning to wonder whether I was trusting grace. Maybe I was bulling along my own way. I tried to remember what had attracted me to Lorenzo's farm. I couldn't imagine what it had been, unless it was that the owner was Italian. Nothing about Lorenzo or his farm seemed traditional, except his appearance—classic Roman with a full head of wavy gray-streaked black hair. The place was fully mechanized, including tractors and bulldozers and rusting pieces of equipment strewn about his hilltop farm. There was a lot of work to be done. The first hour I spent helping his wife clean up the house where I'd be staying. I was starved, as my "friend" in Florence told me I would be, and no one seemed to be thinking of dinner. I kept hoping they would offer a piece of fruit or something, but instead we kept sweeping and cleaning. And I kept hoping and wishing I could think of something to say that would gracefully bring up the subject of food.

Finally we finished sweeping, and I began tasting pasta in my mind. But then we began mopping. Again I said nothing. But I thought a lot of things. Nothing clever or subtle though, so I kept quiet, except for my stomach, but apparently it was loud enough only for me to hear.

After two hours of cleaning and gathering firewood, I discovered that we wouldn't be eating together. Lorenzo informed me I would be fixing my own meals and dining alone—except for the company of a couple of attack geese that thought they were the resident watchdogs, and a cat that I was to feed. I would have chosen, if Lorenzo had offered, to leave the very next morning. I would not have known where I was going, but I would have left. But Lorenzo didn't give me that choice.

Instead he gave me the choice of what food to buy at the *supermercato*. I had naively thought that Italy didn't even have such stores. I was disappointed, disoriented, and hungry. I feel lost in "big box" American stores, and here I was walking around a huge, crowded store, trying to plan meals in a foreign language when all I really wanted to do was to grab a sandwich from the deli and tear into it. But Lorenzo was encouraging me to choose a week's worth of food. I didn't want to. I didn't want to spend so many days cooking and eating alone. I also didn't want Lorenzo to buy food I wouldn't be around to eat. But I didn't have the courage to say anything. So I deferred to his suggestions, just in case the food was still there when I left.

I couldn't figure the place out. It was high tech, busy, and confusing. My wife has always warned against going to the grocery store hungry. I was far past that. I was famished—*fame* as the Italians say, just like the young man in Florence warned I would be. Had I been making the decisions, we would have needed two or three carts. With Lorenzo choosing we got to the automated checkout with one cart half full.

By myself I never would have been able to figure out the self-checkout. Even Lorenzo seemed confused by the high-tech world of buzzers and lights and scanners and messages on the screen. Something we were doing, the technology did not like. Lorenzo had to call in a human to save us from the techno-loop we were stuck in, to the great relief of the long line of people trapped behind us. Not once when I first began dreaming of this journey did I envision such an end to one of my days in Tuscany—trapped in technology.

On the drive back to the farm I learned that Lorenzo, in his former life, was a salesman of farm products and a manager of a large farm. He wanted to put that experience to work. He also wanted to be his own boss. As we were pulling into the farmyard he was telling me that every year, just as he did when he worked for others, he faithfully records income and expense, plots and yields. Then he sits down with his accountant to go over the numbers "and each year I discover once again what my best crop is..." He paused half a beat and gave me a wry smile before delivering the kicker, "red ink."

At that moment I remembered why I had wanted to come to Lorenzo's. He had been funny on the phone too. My love of witticisms was going to cost me. While I put the food away, Lorenzo hummed a strange tune in his deep timber of a voice and sorted through some papers. He found what he was looking for, and then he was gone. I felt alone—so alone I would have loved hearing Pietro's son, Joshua, prance around the room repeating *ad nauseam* his singsong ditty, "The Cock Is Dead," in every language he knows and a few that he doesn't. I desperately wanted to hear Aurora calling me and *Annnnn-aaaaaaa-Ma-reeeeeeee-ah* to dinner, but all I heard was silence. I didn't come to Italy to eat German food, and I didn't come to Tuscany to eat alone.

But on that night I had no choice. I began my apprenticeship in Italian cooking, even though no master chefs were present. I envisioned Aurora cooking, my wife in the kitchen, my mom's favorite tomato-based recipes, even movies with chefs. The food I fixed, much to my surprise was doggone good. Fixing pasta is fun. I recalled a movie I saw when I was a kid in which a man who was trying to impress his girlfriend demonstrated that the pasta was done when it would stick on the wall. I flung a piece at the side of the stove and it stuck. That night I became not only a lover of Italian food, but of Italian cooking as well. While washing the dishes, I thought of my wife and vowed to fix pasta for her when I got home. That thought made me feel even lonelier. I fell asleep wishing Lorenzo hadn't been so darned clever on the phone. Maybe I would have chosen a more traditional farm and a family that would have invited me to join them at their dinner table.

Reverting to my Midwestern upbringing I got up the next morning before dawn, fried myself some eggs, and ate them in silence, with only the cat, a rooster, and two geese for company. Just as the sun began to climb above the nearby hills I headed out for a tour of Lorenzo's farm. I thought I had seen enough equipment for two or three farms scattered about his farmstead last night, but to my surprise, his sheds were also full of farm implements. Lorenzo had been selling machinery to other farmers so long and so well that he'd convinced himself that he too needed all that equipment to make a living farming. And there it sat rusting away. I was looking at the *seeds* that produce Lorenzo's *best crop*.

The description on the WWOOF website (*I work on the farm on my own*) of Lorenzo picking olives by himself, were it not for *wwoofers*, is totally wrong. The first pickers to show up were a couple of young men from India. I began to help them, but they explained that they worked separately. They worked not by the hour, but by the kilogram, keeping track of which *cassetti* were theirs.

They were quite efficient. They used nets and ladders and plastic fingers but no mechanical shaker. Lorenzo also employed another contractor, with six employees, to pick olives. He kept this group separate as well. They were in a grove a half a kilometer from the house. They used three shakers powered by the battery on their car. Each night they weighed their output and gave those figures to Lorenzo.

Lorenzo kept track of everything, "I may know more about my operation than other farmers, but my knowledge does not change the bottom line," he lamented. Unlike Aurora, who said she got into farming without thinking, with only passion, Lorenzo got into farming with much thinking and much knowledge. He thought that if he were willing to change his lifestyle he could make it in farming. But he had come to the conclusion that even if he could cut his expenses to nothing, he still could not survive. "Every year I lose money, James."

Lorenzo was trying to reverse his fortunes by marketing directly. Saturday's market in San Casciano, a small town about fifteen kilometers north, toward Florence, was a bust. He and I spent the whole day in the park at the edge of the town. I sold nothing all day. Any profit he made was probably donated to the vendors' lunch. Lorenzo contributed a couple of bottles of wine, which was more than I had seen him sell.

For me, though, the day was not a loss. I got to see a town living, not off money from tourists, but money from their neighbors. The bakery was twenty deep in customers. I waited in line and discovered the reason for the long line—the bread and the pastries were delicious and inexpensive. I also stopped by a couple of butcher shops to reconnect with the memories and smells of Bob's Butcher Shop from my childhood. The long lines reminded me of a Tuscan truism: *"Better to spend money at the butcher than the pharmacist."* The banter was light-hearted and spirited. But returning to Lorenzo's stand was depressing—no customers, and the bottles were still as I had arranged them that morning—no gaps in the designs.

I ended up staying at Lorenzo's farm for six days. I picked for two and one-half days and for half a day I gathered pruned limbs so that they wouldn't snag the nets that his workers spread under the trees. But I never did come to enjoy picking olives at Lorenzo's like I did at Aurora's.

Conversation is what I most enjoy about picking olives. Lunchtime was pleasant, though. Each day Lorenzo would set up a table in the olive grove and sit down to eat with us. We talked then, but Lorenzo didn't pick with us. His operation required too much management to afford him the luxury of picking his own olives.

It was at Lorenzo's though, that the wisdom of Saint Paul's advice that we should give thanks in all situations hit home. Rather than complaining that I had to fix my own meals, I should have given thanks for the opportunity to show myself that I was capable of cooking up delicious food from scratch. Instead of complaining that I was alone, I should have given thanks that I was staying on the farm of someone as generous as Lorenzo.

On the third evening, after we had weighed the olives, using an old-fashioned scale with counterweights that must have been at least a hundred years old, Lorenzo came into the house, pulled out a map, and began showing me the nearby towns that were in range of a bike ride. His strongest recommendation, if I was up to "a beast of a climb," was to ride to San Gimignano, famous for its many towers—a medieval skyline in the twenty-first century, set high on a hill and visible long before you reach it.

Lorenzo insisted that I bike there the next day, which meant I had three days off from picking olives. He had already told me to expect to help him at farmers markets on Saturday and Sunday. I shuddered at the thoughts I harbored that first night, when Lorenzo's wife and I were straightening up the farmhouse, instead of sitting down to eat.

Strange life, this trusting grace I thought the next morning as I planned the day's ride. My guidebook noted that in the area was a rural church said to be a fine example of sixteenth-century architecture, La Cupola, set high on a lonely hill in the countryside. I programmed it into my GPS, and discovered that adding the church as a "via point" added only ten kilometers to the trip, so I took off on a circuitous route to San Gimignano with just a bike and an all-but-empty backpack.

The route led me through Barberino, where Lorenzo told me I would find a bike shop. For a couple of weeks I'd been riding on a tire with a bubble, unable to find a replacement because of the small wheels on my Bike Friday. I had even considered having one shipped FedEx from the States. It would be an extraordinary expense, but if that tire exploded, I'd be forced to spend the money—and possibly more—paying for a hotel room while waiting for it to arrive.

I found the bike shop, exactly where Lorenzo said it would be, across the street from a beautiful church, San Bartolomeo. The town seemed too small for such a grand edifice, but I was beginning to get used to the grandeur of churches in Italy. The bike shop was also a service station, so while I waited for the owner to pump gas for a customer, I browsed his selection of bikes. I was thrilled to discover that he had a couple of children's bikes with wheels the same size as my Bike Friday. But when I asked the owner if he had a tire to fit my bike, he told me he did not. My heart sank. He spoke no English, but considering that it could cost me as much as a hundred dollars to have a tire shipped to me, it seemed worth a try to push my Italian out of its comfort zone. I searched my mind for the words to ask if he had a tire in the back room that had been replaced on a children's bike. Even if it had only a little bit of tread left, it would be good to carry it as a spare, just in case. Some words I couldn't find in my mind, so I spoke them with my hands. When he turned quickly, and went into the back room, I was pleased that my Italian, aided by some pantomiming, had been able to make him understand what I needed.

I could hear him rummaging around, moving boxes and bikes. Then I heard a melodious whistle, a quick step to the swinging doors, and there he stood, his face sporting a big smile, encircled by what looked like an almost new tire. It was for a kid's bike. It sported a white sidewall, and its maximum pressure was only forty-five pounds, but I wanted to hug the guy. And if Lorenzo had been there, I would have hugged him too. While the tire was being mounted, I headed across the street and climbed the steps to the church. Good decision. Inside were four magnificent paintings that would not look out of place hanging in the Uffizi Gallery in Florence.

Feeling uplifted, I walked out of the church and looked down at the service station far below. My bike was parked outside, pointing down the road, looking like it was ready for more adventures. I tried, but I'm not sure I was able to make the shop owner understand why I was so happy that he had taken the trouble to find that tire. I suppose I could have packed up my bike and traveled by trains and buses, but to me that represented the loss of what I had come to Tuscany to experience—Italians up close and personal.

A stranger's kindness has the capacity to paint a day beautiful. Everything seemed perfect as I set out from that little gas station in Barberino—the sunlight, the clouds, the old couple stretching a bright green football-field-length net beneath the olive trees on the their farm at the edge of town. Everywhere I pointed my camera, it recorded a picture postcard to send back home. And it was not very long before I was reminded once again why I love to travel by bike.

No more than four kilometers from Barberino, on a long, gentle coast down a small country road, I saw far ahead of me, a man with a walking stick. I couldn't figure out where he had come from or where he was going. Wheat fields stretched out to the horizon on either side of the road. I watched him make his way slowly along as my speed continued building. Something about him was piquing my curiosity. I wanted to talk to him, but I had picked up a lot of speed on the hill. If I stopped, I'd lose the momentum that looked like it might carry me to the top of the next hill. I quit pedaling for an instant as I flew by him and called out, *"Buongiorno."*

He yelled out a friendly *"Buongiorno,"* but my mind was focused on getting up the hill. I made a big shift to a lower gear, so low and so quick that the chain flew right off the front ring. My pedals spun wildly, the momentum dissipated, and the bike came to a stop.

I reached into my backpack and pulled out the brown cotton gloves I carry for greasy jobs. I put them on, reached down, and cranked the pedals around while holding the chain in place—ready to go again. I pulled off the gloves and stuffed them back in their plastic bag.

"*Problema?*" Startled, I turned to see the old man with the walking stick standing close enough he could have reached out and hit me with it.

"*Si, Senor, piccolo problema,*" I said and then searched for more Italian words to describe what had happened. But I didn't know the words for "switching" and "chain" and "gears" and "grease," so I switched to pantomime and English. English didn't work for him, so I just said, "*finito,*" then asked him where he was heading.

"*Nessuna parte,*" and he gave me that beautiful Italian shrug that says everything, a jutting of the chin and a lifting of the head and eyes.

"*Proprio camminare,*" I said, hoping the two words in combination would be the equivalent of "just walking" in English. I had no idea whether it was "good Italian" or whether Italians even have that expression. There was so much about the language I didn't know and wanted to. Even a simple exchange with a stranger made me frustratingly aware of the marvelous intricacies of language. Over and over I had studied the words for running and walking, where are you going, where are you from. But the tenses, idioms, and nuances of Italian still confounded me, as did the speed at which Italians speak. I heard not words but sentences, and even familiar words were lost on me because they were embedded in melodious phrases in which the original sound of the word by itself was lost.

I wanted to ask the man where he lived. I think I asked him where he was from, but in Italy more often than not, that is one and the same. He pointed with pride to a hilltop farm about two kilometers away, set back quite a distance from the road. He told me he owned forty hectares. I asked what he raised. His eyes lost their sparkle.

"*Niente,*" he said and shrugged again. His sad face made my heart hurt. He had quit farming a few years ago and now only gardened a little. He rented the land, but wished one of his sons had wanted to farm. He missed the patterns and rituals of farming, but he said he was too old to do it all. I wanted to just keep walking with him, until he turned around and headed back to his farm. Heck, in a few short moments, I had grown to care so deeply for him that I wanted to go and start farming with him, helping him as long as I could. I wanted by the grace of God for one of his sons to come back to farm with him again. I regretted deeply saying goodbye to this gentle man.

I said, "*Ciao*" and began biking away, thanking God that my chain had come off. If the chain had stayed on, I would have learned nothing of that old man's story. I began wondering what would have happened had my chain come off a few weeks ago, causing me to coast to a stop next to the old woman working on her motorbike. But it didn't. Saint Paul, were he here, would tell me to give thanks for that too. And he is right, I should. That day turned out just fine. *In all circumstances give thanks.* I'm a slow learner, but by God's grace, *grazia di Dio*, maybe I will someday develop a thankful attitude even *when bad things happen to good people* and myself as well.

I began thinking about the word I had said to the man, *ciao*. If we had been on a road near my farm we would have said *goodbye*. In America when you meet someone, the expression is *hello* or *hi*, but in Italy the expression is again, *ciao*. Why do Italians say the same thing upon greeting each other as they do when parting? The answer is that *ciao* is not so much a salute or a valediction as it is a pledge. The word *ciao* has been shortened over the years from *Il suo schiavo*. "I am your servant/slave" became *Sciao*, which became the short and cheerful-sounding *Ciao*.

Il suo schiavo brought to mind Saint Francis, pledging to serve his fellow human beings on the road of life. The expression "I am your servant" reminded me also of the words of Saint Paul when he acknowledged that he was but a servant through whom others had come to believe in Jesus. Does that expression go back two millenia? Paul used similar words when he wrote about Jesus: *who made himself nothing, taking the very nature of a servant, being made in human likeness.* Did the followers of Jesus greet each other with the expression *I am your servant*, and was that expression so commonly used that it became a form of greeting throughout the old Roman empire? In the English language, *goodbye* comes to us with an interesting story as well. Up until the sixteenth century, the valediction used was *God be with you.* Within a century it had gone from *God be wy you* to *god b'w'y* to *godbwye* to *god buy' ye* to *good-b'wy* and then to *goodbye.* I am not a linguist, but I'm fascinated by the clues language can offer us as we seek to understand ourselves and our past.

In America, the national pastime is baseball. In Italy it's hospitality. Might it be that at one time there existed among the populace a universal concept of servanthood? Something has to explain the good-natured, love-of-life, helpful attitude of Italians. As Annamarja said over and over to me while we picked olives in Aurora's grove, "Italians are different. I don't understand it. But I can tell you one thing, they are fun to be around. My people are nothing like Italians. We could learn a lot from them."

No way could I offer an argument to Annamarja, especially with the memory of this gentle soul with whom I had just spent fifteen delightful minutes still playing in my mind. At the crest of a long hill, I got off my bike, turned, and looked back. My farmer friend must have turned around at the spot where we talked. He was now but a speck in the distance—but he was halfway home to his farm.

Goodbye and God be with you.

I arrived ten minutes later at the little church in the round encircled by cypress trees—and discovered my first locked church. But the church, modeled after Brunelleschi's dome, was worth the extra kilometers, sitting as it does atop a high hill affording a view of all the land around. When it was built, about a century after Columbus sailed to America, I wondered if the planners thought that a town would grow up around it. Its isolation reminded me of country churches back in Wisconsin, set as they often are far from town or even other farmsteads, lonely but beautiful outposts of God in the countryside. I sat down on the steps of the church to eat my lunch and write in my journal of the kind-hearted man I had just met.

For half an hour I wrote, trying to do justice to this extraordinary day that had only just begun. I finished writing and glanced at the map. My goal was to stay on high ground, dropping into the valley only once. Lorenzo and the guidebooks were right. The town is a lovely sight, worthy of all the calendar shots, picture post cards, and movies. The small town featured in *Where Angels Fear to Tread* and known as *Monteriano* was San Gimignano.

Lorenzo was also right about the final climb up to San Gimignano. It was a "beast" as he said, but not all that tiring because of frequent stops. Around every bend of the road, and with each change of foreground, I felt the urge to take another picture of *the city of beautiful towers*—known as the *Medieval Manhattan* because of the thirteen of its seventy-some towers that still remain. Eventually I arrived in town and was not surprised to find a huge bus disgorging a massive group of tourists, massive in number and in size. Judging by the tourists on the streets of San Gimignano, who were from all over the globe, the 1971 musical dream of Coca-Cola executives has come true. The whole world in perfect harmony drinking Coke—and the whole world getting fat.

Within minutes any lingering questions about why the town was so overrun with tourists vanished. San Gimignano was charming. Many hilltop towns are more authentically Italian and less touristy Italian, whatever that means, but I wasn't sorry I had added to San Gimignano's tourist numbers. It was definitely worth the climb. I fielded questions from all over the world while I ate my lunch by the town's water fountain. My little-wheeled bicycle was proving to be a great conversation starter.

The town was interesting, but I was a tourist and not a participant in the life of San Gimignano. It might be an unfair comparison, because much of the time I was there was during the afternoon *siesta*, when the shops were closed, but I felt it would be unlikely that I'd ever be perceived as a regular at the bakery, as I had already become in Tavernelle di Pisa, a few kilometers from Lorenzo's farm. On my second day in the bakery I was asked which of the two breads I had bought the previous day did I prefer. On the third day all I had to say was *Buongiorno* and my favorite bread was on the counter before I had time to get a one euro coin out of my pocket. "*Grazie, prego,* and *arrivederci.*" "Thank you, you're welcome, and goodbye."

I know it's a small thing, but it is moments like my reception at the bakery that I hope for when I travel. I love to see the beautiful sights like San Gimignano, but what I really enjoy are the simple exchanges of life—being recognized at the bakery, talking to a retired farmer who wishes his son were with him, or meeting a bike shop owner who takes the time to solve a problem. The simple everyday exchanges of life were making me feel that I was getting to know Italians—that I had begun a relationship that just may allow me to get to know these intriguing people.

You go to see the sights and return for the people. E.M. Forster got it right. In the first scene of the first chapter of his first novel, Philip advises Lilia to see the little towns like Pienza, Cortona, and San Gimignano, but then cautions: *...don't, let me beg you, go with that awful tourist idea that Italy's only a museum of antiquities and art. Love and understand the Italians, for the people are more marvelous than the land.*

The photos you show from your travels around Italy may be of the gorgeous countryside, but the stories you tell will be of the beautiful, in-love-with-life people.

The landscapes of Tuscany are a delight to the eye of painters and photographers. I love the subtle interplay of shapes and textures and light on this hillside. I was on my way to Lorenzo's farm and was beginning to get worried that the sun was going to get to the horizon before I found his place. But eventually I did find it and I found Lorenzo to be one of the great surprises of my Italian journey. He was not working alone on his farm as the WWOOF description had led me to believe. His was one of the most mechanized farms I worked on, and he had lots of people working for him. But from Lorenzo I learned a lot about farming and a lot about hospitality as well. Each day Lorenzo would set up a small table in the olive grove where we would inevitably be joined by his "attack geese" who watched the place in Lorenzo's absence—you can see them in the background—you can also see that we have enjoyed quite a few bottles of Lorenzo's delicious red wine.

Lorenzo gave me a wonderful day to explore the region. He pulled out maps and told me of all the special places nearby. After hearing his descriptions I chose San Gimignano although Lorenzo cautioned me that I should be ready for a "beast of a climb" the last mile or so. He was right, but I never got tired because I was stopping to take so many photographs. On the way to San Gimignano I couldn't resist another steep climb, up into the old part of Certaldo where I took one of my favorite photos of the journey. I discovered that even the cats are hospitable. This beautiful animal allowed me get to close enough to capture the composition that would for me define the sweet life of Italy. You can tell that this is a gathering spot—those chairs will soon be occupied and the stories will be flowing.

Chapter Nine

Art is a human activity
which has as its purpose the transmission to others
of the highest and best feelings to which men have risen.

TOLSTOY

🖋

Simplicity is the ultimate sophistication.

LEONARDO DA VINCI

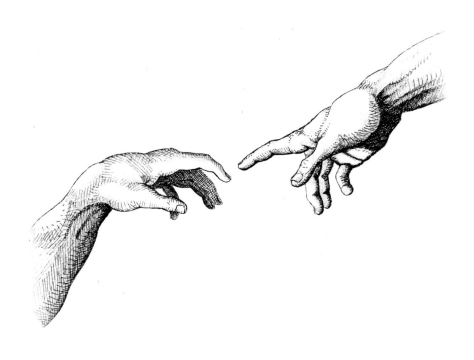

Healthy food and great art have this in common—
they both need patrons. As we began carrying the bottles of wine
and olive oil to his reserved spot on the sidewalk,
I was overwhelmed by how good it felt to be helping
Lorenzo the farmer, the philosopher, the citizen, the neighbor, the
husband, the father, the friend, set up his stand
for a day of selling—a day of connecting
with those who enjoy the fruit of his land and his labor.

A New Renaissance
From Greed to Grace & Thankful Stewardship

If asked how I celebrated any of my birthdays, I would, with certainty, be able to describe in detail very few. The first I remember vividly is my sixteenth. I got my driver's license on that day. God willing, another one will be special too—my one hundredth. But for now, my sixty-third stands out.

The day began before dawn, a Sunday. Lorenzo and I were headed, in a tightly packed Toyota Land Cruiser we had loaded the night before, to the Piazza di Santo Spirito in Florence to sell wine and olive oil. Even the direction we traveled stands out. I expected to be retracing the route my GPS had chosen the day I rode to Lorenzo's farm, but we turned the opposite direction. The road followed the spine of a high ridge.

At a sign for Bargino, Lorenzo turned and we dropped off the high ground, following tight switchbacks cutting across the hillside. The sign troubled me. I wanted to ask Lorenzo about it, but I didn't want to distract him. We were descending very fast. Neither the brakes nor the engine was holding back our heavily laden SUV. The speed on the turns didn't seem to bother Lorenzo. When at last the road straightened I asked, "Lorenzo, did that sign say *Bargino—two kilometers?*"

"*Si*, Bargino is just here, not much to it."

I couldn't believe it. *Twelve kilometers or some other single digit number, but not two kilometers.* That sign was confirmation that with every pedal stroke I took past Bargino the evening I rode to Lorenzo's, I was getting farther away from his farm. I had stopped to check my map at the intersection where Lorenzo and I were now waiting for traffic to clear. Had I not been relying on the GPS, I would have inquired at the tavern and would have met someone who knew Lorenzo, and he would have directed me up this much shorter route. By following the abstractions of technology, I had eliminated the possibility of allowing grace, flowing through people, to get me to Lorenzo's farm.

I wondered if Lorenzo thought about grace, but I didn't ask him. I asked instead about the farmers market in Casciano. During the occasional times Lorenzo had left me in charge, no one bought anything. Many people sampled his olive oil, using the bread he had cut up to soak up some of his precious *olio d'oliva nuovo*, but no one parted with any money. Some people asked a question or greeted me with a *"Buongiorno"*; others just sampled. Most just walked by.

"Some days a farmer makes more money sleeping," Lorenzo said as we pulled onto the highway. During the times when we were both in the stall, I saw Lorenzo sell only one bottle of wine and two bottles of olive oil. "Sixty-five euros yesterday, that's all," Lorenzo continued as he shifted into fourth gear. Apparently during the time I had spent in the village, at the bakery, at the butcher, and just hanging out in the *piazza*, I had missed only a couple of sales.

"Roughly I figure I keep one third, so twenty euros to pay me and to pay for the gasoline and…" Lorenzo quit talking, knowing that I had the picture. I did. I ticked off a few of his expenses, but I didn't mention the two bottles of wine he contributed to lunch, when we gathered in a big circle with all the other vendors to eat. *Sorte fortuna. Mangia, mangia.* Pot luck. Eat, eat.

"Today, maybe will be different. I do not know though. These are tough times." Lorenzo told me that he had been selling at the market at *Santo Spirito* for four years. "Even Rome has nothing like it; there's more tradition here. I have had days of one thousand euros. Now I would be very happy with four hundred, five hundred euros. People are afraid."

Lorenzo continued, energized, "Agriculture is going to die if things do not change. People should be afraid of that, but I do not think most people care. They do not understand the consequences. They think food will always be there. I have been farming ten years. The price of everything has gone up except what I sell. Olives and wine. It is easier making a living doing something else."

The way Lorenzo was talking reminded me of a joke I heard many years ago. I easily imagined Lorenzo delivering the punch line, so I shared it, "An old Texas hill country farmer has spent the better part of a morning complaining about his lot in life. Hoping for happier thoughts, his friend asks him what he would do if he won the lottery. The old guy thinks for a moment, then drawls, 'If I won the lottery, I reckon I'd just keep right on farming 'til the money was all gone.'"

Lorenzo smiled, then he laughed. "Yes, you're right. That's me, I guess—except for the lottery part. I complain, but still I hope things will get better. Someday."

The life of a farmer is tough. There's much to complain about, but it's a good life. And lots of farmers recognize it, especially if they have once, like Lorenzo, worked for a paycheck. Then they love the freedom of working for themselves and with nature. Lorenzo knows what it is to be a farmer and he knows what it is to not be a farmer. And he prefers being a farmer. He likes being known as a man of the land.

"I can't imagine doing anything different. I farm for the *Hell-th* of it," he quipped. "I have tried many roads to make a living as a farmer. I have raised my prices, I have lowered my prices. I sell direct, I sell in bulk. I have accepted subsidies, I have refused subsidies. Will I do like many? Will I take a job for five days, so I can farm for two days—Saturday and Sunday?"

Lorenzo went on to say that farming would not be quite so difficult if his competition didn't have an unfair advantage. We were in the outskirts of Florence, passing by big buildings that reminded Lorenzo of the corporations he competes against. "They can sell eggs for one cent. They cram one hundred thousand chickens in one square kilometer, eating shit and chicken parts—becoming cannibals. And they use propaganda to fool the customer into thinking that their eggs are as good as what I raise. You find yourself struggling against an overwhelming tide, but they have all the money and the power," Lorenzo told me, sounding defeated. "We are losing the war. If we were only fighting against corporations we might win because we love what we do, but we also fight against governments," Lorenzo added.

"Are things better or worse since Italy joined the European Union?" I asked.

He looked at me, wondering whether I was serious. "Much worse. Some things have doubled in price. It's especially bad for the poorer countries, the poorer people."

"What about subsidies?" I asked trying not to reveal my feelings.

"I don't take them anymore. Too much paperwork for the small farmer. The big corporations *farm* bureaucracies, and they make a lot of money doing it," Lorenzo quipped, his words full of humor and truth. "Corporations don't have to make money on food. A penny an egg is enough for them. For those of us who do not have the government filling our back pockets, it is a struggle."

Lorenzo told me that in Italy, when the agri-giants saw that consumers were willing to pay more money for organic local food, they figured out a way to milk the system to make sure they were able to get the higher prices and the subsidies available to organic farmers.

"What can be done?" I asked, impressed by his knowledge and his passion. I was hoping he had an answer I hadn't yet heard.

"I will just keep doing what I have been, and hope enough farmers, and enough politicians—enough people figure out what subsidies and governments are doing to us—what globalization is doing to us. But that may not happen until a lot of people go hungry, until governments go broke passing out all that money to people who contribute nothing, who in fact steal from all of us," Lorenzo said as we double-parked near the Piazza di Santo Spirito.

Of all the farmers I have met in my life, Lorenzo is unique. Not many farmers have the gumption to refuse the money. But he knows that in refusing the money he is also saying no to the control that government has over you when you accept handouts. My Amish farmer friends know that to take money from the government is to lose their autonomy and their independence. If they accepted the money they would also lose their ability to make decisions that are good for them, their land, the people who eat the food they grow. But the Amish have an advantage that Lorenzo does not have. They are not saddled with the debt of tractors and big machinery. Lorenzo is fighting the good fight, but he and his compatriots need the help of the people gathering in this *piazza*, and farmers markets all over the world, to win the war against corporations and governments and politicians that put out propaganda saying that they are trying to save small independent farmers while doing everything they can to make it impossible for them to make a living.

As we began carrying the bottles of wine and olive oil to his reserved spot on the sidewalk, I was overwhelmed by how good it felt to be helping Lorenzo the farmer, the philosopher, the citizen, the neighbor, the husband, the father, the friend, set up his stand for a day of selling—a day of connecting with those who enjoy the fruit of his land and his labor.

In the very city that was at the heart of the original Renaissance, we had come to set up our bottles of extra virgin olive oil fresh from the *frantoio*. Next to those bottles I arranged Lorenzo Rizzotti's wine, bearing his tastefully designed label—the wine I'd been drinking all week. I had grown to love its gentle earthy taste. As I arranged the bottles in an artful wedge, I imagined myself a Renaissance man like Lorenzo, looking forward to the day when wine from my land would accompany meals on my Wisconsin farm.

Similar thoughts about food were on the minds of the Florentines who stopped by our small stand. They liked knowing the farmer who pressed their olive oil and bottled their wine. One man with great flair tried to get Lorenzo to sell at *supermercato* prices, but the rest seemed pleased, even happy to be buying directly from the farmer and to pay him a fair price for his labor and his investment. That very idea lies at the heart of this new Renaissance. In this, one of the most beautiful cities in the world, a city devoted to the most renowned art ever created, it is fitting that the world is witnessing a rebirth—a return to practices that are at the heart of an art-filled, civilized life. City people buying from country people, the necessities of life.

And because of that personal connection with country people whose hands are daily in dirt, city people know the very basic truth that their lives are sustained by teeming-with-organisms dirt. These people want to get away from what Lorenzo calls "chemical farming." That was what I was feeling, and it seemed safe to say that this critical mass of people gathering in the Piazza di Santo Spirito in Florence, Italy, on a mid-November day were feeling the same way.

People living at the time of the Renaissance knew their lives came from dirt. Forgetting that connection was not possible five hundred years ago. The chances that you or a member of your family was a farmer were much greater then. And even if you didn't know a farmer, the markets didn't let you forget the connection. Sterile plastic packaging that hides the fact of dirt was as distant as the moon that Galileo was watching.

But a new way of perceiving the world was being born, what we today call *The Age of Reason*—a move away from God and toward a more materialistic view of the world. But the change was only started and not completed. We remember the Renaissance for the great art that was created, which was possible because of patrons like the Medici family, who paid for the works of artists like Michelangelo, Brunelleschi, Leonardo da Vinci, Donatello, and Raphael. Healthy food and great art have this in common—they both need patrons. We create societies by the choices we make when we spend our money. Those who pay for food and art are co-creators with farmers and artists. Without patrons, farmers and artists starve. As Lorenzo warns his customers, "We need with every fiber of our body to realize that farmers are essential to everyone's survival."

Lorenzo was among his partners and patrons. We took in more money that first half hour, while we were setting up, than we did the whole previous day. With the bottles artfully arranged and our signs in place, Lorenzo put me in charge. He re-parked the car, then disappeared into the crowd, headed for the bakery to buy bread so his customers could taste his delicious olive oil.

My first customers were two college girls with lots of questions about olive oil, from the trees to the bottle. I was happy to be able to tell them about the process, not from abstract knowledge, but from experience.

Consumers no longer trust the propaganda machine that markets food. They want to look into the eyes of the people intimately associated with growing the food they eat.

Did my personal story of picking and pressing the oil close the deal? Hard to say, but the girls bought two bottles. The transaction was gratifying. I experienced a bit of what Lorenzo must feel—a confirmation that what he is doing is important to people. I also enjoyed interacting with the girls on a personal level. I began the story in Italian and stayed with it until the girl who paid for the oil asked where I was from.

"No way," she said. She too was from Wisconsin, a Green Bay Packer fan in Florence to study art and Italian. Her face lit up when she began sharing with me what she was learning from Italians about how to live life, just by being around them all day, every day. What she said, and the happy look on her face as she said it, reminded me of what Annamarja was forever telling me—that Italians just know how to slow down and get the most from life. I took the name of her art program and told her I planned to pass it on to my son Jonathan, who was contemplating his choices for graduate study in fine art. Why not take a graduate course in enjoying life at the same time?

Lorenzo returned with the bread, heard us talking about art and Italians, and promptly sent me on my way to experience both. I left with no specific destination in mind. I figured the city would guide me, revealing to me at each corner which street to walk down. I was pulled immediately to the Ponte Vecchio by the flow of people. The full energy of Florence sweeps over you as you cross the Arno River on a bridge almost everyone has seen a picture of, even if the name is not known. It is indeed an "Old Bridge," some say the oldest. It's covered with goldsmith and silversmith shops and weighted down by locks of love covering the ironwork—and signs posted everywhere stating that it is illegal to attach a padlock to the bridge. Illegal also is the parking of a car in the old part of the city, but that prohibition, unlike the one about locks, seems to be respected.

The absence of cars is the second thing that strikes the newcomer to Florence. The first is the unbridled energy of the people. Everyone is smiling, or if not smiling, they are walking around with a look of mild amusement, an interest in the people around them. People enjoy being around other people who enjoy life, good food, and art, especially if they can do it while walking down the middle of the street looking at exquisitely detailed re-creations of masterpieces like Leonardo da Vinci's *The Last Supper* and *Mona Lisa* rendered in chalk on the pavement.

In other cities most people have a look of disinterest, of being within themselves. In Florence, the passion, the energy, the love shows. People are expectant. With each wave of exuberance that flowed over me, I wanted all the more for my wife to experience this city. I especially want my children to feel the fervor of Florence. The experience could change their lives.

A quarter of a century ago I sojourned in a foreign country. My wife and I, and our friends lived in a small seaside village in Greece and learned to captain a 28-foot sailboat. Each morning we got up when we felt like it and wandered about the village as though we were residents, which I suppose in a way we were. The townspeople certainly made us feel that way. We hopped on no tour buses. We ate among the locals in their restaurants. We bought fruit and cheese and bread and wine from the merchants in their markets. At the restaurant each day we had the choice of "pork chops, lamb chops, chicken, or kabobs." We danced with the revelers until two in the morning. We took naps when the Greeks did in the heat of the afternoon so that we would able to stay up late, and do it all again. We were living the rhythm of the villagers.

We weren't consciously aware of how different that rhythm was until two weeks into our new lives, when we were invited to attend a harvest festival in a nearby town. We would neither be walking nor sailing. We would be riding in our host's car. We thought nothing of it until the car started moving and the speed, even the moderate speed at which our careful friend was driving, was disconcerting to us. Trying to make sense of this reaction, we realized that we had not been moving fast since we arrived in the village. Our bodies and our minds had adapted to a different pace. We'd lost our comfort level with speed. That bewildering feeling planted within me a desire to wean myself as much as possible from a dependence upon the automobile.

Lorenzo's gift of a day in Florence confirmed my conviction that cities should be, to the extent possible, experienced on foot. Only in New York have I come close to experiencing anything like what I was feeling in Florence. In New York though, the energy of the people doesn't show up on their faces. They may enjoy being there, but they manage to do it without looking into the eyes of the people they pass on the streets.

But on the streets of Florence a palpable feeling of happiness enthuses that energy. I had felt it before, and Lorenzo reminded me of it earlier when he said of Florence what is often said of Aspen—*The only way to live there is to make money off tourists or to be extremely wealthy.* Lorenzo was right, but people do make the sacrifices necessary to live in towns that make people feel good just walking down their streets. When my wife and I, and our two boys were young we lived in Aspen. Mardi and I worked in a lodge to get established. We made the sacrifices. Something ineffable attracts people to towns like Aspen, and I was feeling it in Florence too. Cities become places where people want to live when they are a delight for people on foot as Florence was to me on that gorgeous fall day in November.

Florence captivates the visitor first with its beautiful architecture and sculpture. In this city of stunning statues, the most memorable appeared to move ever so slightly as I walked by. And then, when I stopped to figure out what the heck was going on, it winked at me, or so it seemed. I held my eyes wide and focused on the head of the statue. Nothing moved. I stared so long my eyes cried out to me to blink. I walked a few feet closer. It winked again and curled the corner of its mouth, hinting at a smile.

The statue, uniformly colored of weathered marble, even down to the irises of the eyes, otherwise betrayed no movement—nothing. I continued watching, mesmerized by what I was seeing and not seeing. While I was standing transfixed, another person walked by. My eyes were momentarily distracted, but I thought again that I had detected movement. So too did the passerby; he turned his head and looked, and then stopped abruptly, just as I had done.

I focused my eyes, laser-like on the marble. The statue cocked its head ever so slightly. I never did tire of watching others fall prey to this Venus flytrap of an artist as he sucked into his lair yet another unsuspecting virgin of the Florentine streets. With no sign and no admission charge, this subtle artist/athlete captivated us. Even those who had passed by earlier and knew what was happening could not keep from stopping to watch the comedic drama play out again.

I later saw other people plying their trade as statues but not one was as gifted as the street urchin statue, for he was not much larger than the children he never seemed to tire of luring into his sway of influence. Nor did his audience tire of seeing yet another child's face turn from shock, to surprise, to delight. The child being captured brought to me and to the others who stopped to watch, an overwhelming sense of joy, and I'm sure to the performer as well, though not a single muscle would move, until he chose to make it move.

We were captured not just by the surprise of a statue moving, but the grace of the man's movements and his ability to arrest that motion into a rock-steady pose. A man should not be able to balance in such an uncomfortable pose for even a moment, much less for endless minutes waiting for the next *victim*. But he did just that on a pedestal only slightly wider than his foot.

I did discover, however, a way to make him move. Sitting at the base of his pedestal I noticed a small old-fashioned laborer's lunchbox, also the color of marble. I walked up and slid some bills into the slot on the top. Following a machine-like delay while the offering registered and kicked the gears into motion, the statue, in a subtle mimic of a robot, executed a stiff-bodied movement to a new position—there to wait for another offering or another unsuspecting victim to come along.

His lunch pail, by the end of the day, was bulging with enough money to leave no doubt that his subtle dance was greatly appreciated. We, by the simple act of dropping a few euros in the lunch pail of a street urchin, had become co-creators of a delightful art form that colors my memories of Florence.

But I had come to the heart of Florence to see other statues, and within a slingshot's range I found *David*, as the twenty-nine-year-old Michelangelo envisioned him just after he slayed Goliath. When, as an architecture student, I first learned of this seventeen-foot creation in Carrara marble, I could not fathom why it had held such power over people's imaginations for over five hundred years. But having stood myself before it, even though I knew I was standing before a replica, I began to understand. I could not get out of my mind the phrase, *So God created man in his own image, in the image of God He created him.*

In this city in which the movement began that some say turned mankind's heart away from God and faith, and toward reason and materialism, it is ironic that a half millennium after the dawning of the Renaissance, the glory of God still shines through. The Baptistery of San Giovanni is famous for the beautiful gilded bronze doors at its three entrances. In exquisitely sculpted relief the principle stories of the Old Testament glow with a brilliance of light and creativity that startles every person who steps close enough to absorb their paneled depictions.

Florence brings to mind not just art, but the new ways of thinking that accompanied the discoveries of Galileo and Copernicus and Columbus— disturbances of the world's order that still reverberate today. Walking through the streets of Florence makes a person acutely aware of not only where we have been, but also where we are going. Florence made me contemplate my own journey and destiny as well, or maybe it was just the fact that another birthday had rolled around. But for whatever reason, I journeyed back to a time when I paid little attention to God. As I walked around this city which celebrates God and the Bible in its art, and yet celebrates secularism as well, I saw much that reminded me of my journey.

Which is the correct view of the world? Is it the view that overwhelmed me during my college years—the view that pushed God to the fringes and toward irrelevance? Or is it the view that was overwhelming me in Florence—that God should be constantly in mind, just as God and the Bible were constantly on the minds of those who created the great and lasting art of the Renaissance?

From a friendly bookseller at the farmers market, I bought a memento that would remind me of selling Lorenzo's oil in the beautiful city of Florence. The book became a present for Lorenzo as well. I chose to buy the Italian language version, and thus late in the afternoon when Lorenzo suggested that I make yet another venture across the Arno to absorb the culture of Florence and the Renaissance, I gave him *The Mad Farmer Poems* of Wendell Berry to read and absorb, knowing that the new day in farming of which Berry writes will encourage Lorenzo.

Lorenzo had not heard of Wendell Berry, but they are soul mates. Lorenzo is also a Mad Farmer. The Italian language version is entitled *La Rivoluzione del Contadino Impazzito—The Revolution of the Impassioned Farmer*—a title and concept Italians may soon be ready for. I'd cast my lot on the side of farmers in a revolution. I know of no people more capable when it comes to the really important skills. Lorenzo believes a revolution will befall his country when a critical mass of people are starving and the government is broke—then and maybe only then does he believe that subsidies will be eliminated, the playing field leveled for the small farmer, and all of Italy will come to know the high cost of cheap, unhealthy food. And when Italy recovers from its excesses, Lorenzo believes that people will come to his stand and be happy to pay to him a fair price for his oil and his wine.

A price Lorenzo's customers will be happy to pay because gone will be the materialistic mindset that more is better and cheap is better. Gone also will be chemical farming. Farmers will once again be planting seeds in nutrient-rich soil. What Lorenzo calls a revolution, I prefer to call a Renaissance, a *new Renaissance*—a rebirth, a *rinascimento*, that will change a materialistic, usurious mindset from greed to grace and thankful stewardship.

Florence was good to Lorenzo. We sold almost all of his wine, had but three bottles of old oil remaining, and none of the new. He didn't reach the thousand-euros mark, but he got well past halfway. The goal that he said would make him happy, did make him happy. As we were driving home, the reality of having that much money in his pocket made him realize that despite the downturns in the economy, more than enough people were willing to pay him a fair price for his work, for his oil and wine.

And each week when he sets up his wares in the square at Santo di Spirito, that is all the Slightly Mad Farmer Lorenzo wants—just enough people with the slightly naïve attitude, that to pay a fair price for food is a good thing—a very good thing—for everybody. Lorenzo is just enough of a mad farmer to hope that someday what used to be seen as naïve will be, as Leonardo da Vinci said, the ultimate sophistication. What could be simpler than a farmer growing food, which he then sells to the people who eat it.

And they become co-creators of a world in which people pay for food a price commensurate to its value—and for things of little value, they pay nothing, because they will have found that things of little value clutter their lives. Spending money for things we don't need also makes us think we can't afford to pay a fair price for things of precious value— like healthful food, great art, and inspired entertainment that celebrates mankind's creative spirit.

Lorenzo gave me one of the most memorable birthdays of my life. We packed his Land Cruiser with wine and olive oil and headed to the farmers market in Florence. Once we had things set up and the pace had slowed Lorenzo sent me across the Arno to explore what I now consider the most beautiful city in the world. It certainly was the most vibrant city I'd ever been in. Everyone seemed happy to be right where they were, doing what they were doing. And for a good number of them it was enjoying the sensuous flavor of their favorite gelato. The farmers market at Piazza di Santo Spirito was a joyous celebration of colors, smells, and tastes added to the simple, but wondrous idea of a farmer growing food which she then sells to the people who eat it.

As I quickly discovered, the streets of Florence are a delight for both tourists and residents. Everyone was happy. This statue brought smiles to the faces of all who passed by.

The Baptistery of San Giovanni is famous for the beautiful gilded bronze doors at its three entrances. In exquisitely sculpted relief the principle stories of the Old Testament glow with a brilliance of light and creativity that startles every person who steps close enough to absorb their paneled depictions.

Chapter Ten

My father was a farmer and my mother was a farmer,
my childhood was very good.
I am very grateful for my childhood,
because it was full of gladness and good humanity.
ROBERTO BENIGNI

A Radicondoli Reverie

Italians have a way, a very natural way, of making you feel as though you, although a stranger, are the most important person in the world to them. They give as though their reservoir of time is endless. Before long you're laughing with them and then, without realizing it, you too start talking with your hands.

This farm where I now feel so welcome—where I came to realize these things—lies in the Colline Metallifere, the metal-bearing hills of southern Tuscany, rich in iron, copper, and lead. About an hour before I reached the farm, the land rose up and began reminding me of Wisconsin. The road, curving gently through thick stands of pine and oaks transported me to Wisconsin's vacation land, the North Woods. For eight or nine kilometers I rode along feeling sheltered and protected, as though the woods would never end. And then with no warning, the forest opened up to an expansive view of distant hilltops that instantly transported me to southwestern Wisconsin and the rolling hills near my farm. I stayed in that familiar landscape until church bells, ringing out from the towers of Radicondoli, began pulling me back to Italy. Their insistent resonating tones, harmonizing with the rolling, tingling bells on the necks of the sheep grazing in lush green pastures brought me gently back to Tuscany. A scene, much like the one unrolling before my eyes must have been forming in Beethoven's mind when he wrote Symphony no. 6, the *Pastoral*. Every movement of that grand composition was playing out on that hillside—the quiet interludes, the grand drama of approaching thunder clouds—the unfolding, overwhelming grandeur of creation.

Sheep, in the form of a wedge, were eating their way slowly toward a well-worn lane leading to a centuries-old, classic Italian farmhouse. Four big white dogs, Maremmas, were guarding the sheep, so perfectly blended in, I did not for the longest time notice them—they looked just like sheep in the flock. Behind them stood spires and towers reaching up from the high ground of Radicondoli—the perfect backdrop to a timeless scene. In the center of it all stood a massive oak tree in a sea of green, parting the flowing white school of grazing sheep.

I wanted to be a shepherd, sitting beneath that oak, reading a book in the low-angle light of a misty November morning as the sheep jingled about me searching for sweet tufts of grass. The GPS indicated a distance of just over a kilometer to my destination. *Please Lord, let this be the farm.* The difficulty of finding Lorenzo's place was fresh in my memory. I was afraid to give free rein to my joy. I wanted to be picking olives on this peaceful hillside for the next seven days—to walk the same lane the sheep were walking—and to eat my meals in the farmhouse at the end of the lane. I wanted all that but I did not yet know that this was Podere Paugnano, the farm where I was scheduled to work for a week. I saw no sign. I praised God for the grace of it all—a masterpiece of form, color, and movement. The words of Luigi Barzini came to mind: *Italy… is a masterpiece made by God in a moment of special felicity, each mountain shaped, each lake designed, each tree planted, and each shoreline etched in the exact way to achieve some particular poetic or pictorial effect.*

What, I wondered, do atheists and materialists feel when confronted with such wondrous beauty? Surely they too are moved, but who do they praise? The sunlight, the sheep, the dogs, the clouds—all were just where they needed to be to create in those green fields an earthly paradise at the precise moment I coasted into the clearing.

I glanced again at the GPS. It indicated only five hundred meters to my destination. The highway curved, then rose up and over a small hill. At two hundred meters, a turnoff appeared, but still no *agriturismo* sign. I turned with hope, but no certainty, onto the unpaved, rock-strewn road and followed it down a steep, gullied hill. The road leveled and ran alongside the path leading the sheep home from pasture. I got to the farmhouse just before the leading edge of the sheep was entering the barnyard. I still didn't know whether I was at the right farm, but even if I had to climb back up to the highway to make my way to a neighboring farm I would have judged it all worthwhile just to have arrived at the very moment the sheep were coming in from the pasture.

Looking out from the farm was almost as beautiful as looking in. Radicondoli seemed close enough that on a good morning, with currents of rising air, I was confident I could fling a Frisbee across the valley, and it would climb up and out and over the ancient walls and into the *piazza*. I watched its mythical flight until the Frisbee disappeared and then turned to look at the large, inviting farmhouse that strongly reminded me of Aurora's solid house. Which door should I enter—the back or the front? I chose what seemed to be the more public entrance and walked past a large outdoor table with views of the western horizon and through a door that opened onto the world I'd been looking for—a large table surrounded by people overflowing with energy. All eyes turned toward me and arms with open hands flew into the air.

Giovanni, sitting at the head of the table, waved for me to come and sit, pointing to the only opening at the table, a corner spot on the far end. Giovanna, wearing an apron and a shy smile, reminded me of Amish women I've known. She brought me a plate, poured me a glass of wine, then introduced me. Names and hands were thrust at me, as each person introduced himself. I didn't count, but it felt like twenty people, maybe more, were seated around that table. Giovanni, a solid rock of a man, toasted me and welcomed me to his farm. Then the conversations, the noise level, the intensity, and the emotion went right back to where they'd had been when I walked through the door.

Giovanni picked up right where he had left off with Renato, who, because of his broken nose and cauliflower ears, I dubbed *The Fighter*. The name also fit, I was now discovering, because of the passion and conviction with which he expressed his opinions. Even though he was at the far end of the table, I could hear his voice clearly over the others. Sitting at Giovanni's right shoulder, Renato was letting words fly out of his mouth so assuredly, that were this my first day in Italy, I would have thought I'd stepped into the middle of a heated argument that might erupt into a fistfight or at the very least cause hard feelings that would not be softened for months, if ever. But here in Italy, this was just typical table talk, which has no appetite for the banality of political correctness or lockstep thinking. Tuscans—all Italians—have strong personalities, and they have no reservations about expressing their individuality.

The fervor of their opinions stimulated me. I wanted to follow every conversation, but for me, managing even one in Italian is difficult. The young man seated next to me, another Pietro, knew enough English, and I enough Italian, that I learned that he and half a dozen of his friends had been coming to Podere Paugnano from all over Italy for six or seven years to help with the olive harvest and renew themselves around Giovanni and Giovanna's table.

I attributed to grace the fact that I didn't come first to this farm. I never would have left. I would not have rebuilt Pietro's wall, or sold

Lorenzo's wine, or been taken in by the street urchin of Florence. I would have settled into the flow of this family and their guests and would have picked olives for them as long as they needed me. And once that was finished, I would have volunteered to make cheese or shepherd their sheep—whatever it took to earn my keep.

By the time we got to the fruit, we'd been at the table for an hour. I didn't know how long they had been eating before I arrived, but it looked like they'd been enjoying lunch for quite some time. Giovanna noticed that I had finished eating and motioned for me to follow her, saying to me in English, "show you room," and then apologized in Italian for her English. I responded in Italian, telling her not to worry; I had chosen her family because I wanted to speak Italian.

At the far end of the patio, Giovanna led me though a door that opened into a comfortable sitting room. She showed me a bathroom that was bigger than the camper I slept in at my first farm. Then she swung open another door and showed me a large room with a big bed and plenty of storage—the kind of room you expect at a four-star bed and breakfast—a chocolate rested on the pillow.

"*Rilassari un momento,*" she said, "No one will pick olives for fifteen minutes." At that moment I couldn't comprehend why anyone would ever want to leave this farm. I unpacked my bags, took a look out the picture window to the distant hills, then lay down for a moment to reflect on my good fortune.

By the time we began meandering down the lane toward the olive grove, three o'clock had quietly come and gone. The mood was relaxed. Pietro and his friends had been at the farm for most of a week. Tomorrow they would be leaving—today they were giddy. They recalled other years and other harvests and laughed at the memories. They were professionals living in the city who liked seeing the fruit of their labor, something which I gathered they didn't always see in their careers. And they like being with Giovanni and Giovanna, so year after year they keep coming back.

We didn't work very long that afternoon, but we worked steadily—and apparently efficiently because by the time we quit just before five, we had filled two more *cassetti* with olives than I expected.

The sun was still well above the horizon as we made our way back to the farmyard, to the baby lambs Giovanni wanted to show off to his city friends. But Pietro and his friends, like me, were more interested in the wild boar, *il cinghiale*, that Giovanni had raised on the farm since it was a baby—an animal that still looked wild, even dangerous. As he showed us around, pointing out many new buildings and even more on the drawing boards, I got the feeling, similar to what I had felt at Lorenzo's, that Giovanni's farm was under the influence of big business, burdened by big debt. What had happened in America seemed to be happening in Tuscany as well. And just like Lorenzo, Giovanni had not been in the olive grove picking with us.

That night at dinner I learned that Giovanni and his father had bought the place in 1968, a run-down farm that had neither good land nor good buildings. The fields were so depleted and filled with rocks that he found he needed two big tractors on tracks, Caterpillars, to restore the land and make it productive again. He also bought a large John Deere tractor on rubber to work the land, make hay, and plant crops. His father was a shepherd, *un pastore*, from Sardinia. They were not greeted with open arms. The locals thought the Southerners had come to steal things. He is not sure he is welcome, even today, over forty years later. With a wry smile, Giovanni mentions that there is one local with whom he has developed very close ties.

"You mean the banker?" I ask.

"*Si, il banchiare,*" Giovanni says, "*un compagno di sventura.*" I am not familiar with the phrase, but his hands and face tell me that it means something like a partner in misfortune.

Despite the hard times, or maybe because of them, Giovanni is proud of what he and his father and family have accomplished. He seems just as proud of the house he has built as he is of the land he has restored. The house is large enough for extended family. His unmarried daughter, Natalie and his married daughter, Tamara, and her husband Maurizio live with them, and of course guests and *wwoofers* too. He even built a separate house that he rents out for extra income. Joining us at the table that night was its current tenant, Allessandro, a horse whisperer from *Roma*, presently enjoying the great view the house has of Radicondoli. Alessandro has been coming to Podere Paugnano for many years. He uses it as his hotel when he has business in the area.

Giovanni's *agriturismo* is a great model for farming in the twenty-first century. The farm is well diversified—animals, olives, people. A farm near population centers or natural or man-made attractions—or just a quiet place in the country—is a resource that can bring a steady stream of income. Farmers may get made fun of as hicks, hayseeds, and worse, but a lot of people feel a deep desire to remain connected to the land—if not permanently, then like Pietro and his friends, to get a fix once a year.

The farmer who finds ways to harness the energy of people who have a craving for land will stand a better chance of surviving when farming is forced to become less dependent upon fossil fuels. That day may not come for many years, even decades, but in this crazy world the need for repopulating the countryside could arrive before the next olive crop is ready to be picked.

Establishing an *agriturismo* may not be a good source of income for every farmer, but inn-keeping is working for Giovanni and Giovanna. It harkens back to the weekly cash income from eggs that sustained many farm families during the Great Depression in America. The egg money was part of the old model of a well-diversified farm—a model that lost favor when government handouts made the old-fashioned practices of diversity, stewardship, and husbandry less necessary. With money from taxpayers, putting all your eggs in one basket became little risk at all. No longer was there a need to pay attention to the market and to diversified income, if price supports guaranteed you cost of production in your one-crop specialization.

Over the years Giovanni has been feeling the changing winds of economic reform and has turned to marketing directly to the consumer. Cheese is now his primary product at farmers markets, but the farm experience is arguably Giovanni's best-selling product. He has the facilities, and his family has the temperament. In the week I was at Giovanni's farm I must have met forty people, maybe more. Some would show up for the noon meal and never be seen again. Others joined us for every meal. Some provided income to the farm, some provided labor, but all created an interesting, energized atmosphere.

Giovanni and Giovanna understand what today's traveler wants—great accommodations, great food, great camaraderie. The way they run their farm perfectly illustrates one of the paradoxes of life: *If you want to get something, first you have to give it.* They give of themselves and it comes flowing back like a river to them. I feel I could write a promo for Giovanni and Giovanna. In my younger days I would have made a film about their farm—casting it as the farm of the future if governments ever face up to the fact that they're going broke using subsidies to keep farmers subjugated.

People feel a deep desire to be close to the land. Growing up in a small town, I felt a strong affinity for the land. It's not a crazy idea to think that people who have grown up in cities, with no connection to dirt, might want the same thing too. If the world's economy self-destructs, not only will people be wanting to feel connected to the land, but they will also once again see the direct link between life and dirt. When the shelves of grocery stores are empty and food is hard to find, everyone will wish for a little piece of ground, or they will want to know a farmer they can depend on.

I fell in love with Podere Paugnano even before I set foot on that lovely land
—even before I knew I would spend my last week in Italy on that farm. I
came over a rise in the road and saw a flock of sheep grazing on the hillside.
That pastoral scene topped off for me what had already been an idyllic ride
through the Tuscan countryside. What I didn't know then was that there are
four large dogs, Maremmas, "grazing" with those sheep. Can you spot them?

The fog cascading down the valley, and that valley only, was a fascinating
meteorological phenonenon that greeted me several mornings as I walked
from my room to the main house for breakfast.

The camaraderie of Podere Paugnano was outstanding—Giovanna and Giovanni's farm was a tremendous example of what a diverse farm of the twenty-first century will look like. Not only do they raise good food, they raise good times for everyone who partakes of their hospitality. We also did a little "partaking" of wine the day this photo was taken. I also fell in love with the little guest house that Giovanni built to accommodate his many guests. During the week I was on the farm, we were joined at the dinner table by at least forty people—some were there the whole week—others joined us for only one meal. Giovanna was a very good cook but that wasn't the only attraction. Hospitality was the main course at Podere Paugnano.

I was enjoying being forced to speak Italian. But on my second day another *wwoofer* showed up. The moment she walked into the house, the language dynamics changed. Italian began flowing much faster. Anna was from Sweden, but when she was very young, she had lived with her parents in Italy. She'd also lived for a year in Tennessee as an exchange student.

Rather than stumble through on my own, I could now just ask for an interpretation. I understood a lot more of what was going on around the table, but I'm not sure I progressed much further in my Italian. I did, however, learn something about Sweden that I've reflected upon many times since. I've also wondered if it might be true for much of Europe.

At dinner a few evenings after Anna arrived, we were discussing the differences between Sweden and Italy. "We have quit religion," Anna said as though she were discussing what Swedes like to eat for breakfast. "Officially, Sweden used to be Lutheran. We have lots of churches, but they are empty now."

I was shocked. I don't think many Italians would say that Italy has quit religion, but Catholicism does seem to have lost some of its influence on the average Italian. Not once since arriving in Italy had I sat down to a meal at which grace was said.

Anna went on to mention another fact about Sweden that piqued my curiosity. You become a Christian in Sweden not by a profession of faith in Jesus, but by the fact that your mother is a Christian, presumably in the eyes of the state. How Anna felt about the matriarchal succession of Christianity I don't know, but she did convey that she viewed quitting religion as a good thing. And I suppose that shouldn't be surprising if the religion being considered is based on inheritance—not faith.

Anyone who has been exposed to the foundational principles of Christianity would recognize the fallacy of the idea that you become a Christian by being born to a Christian. No surer way exists to kill Christianity than for the state to mandate that Christianity is not a matter of belief, but of lineage. After only one generation, people who are labeled by the state as Christians—as well as those who "self-identify" as Christians—most likely would not be. Despite the fact that a very high percentage of Swedes (between half and three quarters of the population depending upon the poll) say they do not believe in God, they still prefer to be known as Christians rather than atheists. And eighty percent of Swedes back up that desire with their checkbooks—by their willingness to pay a tax to their government for maintaining their membership in the Lutheran Church.

Whenever someone brings up the subject of religion, the distinctions between God and religion are what I hope to find the courage to focus on. I lost interest in religion on December 27, 1979. On that morning, on a snow-covered bridge near Aspen, Colorado, God crashed into my complacent, self-centered, smug life. The mental gymnastics with which I had contorted my mind to keep God out of my worldview instantly began looking silly to me as I lay in the middle of the Castle Creek Bridge with my body pinned beneath the top of the car that only moments before I had been driving. On that morning, as I was regaining consciousness, God became real to me. On that morning all the things I thought I cared deeply about became inconsequential. On that morning family became vitally important to me, and to my wife as well. On that morning we began trusting grace for more children.

I lost all concern about the business contract I had so desperately wanted only minutes before. I became focused only on people. Once I found out that my potential clients, my passengers, were alive, I focused only on one thing. I wanted the EMT who was leaning down next to my face to promise me that he would call my wife and tell her I was OK (I didn't at the time know whether that was true, but that is what I wanted him to tell her) and that I loved her. I didn't, however, ask him to tell my wife that I wanted to have more children.

We had decided two boys were enough. Matthew was five and Christopher three at the time of the crash. Our daughter, Gretchen, was born a year after the accident. She also has another set of brothers, Jonathan and Jimi, and two siblings we won't get to know until we get to the next life—two children who died while Mardi was carrying them in her womb.

On that morning my life was transformed. I could spend a lifetime trying to pass on to you all that was conveyed to me in that moment— that eye-opening moment when I came to see just how ephemeral, how transitory this life is, but I lack the certainty that it is possible for that kind of knowledge to be conveyed, short of a direct confrontation—a Damascus Road encounter with eternity—or the prospect of entering it. To the extent that I am successful, it will be because I have trusted grace, and you have come to see what I mean when I use the phrase, *trusting grace.*

The injuries I suffered that day were mainly to my upper body. The emergency room doctor that morning was the best reconstructive surgeon in Aspen. The stitches he sewed in my head and face numbered in the hundreds. A good friend who brought my wife to the hospital told me later that he almost threw up when he saw me. But within three years, few of the scars were noticeable, and by then I also had a mouthful of new teeth, straighter than those I lost. The physical injuries I suffered that day are now merely minor annoyances, but the mental and spiritual transformations of that day affect me still. In that split second when my car crashed into that guardrail after being hit by an out-of-control Jeep, my life was transformed. Before that crash I hardly ever thought of God—now few hours go by in which I am not aware of God's grace.

When Anna told me that Sweden had quit religion, I didn't ask her how she felt about it, although I certainly was curious. I was letting the conversation take its natural flow and rhythm. But a few moments later, Giovanni stopped mid-sentence in a conversation he was having with Pino, looked at me, and asked in Italian if I liked using a *mechanista.* I didn't know exactly what the word meant, but I felt safe in saying, "Not much" since it was almost certainly some kind of machine. (However I should point out that I have been surprised many times by Italian words that sound similar to English words, but have meanings that are embarrassingly, *un-*similar—for example, Annamarja's use of the word *fastidioso* tripped me up. It means *annoying* not *fastidious.*) To answer Giovanni, I used the Italian words *non* and *molto* together. Whether that translates to the *not much* of English, I didn't know, but by the frown on my face I think Giovanni understood what my words were meant to convey.

The next morning as we picked olives, Pino, Attilio, and Renato, all long-time friends of Giovanni, were in superb form. I was catching only about half of their punch lines, but even if I hadn't understood a single joke or caught the gist of their stories, I would have loved listening to the music of their voices as they sang out their tales.

The grove fell silent, though, when Giovanni drove up in his pickup. We watched as he reached into the bed of the truck to pull out a shaker like the one I had seen Valter use on his farm. Giovanni handed the *mechanista* to Pino—and that's where it stayed all day. Renato and Attilio continued telling stories in fits and spurts, but the words never again flowed with the same energy. The men were closer to shouting than singing. I tried to work as far as possible from the clatter. But on some trees I had no choice but to work right next to the noisemaker.

On the second day Pino grew tired of using the *mechanista* and handed it to Attilio. On the third day Attilio grew weary of being tied to it and handed it to Renato the Fighter. I had enjoyed each day picking olives in the same tree as Renato. I liked watching him—the movements of his large hands were athletic and precise. As he worked his way from branch to branch, he was as careful with the placement of his feet as he was with his hands. Not once did his boots damage the olives clustered about in the nets. He was a delight to have in the grove. I didn't always understand everything he said, but it was fun just sharing his joy.

But with the *mechanista* in his hand Renato became a different person. He was no longer telling stories. His grace was gone. Still, he reminded me of a fighter, but now he was a punch-drunk boxer lumbering around the ring fighting a much taller opponent. He lost all thought of the olives underfoot—his eyes focused only on the olives in the tree. The olives his boots were trampling were no longer important. He could neither hear the squishing of the plump olives nor see the oil on his boots. The grove lost its energy. Renato must have been its life force.

The day before Renato was concerned about making the best olive oil possible. With the *mechanista* in his hands Renato was concerned only with knocking olives from the tree. That became for me the perfect metaphor of what is wrong with factory farming—farming that has as its bottom line doing things as fast as possible. Time is a terrible tyrant. Quality is also a demanding taskmaster, but quality has a *rightness* to it. You feel good about making something as good as it can possibly be.

The following morning the *mechanista* was handed over to Giovanni's son-in-law, but not to shake olives off the tree. Maurizio was stretched out on the ground beside the now-silent stick, attaching and reattaching wires, trying to isolate a short in the electrical system. By his demeanor I could tell he'd been futzing with it quite a while. He put the plastic covers back on the motor, and hoisted the thing up to the branches with an air of triumph. But the feeling didn't last long. Within two minutes the grove fell silent again. Maurizio puttered again with the machine for five minutes. Before long, a pattern developed. The fooling around would be followed by two or three minutes of shaking—then the *mechanista* would fall silent again—a few profane words would be offered, and that would be followed by more tinkering, which would be followed by another couple of minutes of shaking. The machine, I can report with little fear of a contradictory opinion, was on that morning definitely hurting productivity. It wasn't doing much for story-telling either. I did, however, learn some new words.

The question of what to do on Sunday came up. Giovanna suggested that I should not leave her farm without seeing the ruins of the Abbey of San Galgano. The sincerity with which she said it and the words she used brought to mind Pietro's recommendation that I just *had* to see Le Celle. I pulled the heavy *Blue Guide Tuscany* out of my back pack (two pounds I'd been questioning the wisdom of carrying the past three hundred fifty kilometers) and looked up the abbey. The first sentence convinced me Giovanna was right, "The ruined Abbey of San Galgano is one of the most spectacular sights in all of Italy. It has survived for centuries, abandoned and roofless, in majestic isolation, in the middle of beautiful farming country." I didn't know it by name, but I'd seen many pictures of San Galgano, a massive church sitting abandoned in a wheat field, or so it has always appeared to me.

On Sunday morning I left Podere Paugnano at daybreak—early enough that clouds of fog were still hanging in the valley when I arrived. Just as I began riding down the lane of cypress trees leading to San Galgono, the clouds parted and the ruins of the church appeared out of the mist. The effect transfixed me. Adding to the atmosphere was a cart drawn by a horse clopping down the lane leading to the ruins. I slowed my pace, imagining that instead of riding to the ruins on a bike, I was arriving at the abbey via horse-drawn cart. I was reminded again of Le Celle—of arriving there on foot. Clip-clop, clip-clop, clip-clop—the horse and driver pulled me back half a millennium in those two hundred meters. By the time I walked through the doors and looked up to see the hole where stained glass used to be, I was in a full-blown state of praise. The only word that comes close to describing the feeling is *humbling*—the metaphor of a church without a roof was perfect for the moment—nothing in the way of a relationship with God.

The *Blue Guide* had not resorted to hyperbole. This truly is a "spectacular sight." Were I writing the guidebook I might have carried the alliteration further and dubbed it "a spiritually spectacular sight." The early morning ride in patchy fog, the beautifully landscaped approach to the church, and then the moment of stepping through the doors and into a church open to the heavens was truly singular, the kind of moment you never forget. God was not only real at that moment—He felt extremely close. I tried to imagine why such a beautiful church was built and what led to its abandonment. I wondered if it felt then as deeply spiritual with a roof—as it does now without.

Desiring to stay in the moment, I walked outside and around to the back, looking for a private place, and found a very old wooden bench and sat down to eat breakfast. Slowly I realized that I was surrounded by abandoned gardens and what looked like chicken coops. This abbey would have had to be self-sufficient, an independent production unit. Oh, how I'd love to be have been able to travel back in time to see both the good times and the hard times this very special piece of ground had known.

Why was this remote site chosen to construct such a large church? Was that same question asked at the time it was built? I looked up at a nearby hill and saw a small chapel that was still being used. What I discovered up there struck forcefully against the materialistic view of the world I held until I was thirty-three years old. I found a sword sticking out of a large rock—and the answers to my questions.

The Archangel Michael visited an aristocrat named Galgano Guidotti in the twelfth century and asked him to abandon his life of nobility and privilege. Guidotti countered that giving up his worldly riches would be as likely to happen as his sword penetrating a rock. To make his point, he drew his weapon and thrust it at a boulder, expecting the blade to snap. The stone swallowed his sword to the hilt as easily and smoothly as if it were a huge ball of butter. Stunned by the miracle, Guidotti accepted the archangel's challenge and built a chapel around the penetrated rock and never left the hill again, devoting the rest of his life to prayer.

When I learned that Saint Galgano died in 1181, the same year Saint Francis was born, I was further reminded of the power of one man's vision to create a life of service and sacrifice that others follow. Some might view that sword as a hoax—I certainly would have for the first half of my life—but something changed that man's life to cause him to renounce his riches and live out his remaining years in prayer and service. That sword in the stone is a reminder that this world is full of mysteries and that God is, as the Lakota of the Sioux Nation called Him, the *Great Mysterium*. If God is capable of creating this world, then He is capable of causing a rock to swallow a sword, or turning water into wine, or making me to see the futility of seeking worldly wealth and fame.

Is it important that one believes Saint Galgano pierced a rock with his sword? I don't know if it needs to be more than metaphor—death to the material world. The important thing to remember is that a person of privilege, by living a life of sacrifice and service, inspired others to become monks, to live lives of sacrifice, and to build a church in a wheat field. Today, almost eight hundred years later, this church is still helping people to believe in the reality of God, even though those who worship in it look with no impediments to the sky and beyond to the heavens.

When I got back to Podere Paugnano, I tried to convey to everyone what I had felt at San Galgano. Those who had been there already knew it was special. Those who had not may someday go. Will they feel what Saint Galgano felt or what I glimpsed today? Who knows, but I hoped Anna would find reason to go. Her comment that "We have quit religion" intrigued me. Galgano's sword pierced a rock and he bowed down before the reality of God. My face split open on a steering wheel and I came face to face with the reality of God. Both Galgano and I may have been on a journey to *quitting religion*. God intrudes upon the complacency of each of us in unique ways. The possibility of God changing from religion to reality in the lives of other people leaves within me a desire to express the ineffable.

If Anna goes to San Galgano, I hope she too will be struck by the reality of God. For all I know, God is as real to her as He is to me—knowing the really important things about another person is all but impossible. But if God *is* real to her, I hope next time she says "We have quit religion," I hope she will quickly add, "but God—that is a different story. I have not quit God." My encounter with the steering wheel convinced me that God has not quit her.

Saint John told us how difficult it is to find words to express the experience of encountering God. I cannot get my mind around why it should be that words cannot be found—cannot be created—for something that has been happening to people for thousands of years. But the difficulty remains, and I remain in awe of a sword in a stone, a man walking on water, and the most amazing miracle of all—transformed, revitalized lives.

The Blue Guide had not resorted to hyperbole. San Galgano is a "spectacular sight." Were I writing the guidebook I might have carried the alliteration further and dubbed it "a spiritually spectacular sight." The early morning ride in patchy fog, the beautifully landscaped approach to the church, and then the moment of stepping through the doors and into a church open to the heavens was truly singular, the kind of moment you never forget. Not only was God real at that moment—He felt extremely close.

San Galgano will always be special to me. Some places disappoint because expectations are so high. Certainly my hopes had been raised by Giovanna. Her recommendation brought to mind Pietro's words—you can not leave Italy without seeing Le Celle—and now Giovanna had used the same words. But San Galgano did not disappoint. I shall never forget the quiet Sunday morning I spent at this church open to the blue skies of heaven.

Chapter Eleven

Only he can understand what a farm is, what a country is,
who shall have sacrificed part of himself to his farm
or country, fought to save it, struggled to make it beautiful.
Only then will the love of farm or country fill his heart.
ANTOINE DE SAINT-EXUPERY

A Long Day's Journey

Giovanna didn't say whether the dish she had prepared was in honor
of America's upcoming holiday, but for what would be my last meal at
Podere Paugnano, she announced that the meat making its way around
the table was *tacchino*, which I understood to be turkey until I tasted it.
This sumptuous, savory food could not be turkey—beef, lamb, or *cin-*
ghiale—but not turkey. If this was turkey, it was the best-tasting turkey
I'd ever eaten. I checked with Anna, *"Questo che cose?"* She tasted it. She
didn't know. I told her Giovanna had said it was *tacchino*.

"No way," she said. She tasted it again. "No, this isn't turkey. Aren't
you ever going to learn Italian?"

She was right about my Italian, and the meat too. This was too tasty, too flavorful. "Ask Giovanna," I said. Anna knew it wouldn't be the first time I had misunderstood an Italian word.

My eyes were focused on Giovanna as she listened to Anna. Giovanna smiled, putting her hand to her mouth. Anna had praised the dish while questioning what it was. Giovanna recovered her composure, then quietly and simply said, "*Tacchino.*"

Anna thanked her and turned to me, her eyes wide, and said, "Wow. Oh my God." Anna had lived in America long enough to know just what to say when you've tasted something divine. I didn't think before I blurted out, "*Vorrei ricetta?*" Good manners or bad in Italy, I didn't know, but Giovanna humored me and sent me on my way back to America with her recipe for turkey.

I promised, in exchange, that I would email photos I had taken of all of us around the table. The Podere Paugnano family was small and intimate that Sunday night—Giovanni and Giovanna, Renato, Pino, Attilio, Alessandro the Horse Whisperer, Tamara and Maurizio, Natalie, and Anna, the only non-Italian, besides me. Everyone gave me a hearty "*Arrivederci*" after dinner, including Giovanna, even though she assured me that she'd be up in time to say goodbye in the morning. But only Natalie, who had to get up extremely early to catch a ride to school, was awake to send me off. She gave me a couple of oranges to put in my backpack. How fitting—*Siamo alla frutta*—We are at the fruit. Tuscans cap off their meals with fruit. *Siamo alla frutta* is a common saying meaning "We are at the end."

Leaving a farm is never easy, especially one as welcoming and comforting as Podere Paugnano. Two factors are driving the timing. A Thanksgiving celebration with my family is but four days away, and I have to bicycle across Tuscany to retrieve my phone charger before flying across the Atlantic and half the American continent. I could wait one day and leave on Tuesday, but that would leave little time in case anything went wrong. I would have liked to have stayed longer with Giovanni and Giovanna so I could learn more about their struggles to make a living and a good life on the land, and to get to know their family better.

I disliked leaving without hugs for the road, but leaving before the sun was up, even before Giovanni checked on his animals, was necessary if I was going to be certain of getting to Aurora's farm by nightfall. One hundred thirty-five kilometers separated me from my phone charger, which I'd just discovered that I'd left in Aurora's loft the morning I was rushing to catch the train to Florence. And if I made a wrong turn or two, the total could easily add up to one hundred fifty or more kilometers of unknown, possibly hazardous roads with long, tortuous climbs.

Between Radicondoli and Cortona are many routes, but none is anywhere near straightforward. I chose the back roads, through the mountains. It was a riskier route, but I had ridden the twenty-five kilometers from Podere Paugnano to San Galgano the day before in only seventy minutes. I estimated that the trailer and extra weight would add twenty additional minutes to the trip. If that was even close to the pace I could maintain on the rest of the route, I could get to Camucia by mid-afternoon, and have plenty of time to make it the rest of the way up the boulder-strewn road to Aurora's, even if I had to push my bike and trailer the whole way.

Light was just beginning to grace the eastern sky as I finished pushing my bike to the top of Giovanni's steep driveway. I wheeled the bike and trailer onto the highway, hopped onto the saddle, and took one last look at the farm I had grown to love. Only the light in the *cucina* was glowing. I zeroed the bike computer for time and distance and pushed off. Even in the predawn light the roadway was easy to distinguish, delineated as it was by towering trees. At the fifteen-kilometer mark I switched off my headlamp. I had not yet turned on the GPS. The battery life on the GPS is three or four hours at best. If I made a bad decision or two, I might need to pedal for fifteen hours. I hoped I was way off on my estimate, but if I wasn't, I wanted batteries to light and direct the way.

Even though I'd ridden this exact route the day before, I studied the map at each intersection. A wrong turn, even if I caught it quickly, could cost a lot of time, and if I kept riding oblivious to where I was going, it could cost me hours. The frequent stops to study the map, as well as the extra weight and drag of the trailer cost a lot of time. At the turnoff to San Galgano I was almost forty minutes behind my pessimistic schedule and close to an hour behind my optimistic guess. I prayed for good decisions, especially on choosing my route, and for good measure I prayed for a tailwind.

What I got was winding roads through nature preserves and over mountaintops opening up to expansive valley views. I saw more big, white Maremmas guarding sheep. I followed rivers and ridges. Just like Irving Stone wrote, nothing less than a state of grace accounts for the beauty that is seen at every turn of the road in the Tuscan landscape. The cynic can say that Tuscan farmers were just doing whatever was necessary to eke out a living from less than fertile soil and beauty was the result. But I, as a lover of land, and a farmer, know better. Tuscans have an eye for beauty that seems to have been inherited from their forebears, the Etruscans. Everywhere, the land has the look of wisdom and antiquity. And the Etruscans, it might be argued, were given their eye for beauty—and their wisdom—from the land itself.

I had chosen this route for the possibility of spectacular scenery, but time became my driving force. I considered biking through Buonconvento but chose what looked like a shorter route through Suvignano and Montauto and Asciano. I should have taken the names of the towns as warnings—the route was a savage, mountainous ascent. By the time I had climbed to Asciano, much of the day was gone, and I still had at least forty kilometers to go. The shortest day of the year was but four weeks away. I needed daylight, time, and batteries, and I had little of the first two and I was low on the third.

I had to turn on the GPS more than I wanted to keep from wandering in ignorant bliss down the wrong roads, most of which were unmarked. But my biggest mistake of the day may have been in the midst of civilization, in high speed bumper-to-bumper traffic when I turned right instead of left when I hit Highway 2 near the halfway point of the day's ride. By opting to ride the shortest distance on that busy highway I may have chosen a much longer route to Camucia.

I had just made up my mind to turn around, when I noticed a sign designating a little-traveled road as a bike route. I've since wondered whether I might have misinterpreted that sign. It may have instead signified a mountain bike route—a brutally steep mountain bike route. I frequently lost traction on the gravel, but I kept seeing the signs, so I continued, making my way slowly up one mountain and down another. Gorgeous country. Farms small and large. Country estates, and even suburban-looking homes, which seemed very much out of place. Land that should not have been farmed because it was too steep—and land that should be farmed, but was not, because some of the fields were too small for the big tractors the farmers in this area were now buying. The landscape reminded me of the wheat country of the American Northwest, a wide-open vista to distant mountains in almost every direction.

By mid-afternoon I was desperately low on water and hoping I would soon see a town. When I realized that was not going to happen, I began praying for a farmyard where I might fill my water bottles. The climb was cruel. I kept hoping for a paved and gentle road, but what I got was loose gravel and switchbacks carrying me higher and higher. I was staring at the road's surface as I struggled, a sure sign I was exhausted and dehydrated, too tired to lift my eyes from the road. Slowly I became aware that a meandering rivulet of moist gravel had appeared in my vision, working its way down the hill. My eyes, still focused on the ground, followed the moist course up the hill pedal stroke by rough pedal stroke, until at last the wet gravel widened into a pool of wet rocks. In the middle of an intersection of three roads, appearing like a mirage to my weakened mind, stood an ancient cast iron spigot, just like you'd see in a Rossellini movie, with water streaming out onto the ground. *Bella, bella.* I tasted it. Sweet, cool, and delicious. I filled the bottle on my bike, the bottle in my pack, and the extra one I carry in the trailer. I stayed by that flowing water for a long time, slowly drinking in its refreshing goodness, and giving my muscles and my mind a chance to recover. I now had enough water to get to Aurora's. And now that I was thinking clearly again, I could see I was desperately short of time.

I didn't want to turn on the GPS, so I judged my arrival time by how far I had traveled versus how much squiggly line was still left on the map to Aurora's house. I had emailed her two days earlier but had not received a reply. She checked her email once a day—at least I know she did while I was there—so she had to be expecting me. But still I wished I knew for sure. Maybe I should find a pay phone or an Internet café, but I hadn't seen a town in hours, and I didn't want to be wasting time looking that could be spent riding. All these considerations were playing over and over in my mind as the sun worked its way toward the horizon and I worked my way slowly toward Camucia.

Never did I feel I had time to stop at a restaurant, so I ate only the fruit and nuts and bread and cheese and sausage I carried with me. I was happy to be in the countryside. I was among the people, exchanging waves and greetings, and even biking for a short distance with a man on his way to visit a neighbor. Once, after half an hour of climbing, the road seemed to be dead-ending in a farmyard. I panicked, thinking I'd have to turn back. An arrival at Aurora's long after dark looked certain.

But on the other side of the barn, I found a lane leading away from the farm. I coasted slowly down the mountain, riding the brakes, working my way, I hoped, ever closer to Camucia. The long day of slow riding gave me time to reflect. I compared Tuscany to another land I had grown to love, the islands of New Zealand. While biking around Waiheke Island about twenty-five years ago, I saw an incredibly gorgeous farm with sheep grazing on rolling green hillsides with views of the sea. I remember wondering what life would be like on such a spectacular ocean-front farm with what looked like thousands of acres of perfect sheep-manicured lawns on which to ride your horse. I wondered if those ranchers got up every day and recognized the beauty, or did they take it for granted?

But something has changed in the intervening years. Instead of fantasizing about life in a different country with a pace more attuned to nature, I think now about creating a more Tuscan-like existence on my farm in Wisconsin. But quickly I realize how unlikely such a transformation is—even though we grow grapes and have vineyards in Wisconsin, we'll never grow olives.

Olive oil contributes much to making Tuscany what it is. We don't realize how much the food we grow influences the kind of people we become. We're not only what we eat, but what we grow and raise as well.

Gathering olives requires a lot of people to take care of the land, and that results in a connubial relationship that leads to a beautiful countryside and healthy communities.

During my last meal, that turkey feast at Podere Paugnano, Giovanni directed a problem to me about butchering a boar. He wanted me to figure out the amount of meat to reach the table as a percentage of dressed weight. I was sitting at the far end of the table. Everyone paused their own conversations to let Giovanni and me talk. He presented the problem to me in Italian. I felt kin with him, as a farmer, and as an honorary Italian.

That short conversation with Giovanni was as memorable—as significant—as any I had while I was in Tuscany. We were talking farmer to farmer, man to man, one father to another about putting food on the table for his family. I want to bring a Tuscan-like connection to food and the land back to Wisconsin. We who live in the land of big tractors (monster tractors live farther south) have a long way to go, but I will do what I can a little bit at a time. What meat I don't raise myself I'll buy from my local butcher who cuts the meat in my town—not meat that's been processed in a factory hundreds or thousands of miles from my home. What vegetables and fruits I don't raise myself I'll buy from my neighbors whenever possible. We create our communities with every dollar we spend locally. And we destroy our communities with every dollar we spend carelessly—every dollar we spend eliminating our neighbor, and every dollar we spend buying more land than we can take good care of.

Most nations on Earth, including Italy, are in financial trouble. Getting out of debt will be the road paving our way to understanding. Just about every country is going to have to adapt to a saner, a more food-oriented standard of living. My experience in Tuscany tells me that having fewer material goods does not translate to a less enjoyable life. The standard of living, as such things are measured, is lower in Tuscany than America, but the enjoyment of life is not. The simple things of life, which typically translate to the God-given things of life, bring us the most lasting pleasure and comfort. I learned about such things in an instant on that bridge in Aspen. Some people are born wise, but for others it takes a whole lifetime to learn simple truths. Of course some people don't live long enough learn such truths. Many people believe that the things of God are only for naïve, simple-minded people. Smart people, industrious people, the educated elite have better things with which to occupy themselves. And many people stay concerned with those *better* things and those thoughts their whole lives.

I'm still not sure why Italians have learned the lesson of simple pleasures so well that generation after generation is blessed with that wisdom, but learn it they have. Focusing on people, not things is so ingrained in their way of life that they would not stoop to call it wisdom. It's just the way they live. Even though many, particularly the young people, say they want out, the Italian way of life persists. The young have visions of what are supposedly the better things. Many of them want a more materialistic way of life. And I suppose it should always be that way. Each generation has to learn anew what the most valuable things in life are. Mankind is free to choose many paths. Italians choose the path of people, family, and relationships. Only in those societies where people have lost the freedom to choose, is it impossible to learn these lessons.

I chose that day a path that took me down and up many difficult roads to get to Camucia. Google maps informed me that I could have chosen a dozen routes with similar estimated travel times, routes in the real world that may have gotten me to Aurora's many hours earlier. I might have enjoyed better surfaces, fewer hills, and less distance. But that route, leading me over mountains and through farmyards was the route I traveled—and just like the paths we go down in life, we can only try to imagine what different roads in life might have meant to us.

The woman I married is the upshot, from my limited perspective, of a change in my schedule on just one day of my life. Had I not altered my routine on the final day of summer school of my senior year of college, going to the Union instead of the library, I do not see how I would have ever met her. But that was the choice I made that day. And soon we will celebrate our forty-second year of marriage.

Strange life this. I made a lot of decisions getting from Giovanni's farm to Aurora's farm. I marvel at the way the day turned out. That day is a microcosm of life. When I was in college, mapping out my life, I envisioned I'd be an architect and have two children—a boy and a girl. At Aurora's I envisioned a warm welcome, the chance to tell everyone my stories, and an opportunity to listen to theirs. I didn't know I had one more farmer I needed to meet.

During those long, tiring fifteen hours on the road, I had a lot of time to think of all the people I had just met, and what those relationships meant to me. But on that day, one conversation was like a song stuck on repeat. Over and over I kept hearing Anna say, *We have quit religion.* Finally the reason hit me. Her response was eerily reminiscent of an answer I had once given to a question about religion.

The year was 1970 and I was just twenty-three years old. I'd been told to sit in a cold-looking cubicle. While I waited, I began questioning what I had just done. A private first class, dressed in fatigues, walked in and began asking me questions. The answers I gave would be imprinted on my dog tags. These metallic ID's, I was informed, were never to leave my neck. In case I was killed in Vietnam—I could be identified and given last rites. *Whoa.*

Social Security Number? Blood type? Religion?

The first two were quickly and easily answered, and the third should have been, would have been, if I'd joined the Army right out of high school. I would have responded, "Congregational." The PFC would have written down Protestant and that would have been that. But I had spent four and one-half years, plus two sessions of summer school in college, and such things were no longer simple for me. The young man saw that I was having trouble answering the question, so he offered me some alternatives. "Are you Roman Catholic?"

I shook my head.

"Are you Protestant?" I didn't shake my head, nor did I say anything. I'd been away from church a long time and I'd taken a lot of classes that seemed to have little use for God, Jesus, or Christianity. I'd rubbed shoulders for almost half a dozen years with hundreds of people who also had little use for anything remotely connected to "organized religion," so I figured they must have a category for people like me. Surely I wasn't the only guy having trouble with this question. And I was right. I don't know how many other choices the PFC skipped over to get to the one he thought I might be looking for, but he threw me a home run ball for the next pitch and I hit it out of the park with barely a thought given to how I might feel about my answer years later.

On that day I branded my dog tags and myself with the religion of "No Pref," short for "No Preference." For the three years I served in the U.S. Army I operated in that realm of weak belief. I never descended to a consideration of the term *atheist*. Even in my periods of weakest belief, it seemed too prideful to say that God does not exist. But *agnostic* occasionally came to mind as I tried to resolve the materialism that kept darkening my worldview. The process that began my freshman year of college continued until my window on the world became so clouded I could no longer see to the other side. I saw only this world and what I was going to make of myself. I was *a self-made man worshipping his creator,* as a newspaper cartoon clinging by a magnet to my mother-in-law's refrigerator reminded me.

I did not at that time know that a man who knew so little, could think he knew so much. Maybe college graduates today think of themselves the same way, but I think not. In the late 1960s even adults aided us in our self-deception. We young people were given far too much credit. Far too many people were convinced we were going to be able to solve the world's problems. Those of us born in the heady days after World War II were told that we were unique in the history of the world. We were going to be the culmination of a journey that began in the pre-biotic soup and was now being consummated in the perfect man, the perfect society. We baby boomers had been taught that life is a continual progression. When I was a teenager, General Electric created a slogan out of the pride the whole nation felt—*Progress Is Our Most Important Product.*

We lost sight of boundaries. Then we put a man on the moon and became convinced that boundaries no longer existed. What we *could* do, we thought we *should* do. We even lost the ability to ask ourselves whether something was right or wrong. Nature existed for us to manipulate in whatever way progress dictated. Since the Renaissance, and certainly since the Industrial Revolution, we were on the way up. Nothing could stop us.

A few people urged caution by pointing out that progress involved ethical questions. The first I remember paying attention to was Rachael Carson. She helped me to question our unfettered manipulation of nature. But I was still a long way from the realization that our views of life and the universe involve presumptions or assumptions. I was thoroughly educated into the concept that only one view of reality exists. My college education was complete. I was a through-and-through materialist. I just didn't know it. I thought of myself as a realist, looking at the world just as it was. The idea that an intelligent person might have a different concept of the world had not yet occurred to me. Intelligent, educated people all over the world thought alike. And if you didn't think that way, you were either not intelligent, not educated, or both. That's what I was educated to believe, and I numbered myself among the faithful.

Not once during my college courses did a student or a teacher offer an opinion that was not perfectly in line with the materialistic view of the world. Occasionally on television I would hear about people who didn't accept the materialistic view of the world, but they lived in places like the hills of Appalachia or were sequestered in compounds in the hardscrabble outback of Texas, or so I was taught to believe. I did not yet know any Amish people. At that point in my life, they were just an oddity—a group of people stuck in the nineteenth century. Only people like that mentioned God anymore. Certainly no one did such a thing on a major university campus in the 1960s. So it was from that background I came to believe I'd done a very clever thing in letting the world know, or at least the Army, that when it comes to God and religion, I had no preference. I was an open-minded kind of guy—just what my college years had taught me to be.

I wasn't an atheist, but I wasn't a Christian either—at least not in any sense in which being a Christian made much difference in my life. I had never read the Bible, not all the way through anyway—not even one complete book. I believed what I was taught in school and in the media with more conviction than I believed what I'd learned as a child in Sunday

School and church. At college I came to accept the view that Christianity was a crutch for the weak, and I was no longer among the weak.

I was so ambivalent about tradition that I petitioned the University of Nebraska to allow me to skip the graduation ceremonies. Since I no longer had a student deferment I'd soon be receiving orders and I didn't want to waste time doing establishment stuff. It didn't take the draft board long to notice my new status—within a few weeks I had my orders. The polite language informed me that the day for raising my right hand to take the oath of induction into the United States Army was 7 May 1970.

That girl I met in the Union on the last day of summer classes married me on May 5th. I didn't see our marriage as a covenant made with God, but as a contract with the government that would provide us with a little more money and make it possible for me to live off base during my MOS training, the schooling that would prepare me to be a motion picture cameraman for the U.S. Army. Marriage was good. It was expedient. I was making more money than the single guys, but the covenant before God part—I didn't even consider.

I planned to chart my own course and not adhere to the tradition of graduation ceremonies, or the conventions of a church wedding. I was doing it my way. I believed things happened for a reason, not because God had made it happen. God may not have been dead in my world, but I sure didn't see where He had done much or for that matter had much to do, now or ever. I'd been educated to believe that God was of no consequence in our lives—an unnecessary hypothesis.

I mention all this to set the stage for what happened to me. It is obvious that I now believe in God—that God is very important in my life. How does a person change so much in one life? How do you go from disinterest to certainty about God? It's one of those great mysteries. I've come to see that I may have different beliefs about God than you do or anyone else does, but what I believe about God in no way changes Him. God is God. People approach God through different religions, call Him by different names, and have different beliefs about God, but there is only one God. My God is the same as your God. We just have differing ideas about Him.

I was surprised when I heard President Obama say, "I don't know of any gods who would condone..." at a National Prayer Breakfast—and then again a few weeks later when he announced the killing of Osama Bin Laden by saying, "No matter what god we pray to..." These references to multiple gods were obviously not a slip of the tongue. He was repeating a theme. Such use of the word *god* is a natural outgrowth of the beliefs that have held sway in America's colleges for a half-century or more, as are the actions of a television network that edited out of the Pledge of Allegiance the words, *One nation under God, indivisible..."* The educated elite have little use for the singular God.

I no longer understand how I once believed materialism's story. The only excuse I have is that I bought the story that scientists were somehow smarter than the rest of mankind when they told us we just appeared out of a *pre-biotic soup*—that's just a fancy word for non-living, which means *dead.* I didn't realize that smarter—that higher IQ—does not translate to wiser. I cannot believe I was so gullible that I bought the alchemist's dream—of base metals turning into gold and life coming from non-life. During my "education," Jesus transformed from the Messiah into being simply a good man and a good teacher. My philosophy was anchored by this question: *If we evolved, if we began life's progression in a pre-biotic soup—what influence can Jesus have on my life except as a good example?*

I have a lot of sympathy for the non-believer, even for the person antagonistic toward God. I don't know how old Anna is—certainly somewhere in her twenties, and a college graduate. In many ways she's similar to me in 1970 when I said of religion, "No preference." I also understand Pietro, even though his antagonism seems directed at the Church. And I understand Aurora asking, *How can you believe?* Life today has many impediments to belief in God.

Despite the hardships—or maybe because of them—the brutal ride across Tuscany was the right way to end my trip. I saw much and thought of much. I saw parallels to my journey from belief to unbelief and back to belief. My GPS lost all power in the last few kilometers. I had to trust my memory. This would be the third time I had ridden the route from the round-about, but it would be the only time finding the route on my own and pulling the trailer. I had followed Pietro up the hill on that first day. I followed the GPS track on the day I returned from Valter's farm. On this evening I rode from light into darkness and got lost.

After riding far enough to be sure I was on the wrong road, I turned back and found the right road—the winding lane to Aurora's. And once again I struggled up her steep, boulder-strewn road. Suddenly, the headlights of an unseen car lit up the slope above me. I pulled off the road onto the grass and waited, watching the dance of the light on the hillside above my head. When the car was right beside me, it stopped. "*Buonasera*, James," a voice called out. I was surprised to hear my name. The voice was Pietro's. "Aurora is expecting you. I'll be back before you get all the way home. I must go get Joshua."

I didn't race Pietro home that evening. I mustered the last of my energy and made my way slowly to Aurora's farm. I walked when necessary, rather than push past my limit of strength, balance, and energy. But even so, Pietro didn't get back before I got to Aurora's. Despite being near exhaustion I willed myself up that long, grueling hill pulling that fifty-plus pound trailer, and wearing a twenty-five pound pack. As I crested the final rise and pulled into Aurora's farmyard I gathered the strength to shout, "*Come va, Aurora?*"

"Terrible, James, just terrible," Aurora called out from her front porch. She was sitting by the table, agitated, my phone charger in her hand. "You cannot stay here," she said as she got up and began walking in my direction. Her trembling voice and her words stunned me as she handed me the charger. "I almost left today. I cannot take it anymore. Pietro is driving me mad."

"Oh, Aurora, I am so sorry." I reached out to hug her, but she was moving past me toward her car. She was so worked up she didn't even think to greet me. I'm sure it hurt her to not be able to welcome me to her farm. I know it hurt me.

"Dino has a place for you. He is expecting you." My mind was searching, reeling. If only I had been able to reach Aurora by phone. Maybe she wouldn't be so agitated. I certainly wouldn't be so exhausted.

Ironically, I'd been in Dino's driveway well over an hour ago. The sight of Dino's place made me realize I had made a wrong turn. I was keying in on the wrong landmarks—houses and bridges I had seen before, but not on the way to Aurora's. If only I had called Aurora. I could have wheeled into Dino's, taken a warm shower, eaten dinner, and been relaxing this very minute. But instead I had spent the past hour and a half climbing, with the last of my strength, slowly up Aurora's mountain.

And now I was going to have to ride back down that rock-strewn road in the dark. But Aurora would not have it. She insisted that I put my bike and trailer in her car. Most of the bike fit inside the car, but the trailer hitch was hanging out of the hatchback. With bungee cords and ropes I secured it while I listened to Aurora tell how she'd suffered in the weeks I had been gone.

The feeling of not being welcome at this farm where I had once felt so appreciated was odd, disconcerting. Pietro drove in just as I was tying the last knot. I realized too late that Aurora had wanted to be gone before Pietro got back. Annamarja came out of the house when she heard Pietro drive in. We had time only to exchange hugs and say goodbye to each other. I walked over to where Pietro was getting things out of the trunk of his car. "Arrivederci, Pietro." I reached out my hand. He shook it. We didn't hug, but I would have liked to.

"Arrivederci, James," he said. He was not smiling, but neither did he seem angry. I couldn't tell whether he was embarrassed. I wanted to share the stories of my last three weeks with him, but for whatever reason, it wasn't meant to be. Pietro turned and walked into the house. I was sad. I wondered what Pietro was feeling as I waved goodbye to Joshua.

Aurora and I crawled into her little Fiat, curled ourselves under the projecting bike parts, and scraped our way over the boulders to Dino's. Aurora kept repeating herself, saying only that Pietro had been awful, but saying nothing specific. I was tired, but even with a rested mind, I wasn't sure I could have come up with anything that wouldn't have sounded like an idle platitude.

As I looked back on it, I believed that it was good I climbed all the way up Aurora's hill. I was made to see and feel her anguish. I too was now persuaded that Aurora, for her own peace of mind, was going to have to turn her farm over to Pietro.

As we bounced down the road I wondered how Aurora felt about trusting grace. She was tired. She was frazzled. She seemed fearful. She was angry with Pietro for what he had put her through for the past three months. She was worrying about what an old woman would do—an old woman who could no longer stand to live under the same roof with her son. I wondered about all these things, but I could find only the words and the strength to say, "I'm sure it will work itself out, Aurora."

Our goodbye was much too short, considering how much she felt like family to me. As she pulled away, leaving me at Dino's, I regretted not being able to sit for three or four hours talking. The part that I was playing, or might play, in God's grace for Aurora, was for the moment, over. But I made a vow that night, as I watched her tail-lights disappear among the trees in the olive grove, that each year, just as the last of the olives are being pressed, I would email Aurora and thank her for the basket she gave me *to remember the good times* and ask her, "*Come va, Aurora? How's it going?*" Maybe someday she'll believe me when I tell her that I really did enjoy being on her farm...not in spite of Pietro, but because of Pietro.

He is, after all, a good boy. He just says bad things about his mother.

I learned a lot from Pietro.

Riding across the breadth of Tuscany in one day, on roads that were sometimes marginal, on a route I knew little about, was a monstrous, possibly foolhardy undertaking. But it felt right to see a "new" part of Tuscany. I didn't know what to expect and that made the ride even more of an adventure. I didn't even know for sure that I could ride that far in one day pulling a fifty-pound trailer up mountainous roads. What I found didn't disappoint. I got a broader view of Tuscany. The land was drier, the farms were larger, and the equipment used to cultivate the fields reminded me of the middle west of America. Some land was so hardscrabble that the landscape looked like Utah or West Texas— but still to my eye the beauty that Italy is known for prevailed—even in this dry land the care of the Tuscan farmers beautifies the countryside. Those sinuous lines are mini terraces plowed into bare fields by the farmer to prevent heavy rains from washing away precious topsoil.

*Dino climbed barefoot into the tree to get to olives
that had eluded me. His movements were pure grace.
He was at one with the tree—atonement. Take off your sandals,
for the place where you are standing is holy ground.
I was watching a man who loves what he is doing—picking olives
from the same trees his grandfather and father cared for.*

Chapter Twelve

Organic farmers cannot put farming
on the path of peace with nature by themselves.
All of us who eat have to become
conscientious objectors to the war against nature.

RON KROESE

🖊

Funny how nature just knows how to make things
that are good for you.

TV AD FOR V8

Barefoot with Dino

As I glanced around at my bags and bike parts strewn about Dino's disheveled front porch, contemplating signs of a rather ignominious ending to my seven weeks in Italy, it hit me that I would have scripted a far different ending. Which goes to show, yet again, what a slow learner I am.

Twenty-five years ago—about five years after I woke up with a car on top of me—I noticed the verse in Proverbs that reads, *In his heart a man plans his course, but the Lord determines his steps.* I figured the Bible had it wrong. I could imagine God influencing my heart, my desires, but thinking that God determines my steps is ludicrous. I was still enough of a materialist to know that *I* was in charge of my destiny. *I* planned out my days.

But the longer I live, the more I see the wisdom of this Proverb. I have carried in my heart the vision I have for my life, but God has taken me through the steps to get me where I wanted to go. Had I been aware of this Proverb when I was in my twenties, I would have argued against it with passion, but not now. Over and over I see God taking me down paths I did not foresee—steps I would not have chosen. Looking back, I'm glad I didn't know beforehand about Pietro and Aurora's falling out. I most likely would have stayed in a hotel somewhere and missed out on a very special and very unexpected last day in Tuscany.

I had been to Dino's farm before, twice—no—three times counting the turn-around in his driveway. Aurora and I stopped by the day we pressed her olives. She wanted to show me a different kind of farming operation. Dino has carved for himself a unique niche. He encourages artists to come to his farm, and then he encourages farmers and neighbors to come to see their work, their creations. Which is what Valter and I did after we finished eating my one and only German supper while I was in Tuscany. Valter drove me to Dino's for a night of tango. Two musicians from Buenos Aires were playing, one on a piano and the other on a *bandoneon,* an instrument I had neither heard, nor heard of. The thing looked like a poor man's accordion—a skinny, stretched-out bit of a box draped over the man's knee that put out a sound like a cello. I also heard, for the first time, the music of Italian-born composer Astor Piazzolla. These two Argentinians played Piazzolla's music as if it was their own. Their get-up-out-of-your-seats rendition of *Libertango* brought everyone in the barn to their feet, and most to the dance floor. Dino had billed the night as *not* just for listening. He made sure dancers were there who could also teach the tango. We were *wwoofers* and farmers coming together in community to entertain ourselves. The *bandoneon* artist and the piano player were there because they were friends of Dino. And I was there thanks to Valter.

Despite the pleasant memories of Dino's farm, I didn't want to be there. I wanted an evening of talking to Aurora and a sweet night of sleep in her loft. It was *Lorenzo déjà vu*, especially when I learned that I would be sleeping in a cold air dorm. But unlike that first night at Lorenzo's, I didn't have to spend the evening alone nor did I have to fix my own dinner. Fabio, an artist Dino was encouraging, prepared a delicious pasta using the Tuscan sausage I had carried over the mountains, and shared with me his love of theater.

As Fabio told me of his dreams to produce a play about college life, and to eventually become a film director, it hit me once again that farms don't just raise food—they grow people and families. Dino has unused space, and he is making it available as studios, theaters, and performance halls. Every farm and farmer has unique attributes that can contribute to the wealth and health of the community. The definition of a farm in the twenty-first century is going to grow and change. Dino's farm is raising the entrepreneurial spirit of artists.

The next morning Dino affirmed my suspicion that every Italian is born with the spiritual gift of hospitality. Even though I had been dropped into his life, Dino took time to invite me to join him for *una tazza di caffe*. Tea is my typical start for the day, but if every morning Dino's *caffelatte* were available I might be persuaded to switch. Dino didn't stop being a good host with the coffee. He asked what I was doing in Italy. When I told him this was my last day, he looked over my train schedule and suggested that I switch to a train that didn't require transferring in Roma Termina and would take me all the way to Fiumicino. He then turned his attention to customs and went to the trouble of re-bottling my olive oil with a better, more professional-looking cap so it would not be confiscated by some over-zealous customs agent. He also cautioned me to expect extra scrutiny from customs because I had worked on farms while I was in Italy. He advised me to make sure my shoes had nothing on them that looked or smelled anything like manure. Dino perfectly illustrated the spirit behind the greeting of *ciao* in Italy. I showed up on his doorstep and he set about trying to figure out how he could be of service to me with not a thought of what I was going to do for him.

Dino, like Lorenzo, is fighting the good fight to save traditional farming, but unlike Lorenzo, he uses very little machinery. He does battle with those who preach that farming can only survive by adopting the practices of factories. Dino feels that farming is unique, and that treating farming like a business will not be its salvation, but its damnation. He told me that because of its link to living things, farming must be tied to natural cycles, not the abstract motivations of business, money, and efficiency. Dino returned to farming because he understands these things and because he loves the land. He likes the sense of place that comes with being a farmer.

He fell in love with farming as a boy, helping his grandfather who farmed during the *mezzadria*. Dino explained to me that the owner provided the land and a good house for the *contadini*. Tradition dictated that the land was not raped, but was taken care of by a gentle steward. The farms were icons of self-sufficiency.

The future of Tuscany depends upon the return to the land of people like Dino and Aurora, who want to preserve the traditional, non-mechanized ways of farming. Farmers like Lorenzo, Giovanni, and Valter will continue to seek an appropriate balance between farming as a business, and farming as organic process.

I asked Dino what the biggest change in farming has been in the last fifty years. Dino told me that he remembers when his farm supported lots of people. He knows that those days involved hard work, but Dino is not one who views hard work with disdain. He reserves his contempt for the state of agriculture in Italy today. "Italians are no longer farmers of the land—they have become chemical farmers," he said using the same term Lorenzo uses to give voice to his scorn for agribusiness and monocultures. Dino is trying to bring diversity back to his grandfather's land because he knows it will improve the soil and the water.

Dino knows what he's talking about. In his previous life he was a biomedical research scientist. He's lived in both worlds—the world of technological progress and the world of natural rhythms. He knows that farmers under the old system depended upon organic nutrients to feed the crops that eventually feed us. But today's food chain starts with petroleum. Dino connects the dots and tells me that when the *mezzadria* system died, *chemical farming* was born. I am old enough to have witnessed the same transition in America. I thought it was a good thing. But back then I wasn't counting the cost. Few people were.

Dino did not foresee the problems associated with moving people off the land to the factories. In the 1960s he too was caught up in the belief that the inexorable march of progress was for the good. Only a few people questioned the path we were on and like me, Dino wasn't one of them. He too thought that using anhydrous ammonia to grow food was a good thing. He changed his mind when he discovered that chemical farming kills the soil and the organisms in it that create natural fertility.

Dino and I found that we had much to talk about. He feels the excesses of petroleum farming are finally being exposed. He said that for too long we overlooked the fact that nature has limits on how much it can be manipulated. His mention of limits reminded me of my childhood and how different attitudes were then. I remember the excitement in the voice of a radio announcer as he was touting an amazing scientific breakthrough called DDT. He spoke glowingly of all that it was going to do for mankind. His enthusiasm for it was so total that to this day I remember exactly where I was in my yard when I heard his gushing report over my brand new transistor radio.

I also remember that it took someone who thought like a poet to warn us that something was wrong. She was also a predictor, a prophet, and someone trained in the sciences. Despite a lot of opposition from the scientific community, major chemical companies, and even the USDA, people eventually began listening to her. Mostly, what she said was born of common sense, so the general public helped her ideas win approval in the court of public opinion. She was able to look at the interconnectedness of life and caution scientists to look beyond their area of expertise to better understand the dangers they were unleashing on all life. Rachael Carson warned us in her aptly titled book, *Silent Spring*, that we need to start asking more questions. *If a poison kills insects, what will prevent it from eventually killing the birds that eat these insects?* It seems like a simple question, but simple questions seldom get the attention they deserve when our focus is too narrow or we're worshipping *progress*.

I too was then in the camp of unfettered progress. I didn't understand what George Bernard Shaw meant—that he wasn't resorting to hyperbole—when he summed up our pride by writing, *Science never solves a problem without creating ten more.* I would, however, quibble with his use of the word *science.* We all do it, though. We speak of science as though it were some living, breathing, intelligent entity. If we were precise in the use of language, we would point out that *science* is but another word for knowledge, specifically knowledge about the created order of the universe—and knowledge is not the problem. The problem is an attitude too often held by those who practice science. When we attack nature, or when we feel we can improve on nature, we often discover that we have created a cancerous tumor that unleashes upon an unsuspecting public a string of unintended consequences. This is especially true when we attack creation with incomplete knowledge, which is, if we are honest, our usual condition.

Our pride though, is losing a bit of its uppitiness. Our mistakes of the past few years—our excesses—have given us a touch of humility. Another "scientific breakthrough" known by a three-letter acronym, BGH (bovine growth hormone) may have unwittingly led to the burgeoning demand for "organic food" and the growth of farmers markets—a move away from excessive manipulation of nature, the excesses that George Bernard Shaw warned us about. In the 1990s when Monsanto was attempting to re-engineer cows by ingesting them with hormones to make them produce more milk, the public began saying, enough is enough. People became concerned about the health of cows and humans. We became more interested in the food nature produces. Writers like Wendell Berry were helping us see that within animals and seeds and dirt are mysteries we will never understand.

A growing number of Americans are beginning to take a Tuscan-like approach to food. But powerful forces are arrayed against us. Mass purveyors of food force unhealthy methods of production on food factories to supply our seemingly insatiable demand for lower and lower prices. Not reflected in those cheap prices is the collateral damage to the health of our bodies and to America's soil and water that the rest of us, and future generations, must pay for. The task before us is to collectively take the production of food away from industrial agri-giants and place it back into the hands of agrarians who will honor not only the food, but also the land on which it is produced.

Even the tourism that has become such a vital part of Tuscany's wealth is dependent upon people like Dino and Aurora, and their dedication to the preservation of the land. Today more people are recognizing the inherent rightness of a good livelihood on the land and they're willing to pay a lot of money to come experience it. Tourists come to Tuscany to see the beautifully cared for fields of the small farmer. They don't come to see the workings of monstrous tractors upon the land. The conversation with Dino reminded me of tourism in the Amish country of Pennsylvania. People come from all over America, and even the world, to see and feel what the land looks like when people farm small with the sensibilities of a thankful steward—when the earth is a canvas for creating a masterpiece of art.

The traditions of centuries ensure that Tuscans feel and care for their land, but pressure to farm big can be found wherever fields are sufficiently large. Farming big does not necessarily mean farming bad, but a change in focus occurs when the hands of the farmer become tied to a machine—just as Renato no longer looked at the damage his feet were inflicting on the olives when his hands were gripping the *mechanista,* the big farmer tends to change his focus from the land to the number of acres covered when he is driving an expensive machine and pouring tons of man-made fertilizers and poisons on his land. He tends toward monocultures, something that nature abhors. The payments for the equipment and chemicals drive the farmer's decisions. He sees that his yields have increased, but he doesn't see the damage that poisons, excessive fertilizer, and single-crop farming are doing to his land and water. He doesn't count the cost, such as the die-off of bees. He fails to notice the earthworms and songbirds his poisons are killing. He forgets about the interconnectedness of life—the connubial nature of farming and living.

I learned in Tuscany that the answers to the questions of how to farm and how to make a living farming are not easily answered. Many farmers, like Dino, are returning to the land to pursue a life well-lived. Even if his life involves hard work and uncertainty, Dino feels that it is preferable to a life without land if the economy falters—or even if it doesn't. Both he and Lorenzo have worked in the corporate world and both have worked as farmers, and as inexplicable as it is, they both prefer being farmers. Both made a lot more money in the corporate world. But they prefer life with their hands in dirt.

It comes down to a rightness of living. What will we forgo to obtain it? Life is a series of choices about what we are willing to give for what we get. Our choices of late have been particularly wrong-headed, but we're beginning to listen to those who are advancing the idea that we should choose a different yardstick. We have been rightfully humbled by the recent failures of our greed-oriented economy.

We find it is easy to envy the person who has a lot of money and flaunts it. I remember the envy I felt when a boy from my high school came to town driving a new car. I was certain I too would be happy if only my father had enough money to buy a new car. My friend's car, like my dad's, was a Pontiac, but it was a 1961 and my father drove a 1959 Pontiac. When I was a kid, people who wanted to appear rich bought a new car every year. Before the used '59 Pontiac, we'd been driving a '55 Pontiac, and before that a '51 Dodge. I knew I wasn't rich and I had the cars to prove it.

The worship of consumerism is tied strongly to our self-image. I felt inferior to that boy. Thank God, I no longer feel that way. The car we are now driving was new when our youngest son was fifteen, the same age as I was when my friend showed up driving his dad's just-off-the-showroom-floor Pontiac. But we're still driving that car, and our son is now twenty-two.

I now recognize that what car we drive and its age are determined by many factors, the least of which is our self-worth, or even how much money we have. Life is full of mysteries and choices, but the life that I've been privileged to live is teaching me that spending money on status seems sillier every year. I appreciate fine craftsmanship, and even new gadgets and new technology, but now that I'm officially old, I want to spend money on what my neighbors provide, produce, grow, and sell. Does such wisdom come only with age? I hope not. I hope that at least some of my kids do not feel the envy I felt at age fifteen. I hope that I taught them at least that much.

Community and family are the yardstick by which we should base our decisions. Tuscany confirmed that belief for me. When you see communities and traditions that have existed for centuries, you begin to recognize the power of stewardship. Tuscans are grounded in ways that most Americans cannot comprehend. We've been on the move so long that we've forgotten what it means to be from somewhere. The sight of Dino picking olives in the trees his grandfather harvested drove that point deep into my being.

Frances Mayes, when she was getting to know her part of Tuscany near Cortona, was surprised to discover how strongly people identify with place. One market day she was in the *piazza* and wanted to practice her Italian. She asked the owner of a *trattoria* "if she was local and she said no, she was from Castiglion Fiorentino, five miles away." Mayes wrote that she was shocked by the distinction. When you know the two towns and know the time it takes and the ground covered to travel between them, the terrain of Castiglion Fiorentino and the terrain of Cortona, the restaurant owner's answer does not seem surprising. Each night when she went to bed in Castiglion Fiorentino, I'm sure she felt a world away from her restaurant high above her in Cortona, separated not just by distance, but elevation and the city's walls as well.

I now know where Castiglion Fiorentino is, and what a long way to Cortona it is, despite being only a short distance on a map, just under twelve kilometers. I have traveled the distance between the towns, on foot as far as Aurora's farm and the rest of the way by bicycle the morning I rode to Valter's farm. It does not seem odd at all that the woman said she was not local. Land does that to you; it defines you. The land and people of Castiglion Fiorentino are very different from the land and people of Cortona. There is no mistaking one for the other. We are creatures of the land we inhabit and the neighbors we come to know, love, and help. Neighbors define us, just as the land and our families define us. Every field, no matter how small, has unique characteristics that farmers must get to know if they are truly going to care for the land. Wendell Berry cautions us to be wary of how far above the earth we sit when we are on tractors, when our feet no longer touch the ground: *A healthy farm culture can be based only upon familiarity and can grow only among a people soundly established upon its land; it nourishes and safeguards human intelligence of the earth that no amount of technology can satisfactorily replace.*

Folks around here, my farm in Wisconsin, don't identify themselves as being from one of the many towns scattered every five to ten miles, but by the ridge or valley or town road they live on. In our case, we tell new acquaintances that we live about a half mile east of the bald eagle's nest. Most everyone in the county has stopped to watch those eagles hatch their young each spring. But if by chance they haven't, we add that we live at the lower end of Snow Valley, where it intersects Hawkins Creek. And if that doesn't do it, we'll mention the five old silos, relics of the old way of farming. That's the land we're from—the land that shaped us.

We can get to know a place by walking on its land, by learning from its people. We can also get to know a place by learning what grows there and when. Michael Pollan knows the value of immersing yourself in the local food: *Eating's not a bad way to get to know a place.* He is referring not just to food in his book *The Omnivore's Dilemma*, but to the act of dining with local people as well: *The talk at the table was mainly about food. Yet this was not the usual food talk you hear nowadays; less about recipes and restaurants, it revolved around specific plants and animals and fungi, and the places where they lived.* Local food, local people, local stories is what the art of eating is about. In southwestern Wisconsin, many of our discussions in the spring focus on morels—and this past year has been the worst year in memory. When we get together, we commiserate with each other about how few mushrooms we have found.

Getting to know farmers and villages in Tuscany reminded me in myriad ways of growing up in my small southwestern Nebraska hometown. The experience of being in Tuscany made me think that it will be possible to import a Tuscan way of life to America. It wasn't that long ago that many of us in America were closer to the Tuscan ideal, even if we didn't have all the pleasures of Tuscan living. We loved our food, but even at our harvest festivals we didn't celebrate the art of eating to the extent that Tuscans do today. But we *did* delight in the taste of tomatoes and corn picked moments before dinner, still warm from the sun. In *The Hills of Tuscany* Ferenc Máté noted that sun-warmed tomatoes are *Perhaps small things, but small things make a life, and a town, and a livable society.* Those small things—caring for the land and for our neighbors—create a life very much worth living.

I hold Italy up as a worthy model to follow to a better life. In Italians I find the best example of the celebration of family, friends, food, and life. Dino and I picked olives together in his trees and talked of farming—the old ways, and the new ways, and then we came back to the old ways again. For that is what Dino wants to do. Dino feels so close to the land that he chooses to pick olives in his bare feet, to touch the soil with his toes, and feel the coarse bark of the branches. Dino climbed barefoot into the tree to get to the olives that had eluded me. His movements were pure grace. He was at one with the tree—atonement—*Take off your sandals, for the place where you are standing is holy ground.* I was watching a man who loves what he is doing. He was picking olives from the same trees his grandfather and father cared for. Even high in a tree, Dino is as much as anyone I have ever met—grounded.

And he was not tied to a *mechanista*. When I asked him why, he mentioned first the money. He didn't want to be tied to the costs associated with farming fast. He did not get into farming because he likes machinery, but because he likes the land and the people. He was a farmer and he was harvesting his own olives. That is what he got into farming to do. He was tied through his bare feet to the earth and the tree. And the sight of him working barefoot confirmed that the connection was important to him. His grace in the tree was efficient too. He was a thankful steward intimately caring for the health of his trees.

As Dino was picking the last olives from the high branches, I noticed Fabio and a young woman walking toward the grove, each carrying a large basket of food. Like Dino, she too had a look of not being tied to now. Fabio introduced me to Alissia as they spread a folded olive net on the grass and invited us to join them for *pranzo*.

I looked again at the girl as she passed me a plate of pasta. The way she was dressed was timeless. She was wearing no make-up; nothing about her except the tread on her boots said she belonged to the twenty-first century. I don't know that the effort was conscious, but she looked to be from the Renaissance era or even centuries earlier. No radio was playing, we were relaxing in an olive grove enjoying the bounty of nature—the tastiness of God's grace. After lunch we leaned back and told stories.

I was getting to know one more Tuscan farmer. Dino was the sixth. Each had fallen in love with farming. In Dino's case he was very young when he fell in love. And now he was living his dream of making a living on the land, just like the farmers and families who worked the land for his grandfather. People who earn their livelihood from the land, in partnership with creation, are good people to be around. If I were to guess a reason I would say that people who are at the mercy of nature most likely have suffered. At some point in their life, they've been humbled.

Dino mentioned all the animals he remembered from childhood. I thought of the children's song, "Old MacDonald Had a Farm," and the variety of animals that used to be on farms—the cows and their moo-moos, the pigs and their oink-oinks, the sheep and their baa-baas—and I thought that yes, it's true, farms are once again becoming more diversified, more like a natural symbiotic system. But Dino was demonstrating that new choruses may need be added to the song. On Old MacDonald's farm of the twenty-first century I suspect that a new breed of farmers will be making their own distinctive *moo-moos* and *baa-baas*—well-diversified farmers like Giovanni and Giovanna, who are using all of a farm's resources, will lead the way. Artists, musicians, and entrepreneurs who want to partner with nature, not overwhelm it—are going to be nurtured back to life on the land. We have tried too long to deny our dependency. In this century we are going to celebrate our connections to the earth—our absolute need of soil. Like Dino, we may be reminded just how good it feels to once again to get our fingers and toes in the dirt—beautiful life-sustaining dirt.

It wasn't how I envisioned it, but a Hollywood writer could not have scripted a better ending to my adventure in Italy. I got to learn more about Dino and his farm on which he grows olives and grapes as well as creative entrepreneurs. Two of the young artists who were "in residence" at Dino's farm prepared a delicious lunch and carried it out to us to enjoy in the olive grove. They told me their stories and I shared with them some of mine, like the day Lorenzo sent me off to bike through the rolling countryside. I'll never forget the ride through vineyards and olive groves set off by the towers of San Gimignano— or the hospitality of Aurora, Valter, Lorenzo, Giovanni, and Dino.

Chapter Thirteen

When the solution is simple, God is answering.
ALBERT EINSTEIN

Arrivederci Italia

Seven weeks ago I boarded an Airbus A330 in Philadelphia to fly to Rome's Fiumicino Airport with the hope that I would find a Tuscan farmer willing to let me pick olives. In exchange I wanted only a place to sleep and a seat at the kitchen table. I was fortunate. Six families invited me onto their farms and into their homes. I learned a lot working alongside Italians and eating three meals a day with them. The experience confirmed my suspicions that Italians do indeed know how to live the good life. But I had hoped to learn *why* Italian life has captured the imagination of the world.

Italian food is linked to the answer, but it is not the complete answer. Having lived closely with Italians in their homes, I now know that Italian food and Italian people are inseparable. The food makes the people and the people make the food. But whether food or people, the question remains, *why?* Why do Americans and much of the rest of the world consistently put Italy near the top of their must-visit lists?

When my wife and friends asked why I had chosen Italy I gave answers that must have been unconvincing. Why was I willing to work as a farm laborer just to eat with Italians? The more adventurous among them were intrigued, but even the most highly charged people couldn't see laboring in the sun day after day picking olives. When pressed, I shrugged and told them that I didn't totally understand it myself. Neither did I have a convincing answer for those who wondered why I was not going instead to County Cork in wee Ireland, to get to know the land where me great-grandfather John lived 'til he was near thirty.

It certainly would have been easier—and probably less embarrassing. I was, however, convinced that if I hoped to discover the *why* of Italy, I would need to learn to speak and understand Italian. When we were young marrieds sailing around the Ionian Islands, I had seen the benefit of my wife's knowledge of a little bit of Greek—how just a few words opened doors into the hearts of the Greeks, especially the older people. Learning Italian would not be easy, especially at my age, but I stretched my synapses, and gave it a go. For five months I treated it like a part-time job, dedicating my brain to three or four hours of study a day. I managed to get through the complete Rosetta Stone Italian course and thought that I was ready to speak "tourist Italian" with some measure of success.

But as I was gathering my carry-on bags to get off USA Air Flight 718 in Rome I lost my confidence. I had not brought a phrase book and I wanted to ask the ticket agent in "casual Italian" the name of the first train station in Tuscany, so I looked around for help. My eyes settled on a beautiful Italian girl. Within that assessment was an assumption, but I was willing to take a chance. I wanted to get off to a good start speaking Italian in Italy. I introduced myself in Italian, but quickly lost my nerve and asked if she spoke English. Bingo. Not only did she speak English, she also spoke Italian—and both perfectly.

She was also very helpful—an Italian student studying at an American university. I guessed that maybe she too had once felt the panic I was feeling—of wanting to make a good impression after months of study. She told me that she would not even bother with the question but just say to the ticket agent: "I'd like to buy a ticket on a train that will take me to the first station in Tuscany." I began repeating the phrase, in the cadence she used, over and over. I shouldered my bags, thanked her, and began rehearsing my part. I didn't expect to see her again.

But after gathering my two huge suitcases from baggage claim, and following the arrows to customs, I saw her standing at the back of one of the lines. I chose to get in it. It was a pretty easy decision. It was a line of one. Looking back on my time in Tuscany, and after listening to the tales of other travelers, I realize it was one of the better decisions I made while I was in Italy. The young customs agent at the head of that short line decided he wanted to spend a little extra time checking her form and he didn't want me, the only other person in his line, watching his every move, so with a flick of his wrist and upraised chin and eyebrows, he sent me on my somewhat bewildered way into Italy. I thought I was being funneled to another customs agent, but within a minute, or at the most two, I was standing in front of a *Trenitalia* agent, about to embark on my adventure. I smiled as I thought of the young man and the beautiful girl and realized it had taken me all of thirty seconds to clear customs. I stuffed my passport into my backpack, joined the queue, and continued repeating the phrase the young woman had suggested.

I got to the front of the line and said as nonchalantly as I could, "*Vorrei acquistare un biglietto su un treno che mi portera alla prima stazione in Toscana.*" To my great relief and surprise, the attendant quickly responded in Italian, not English, asking whether I wanted a first or second class ticket to Chiusi—and that was that—the beginning of my Italian journey.

Looking back over my seven weeks in Tuscany, it would be nice to remember that every time I spoke *italiano* it was quickly and clearly understood, but that is not the case. However, I can say that with few exceptions the effort to speak Italian was appreciated by just about every Italian I met. The main exception to that was my first farm. I now see I should have acted sooner on that clue.

The train ride had been fast and very civilized to Roma Termina in the heart of Rome where I transferred to an even faster train servicing Tuscany. I had read about the extensive network of trains in Italy, but until you experience it for yourself you're not prepared for how civilized it makes you feel—how absolutely right it is that you should be able to wheel your luggage from plane to train, settle back, relax, and actually enjoy the act of getting from one place to another on public transportation.

The sight of the graceful cypresses reaching to the sky, ancient hilltop towns actually in the sky, and field after small field lovingly tended convinced me that it was right that I should be in Tuscany—that I had come to the right place to get a feel for a better way to live. The fields, the crops, the trees seemed fitted to the land and its contours rather than rigidly and mechanically imposed on the countryside. Tuscany looked like a good place for people—not machines. I had come to Tuscany not to be a tourist, but a farm laborer, but I couldn't help myself that first day. I looked the part of an awestruck tourist as I took photo after photo of lush vineyards and ancient olive groves lovingly caressing the hillsides. Train travel is especially geared to absorbing the countryside and I took full advantage as the train carried me to Chiusi.

I had made two major purchases in anticipation of my trip to Tuscany. One was the Italian language DVD course on which the jury is still out. But I have no doubts regarding the second purchase. The Garvin Nuvi 275T with maps of North America and Europe preloaded was indispensable. I can imagine doing what I did without Rosetta Stone—depending upon independent study, a phrase book, and the kindness of strangers, but I cannot imagine biking to small farms throughout Tuscany without a GPS. I mention the specific number because I am so grateful for the man whose name I don't remember who wrote up a personal critique of his GPS and posted it on the web—without his advice I never would have bought the 275T—and I would have suffered.

It can be gathered from my respect for things Tuscan that I am a bit of a traditionalist. But I am thankful for innovations and innovators—and two of the most farsighted are the visionaries who made it possible for that GPS to be on my doorstep less than twenty-four hours after I learned of its existence, which was also only hours before I was scheduled to leave for Italy. I owe a big debt of gratitude to Jeff Bezos, who founded Amazon, and Frederick W. Smith, who envisioned FedEx and submitted it as a class project at Yale—for which, I might add, he received a grade of "C". Credit should be given where credit is due, and looking back over my trip, I couldn't help but see that GPS as a godsend.

Without it I never would have gotten to that first farm, at least not at the time I had told the owners I would arrive. I got off the train in Chiusi, wheeled my Samsonite to a small park in front of the station, put my Bike Friday together, transformed the suitcase into a trailer, typed the address into the GPS, and set off to discover what Tuscany had to teach me. The first thing I learned was that I was heading in exactly the wrong direction. The GPS knew it and began chiding me with that irritating voice within a few cranks of the pedals. I admitted the mistake, turned around, and began riding in the right direction. A few kilometers later, Friday and I, with the trailer tracking nicely behind us, were leaving the varied collection of earth-hued, closely-spaced homes on the hillsides of Chiusi and were winding along the tree-lined roads of Tuscany. It was just the picture I had envisioned all those years dreaming of Italy—the vibrant fall colors, the warm sun, and the cool air of the Tuscan countryside. Topping it all off was a quartering tailwind carrying me to my first farm—the farm where, now that I'm looking at it with hindsight, I'm still wondering why I did not act on the clues that confronted me.

However, I did immediately recognize the benefit of the GPS. By trusting its guidance, I was free to fully enjoy the land. I wasn't worrying about my route. I wasn't stopping to unfold and fold maps—I was just following the moving blue triangle on the GPS display. I also began seeing that Tuscany was not going to disappoint. The land really does have people on it—just like all the books I had read informed me that it would. Farmhouses were often only a stone's throw from each other.

The shape of the fields was dictated by the lay of the land, and they were separated by meandering stone walls or wooden fences, rather than the straight lines of efficiency. The landscapes were mesmerizing, even intoxicating, as the patterns of the grape vines and olive trees whizzed by—my eyes never quite knowing which lines of beauty to follow. It was now no mystery to me why so many people come to Tuscany for a visit, fall in love with the warm, happy people, the ancient, sensible farmhouses, and the luxuriant, sensuous farms, and want to move to Tuscany to begin again.

But I had not come to Tuscany to fall in love. I had fallen in love with a farm in the hills of Wisconsin a half dozen years before. I was familiar with how and why a person wants to begin again on a stunningly beautiful piece of land. I had come to Tuscany to learn how to live better with the love I had already committed to. My goal had been to become a better farmer of my one hundred sixty hilly acres and in doing that, to become a better citizen of my community. Tuscany, I felt, could also teach me to enjoy food more fully—the growing, the buying, the preparing, the eating and the sharing of food. I had traveled to Italy convinced that Tuscany could teach me all of these things. And now on my flight back to the USA, I was leaving this beautiful land feeling that it had done all I had expected of it and more. But still I wondered if I had learned all that I should have. Many of my misgivings concerned that first week I had spent in Tuscany.

My recall of that first afternoon biking through the hills of Tuscany seems total—the smell of the earth, the way the light made the vines glow, even the silence of the countryside. But Tuscany was also full of surprises and on that first day I was dealing with the surprise of finding no sign pointing the way to the farm. I became especially concerned when the GPS directed me to turn off the main road onto an unnamed dirt road. I had been seeing official-looking government signs for *agriturismo* after *agriturismo* all the way from Chiusi, pointing to one farm or another, and I was fully expecting to see one when the GPS directed me off Highway 146. But there was only a lonely-looking road. Getting lost is always frustrating, no matter how you're traveling, but it is much more serious when traveling by bike. Cyclists hate to spend any effort biking down the wrong road and that is exactly what I was fearing as I ventured farther from the main highway with absolutely no indication that there were any farms catering to tourists down that rock-strewn trail, let alone the very farm I was seeking.

But if a machine can appear confident, the GPS was exuding it; so I followed it. It was only when it told me to bike five kilometers down another unnamed, unpaved road that I began questioning it. When it then told me to turn left and bike another three kilometers down "unpaved road" followed by another turn onto "unpaved road" I began to feel that its confidence was instead confusion. I was not yet going in circles but it was beginning to feel like it.

I saw no one to ask for help. After about the twelfth kilometer of unpaved roads I saw parked at a particularly nice looking farm a "caravan"—what we call a small motor home in America. The GPS indicated I was less than five kilometers from my destination, but I still had seen no signs, or anything which confirmed I was that close.

I pulled up alongside the cab, greeted the driver and timidly mentioned the name of the farm, not expecting that he would be able to help. I was certain that I would be talking to a tourist who quite possibly would be just as lost as I was—who would have no idea where I wanted to get to. But not only did he know of the farm, he had stayed there the night before. He pointed into the valley and said in American, "See that plow in the field—turn left there and follow that road, it's very rough, until you come to a driveway veering off and up a hill to the left. I checked the GPS and as best as I could determine from the squiggles on the "unnamed roads," that was exactly what it was telling me to do—amazing.

Still skepticism ruled. I couldn't believe the GPS maps could be so complete that they would have directions to all the farms in Tuscany. "Will I see any signs for the farm?" I asked.

He started to shake his head, but first he looked at his wife. Almost in unison, they said, "Not until you get there." They went on to tell me that they had arrived after dark the night before and had an awful time trying to find the place.

"Did you enjoy it once you got there?" I asked.

Their delay in answering and their glance once again at each other before they answered sent a very clear message. But the only thing they said was that the farm wasn't equipped to handle caravans so they decided to move to a neighboring farm. They then went on to rave about their current hosts, how friendly and accommodating they were, and the delicious food and wine they were "served and served."

"We've never sat at a table so long, or enjoyed it as much."

Armed with their information I made my way with renewed confidence, even astonishment, with the capability of the GPS to lead me to the farm. But I was arriving with less confidence about finding what I was seeking. The GPS led me right to the farmyard, but it didn't tell me what door to enter. Nor did the lady who noticed me wandering about. I started to call out to her but she scurried off so I assumed she was a tourist. I stuck my head into a doorway, but it didn't seem to be the right one, so I continued walking about.

I had expected a warm, even enthusiastic greeting. I had told the hosts that I would be arriving via bicycle. They had told me that I was being optimistic about traveling by train and bike all the way from Rome to their farm so quickly, but I biked into the farmyard at almost the exact minute I had told them to expect me.

But farming is not always that predictable so I continued to wander about. Something had probably come up and the farmers were, I was assuming, dealing with that crisis. But the longer I wandered the stronger the feelings became that I just may have chosen the wrong farm. I began trying out words that might be appropriate to tactfully and gracefully bow out before I got stuck there.

I began rationalizing. I was volunteering to help on their farm; why could they not have been around to offer a warm greeting? I only had seven weeks; why should I spend that time helping people who were giving indications of being the exact opposite of what I had expected to find in Tuscany?

While I was trying to formulate my excuse for leaving I began thinking about first impressions. How useful are they? What can you tell about people by the expression they carry on their face when you first meet them, when you observe them walking toward you? While waiting I decided to write down a few notes regarding my first impressions—so that they would truly remain first impressions and not be colored in my memory by subsequent impressions—if I stayed around long enough to form second impressions. I noted what the lady I had seen first was wearing, and the expression on her face when she looked at me, then turned away. Then I turned my attention to the farm itself.

The farmhouse was as I had expected, very substantial and very beautiful. Even when Tuscan farmhouses have been recently remodeled or rebuilt, they maintain a look of antiquity. Tuscans value age and tradition and the wisdom that comes with it, so they have invested heavily in a bureaucracy that gives latitude for changes inside the house that will be seen by few and very little latitude in making changes that affect the exterior of the house or barn, which in Tuscany is often one and the same.

I looked for evidence of walls recently rebuilt, for evidence of where animals slept one hundred years ago—generally it was on the ground floor and the people slept above where they could take advantage of the heat from composting manure and straw, and the warmth of the animals. Our present sensibilities balk at such an idea because of our loss of knowledge, of wisdom. It was a very sensible arrangement, strongly conserving of resources. Today, we recoil from the idea because of the presumption of the stench. I had learned, taking care of my animals, that properly managed with enough straw or hay, manure from farm animals generates very little odor. Large concentrations of animals defecating all over each other on concrete instead of straw, as they do in confinement operations, is a very different situation that stinks all the way to high heaven and nobody who is not forced by poverty or greed or debt—singly, in combination, or possibly all three—would want to live within five miles of such an arrangement.

But the traditions of Tuscany, in the form of using nature, not abusing nature, were the guides in the layout of the farms and farmsteads. The sensibility of that era can still be seen in the beautiful homes that grace the hills of Tuscany. Everything I saw about the buildings on that farm spoke of what I was seeking in Tuscany.

After I had wandered about the farm for a half hour or so, absorbing the views of the rolling hills and undulating fields, an unsmiling man drove a tractor into the farmyard. I assumed he was a hired man since he ignored me, but I decided he could most likely provide me with some information or tell me where to find it.

As he was getting off the tractor I greeted him in my friendliest Rosetta Stone Italian. He ignored my *italiano* and spoke to me in English. Turned out he was not a hired man, but the owner. He unenthusiastically informed me that he was going to town at the moment and would be back in forty-five minutes or so and would then show me where I would be staying. I had by then lost track of the number of clues I had been given, but still something was keeping me from hopping on Friday and pedaling down the road.

After he drove away I wrote in my journal "decidedly lacking in the gift of hospitality." While waiting, I continued writing down my impressions of the farm and my first day in Tuscany. About the time I was expecting the man to return, the woman I had seen earlier walked up and asked me how long I was staying. She was not a guest, or an employee, but was the wife of the dour man I had just met. I was taken aback by her forthright manner, but I opted to give her a large benefit of the doubt and answered without thinking, "about a week." As soon as I had let go of the words I wanted to grab them and stuff them back in my mouth. But it was too late.

It was an answer I regretted for all but a few hours of the seven days I spent there, but I stayed with it because I had said I would and because my optimism and pragmatism took over and told me that I would learn just as much on that farm as I would on the farms that modeled the ideal Tuscan living that I was expecting. I rationalized that it is not really possible to appreciate spring if you don't have winter to compare it to. At the very least I hoped I would be able to improve my Italian. And as an added bonus, I figured I would arrive at my second farm no longer a grape-picking, olive-picking virgin. These were all good things, but they were going to come at a cost—the cost, I was just about to discover, of a warm place to sleep.

For that I didn't have to wait for her husband to return. She informed me, just after I told her how long I would be staying, that she would show me where to sleep. She then began walking toward the fields and away from the big house. I thought that maybe I had misunderstood her rapid-fire delivery of Italian and English—that she was instead going to show me how to pick olives. I hadn't noticed that we were walking toward a rusted-out hulk of a travel trailer. I wasn't expecting a four star hotel room—but I was hoping for some character with my accommodations. I was traveling with a sleeping bag, just in case a centuries-old barn was offered, but the last thing I was expecting in Tuscany was a run-down mid-twentieth century caravan. As I contemplated the sad state of my very un-Tuscan quarters I became acutely aware of why this *agriturismo's* website relied so heavily on drawings and cartoon-like representations of the farm. The humor made the place very appealing, but it also masked what photographs would have revealed—that this farm someday hoped to be, but was not yet totally Tuscan.

The shower however was warm, and it was inside a building dripping with Tuscan character. I very much like the Italian tendency to make the whole bathroom a shower. They are frequently all tiled and the floor is sloped toward a central drain. Cleaning an Italian bathroom is quick work. An Italian meal however is never quick work. It begins with conversation long before the first of many courses is set on the table, and lasts all the way through the meal to the strong Italian coffee.

I have lots of vivid impressions from that first day in Tuscany but one of the strongest was the fervor with which the husband and the wife spoke to each other. In America, if a husband and wife were speaking to each other with as much energy, emotion, and volume as our hosts did that first night you would be certain they were headed for divorce court. The more they talked, the faster they spoke until my Rosetta Stone Italian was overwhelmed. Not only wasn't I picking up the sentences, I wasn't even understanding the words. Much of the time I had no idea what they were talking about, but the passion was unmistakable. And their children spoke to each other, and to their parents with equal intensity and with what, at times, seemed like rancor, but never did it seem that any of them took offense.

The guests staying at the farm were seated at a separate table, talking among themselves but rarely were they engaged by their hosts. We, the volunteers, were seated on the far end of a long wooden table. The family and permanent employees were on the near end, but no introductions were ever made—the family barely acknowledged our presence. It was a strange situation, my first meal in Italy. I was enjoying the food and loving the energy that was flowing within the family, but it was uncomfortable to be almost completely ignored. I rationalized that the family chose not to engage the volunteers because they knew that they would be there only a short time, so why bother.

But I wanted to be bothered. I wanted to learn about this family, about farming in Tuscany, and I wanted to speak as much Italian as I could muster. So as the meal was winding down I began asking questions about the farm, how long they had been farming, the changes that had taken place in farming since they had begun. They told me of the years of work that went into turning abandoned and dilapidated buildings into useable space, but the most frustrating part of the effort to reclaim the farm was not the physical work or the expense of the materials, but the endless forms and the inspections. They admitted to being cynical—none of what they were required to do seemed to be for the good of the farm or the land, but rather designed to insure that the bureaucrats would always have a job—with salaries paid for by the taxes levied on the improvements to the farm.

The list of hurdles they mentioned that they had to overcome seemed endless. In their minds all the rules, regulations, fines, and taxes were meant to do but one thing—make it impossible for them to compete on the world market against subsidized products of other nations.

Even the improvements to the land were taxed so high that they thought they were better off not taking care of the land. To them, it came down to the fact that they felt they couldn't afford to be good stewards of the land—in terms of both the time to comply with the regulations and the additional taxes levied on the improvements.

They had learned how to live with the "nosy inspectors" and they had accepted the fact that those people were, in effect, on their payroll, but they were not happy with the situation. They longed for the time when "farmers, not bureaucrats, were making the decisions of how best to care for the land."

Eventually only the husband and I were at the table. He told me that when he first came to the farm, the room where we were now seated had no roof. It was a story I was to hear frequently—the story of farms falling into disrepair because of government policy encouraging, even forcing farmers from the land to work in the cities on assembly lines. It was eerily reminiscent of the tale of American farms and farmers and was a precursor to the stories that I heard at each of the farms I visited in Tuscany.

Obviously there was a difference and that is what I wanted to explore. My host, however, was only mildly interested. He didn't engage me; he only answered my questions. As I said *buona notte*, my thoughts went again to first impressions. My first impression had been that he and his wife were focused inward. But now that I knew more about them I was beginning to sense that the burdens of dealing with the bureaucracies had worn them down. However, my first impression remained; they seemed to care little about hospitality, which struck me as odd—very unlike the Tuscany I had expected.

But that was just my first day in Tuscany, the first day of my first week in Tuscany—a week that was very unlike the other six weeks. At Dino's farm, on my last day as a *woofer* in Tuscany, I was quite surprised to be taken back to that first day, to what seemed such a long time ago and so very far away. While Dino and I were enjoying his delicious *caffelatte* he asked me to tell him about all the farms I had visited. When I mentioned the name of the first farm, Dino, without waiting for my assessment said, "Oh yes, I know them. Unfriendly, aren't they?" I tried to put a favorable spin on my comments, but as I searched for nice things to say,

I was struck by how closely my first impression mirrored Dino's lasting impression. I ended up telling Dino that I would remember the farm as a gate, constantly opening and closing as volunteers and guests quickly came and even more quickly left.

Dino noted, as I had discovered that first night, that the owners were not Italian, but had come to the area about twenty years ago. They had moved to Italy seeking what Tuscany had to offer—a good life. And to a certain extent they had found it. They were seeking to improve the buildings and the land, but the evidence of their years on that farm was confirming that until they began giving what they were seeking, as Giovanna and Giovanni were doing, they would not find the good life of warm loving relationships—they would forever be wondering what each person who came to their farm could give them instead of giving of themselves openly, and then in return, surprisingly finding that they had received more than expected. On my journey around Tuscany they were the winter to Giovanni and Giovanna's eternal spring.

They may have known about Italian hospitality but it had not yet seeped into their souls. I'm certain they were trying to adopt the traditions of their new homeland but some of them had never taken root. They were playing at being Italians. Their food was sometimes great, but often it was bland, without that special zing of Italian cuisine. And now that I have truly Italian meals to compare them to, I know that their meals, although sometimes energetic, lacked the camaraderie of the celebrations we enjoyed at Podere Paugnano—at Giovanni and Giovanna's table that played host to dozens of simultaneous conversations. I knew already as I was flying back home that I was going to miss those times—and miss them deeply.

Flying against the jet stream took a couple of hours longer than the flight to Italy. And just like on my long bike ride across Tuscany, I had a lot of time to reflect on the people I had met and the things we had talked about and done. I thought again of Anna and Aurora and Pietro. I fell asleep thinking of them; and I woke up thinking of them. We were still three hours from Philadelphia.

I thought too of my favorite writer, Wendell Berry, who wrote: *It is not from ourselves that we will learn to be better than we are.* I realized I was returning from being with a people who, because of tradition, and what Dante and Saint Francis taught them, learned to be better than they were. I learned this from the old man walking along the road near Barberino, though I spent only fifteen minutes with him. I learned it on my journey from Pienza to Aurora's farm when a woman took it upon herself to find me (a stranger she had just met on the road of life) a place to sleep in a town where I knew no one. I learned it from the gentle and trusting priest in whose church I slept that night. In Italy, the visitor finds everywhere a strong sense of the gift of hospitality. Now that I had experienced Italy I was even more perplexed. *Why is every country not as hospitable as Italy? Why is America not as warm and inviting?* Only in parts of the South, most notably Mississippi, have I encountered people who come close to exuding the hospitality I enjoyed in Italy. What, I was wondering, is the downside of hospitality, of looking at the world as Italians do?

I had no answer but I did now know without a doubt that Italians rejoice in the gift of good food, and the gift of good land that good food come from. Long days and long hours of picking olives gave me the eyes to see the world as Aurora sees it—connubial—a cooperative venture between the thankful stewardship of man and the creative manifestations of God. Every photo I've since looked at of Tuscany sings the praises of Aurora's vision.

Italians have been shaped by their land, their climate, and the food that grows there—and by an attitude. An attitude that has formed their unique character even more than the land has. As I landed in Philadelphia, I knew that I had learned a lot about Italians and from Italians, but still I was confronted by a mystery. I had come to truly believe that Italians are special, but I still couldn't say I fully comprehended what moved Forster to write: *Love and understand the Italians, for the people are more marvelous than the land.*

The People of Italy and The Land of Italy
Together they have created what the
world has come to regard as the Sweet Life!
What Aurora taught me to see as connubial,
the marriage of the creativity of God and man.

Chapter Fourteen

Art can make you understand through emotion
what you are absolutely incapable of understanding
through the intellect.

ROBERTO ROSSELLINI

🖋

All truths are easy to understand
once they are discovered;
the point is to discover them.

GALILEO

BELLA SCOPERTA!

Almost two years have passed since I bicycled in one day across the breadth of Tuscany only to discover that I was not welcome at Aurora's farm. Two years in which I have constantly tried to figure out why Italians are so openly friendly and hospitable—so endlessly fascinating—and why they command so much attention on the world's stage. To say that my trip to Tuscany has affected my life would be, and my wife will attest to this, a monumental understatement.

I have read dozens of books about Italy since returning from the olive groves of Tuscany. Inspired by Roberto Benigni's rendering of *Pinocchio*, I turned to the original, Carlo Collodi's *Pinocchio*. In the introduction Nicolas J. Perella wrote, "*Pinocchio* is the testing ground for foreigners; whoever understands the beauty of *Pinocchio* understands Italy." Collodi told a penetrating story about how strongly Italians believe in truth-telling and hard work, but this didn't answer my *why* question. So I re-read *The Italians* by Luigi Barzini, thinking that the experience of having just come from Italy would help me comprehend things I might have missed the first time I read it.

Barzini, just like the Italians I met, was uncomfortable with the attention of non-Italians: "Either they love us or hate us too much." In his writing he tried to paint a less-than-glowing portrait of Italians. To that end he often criticized Italian society, mostly in relation to its bogged-down bureaucracies, left-leaning government, and its failures in wars. But his purportedly critical book about Italy ("astringent," as one reviewer called it) is an almost-four-hundred page treatise in which the glory of his country shows through—"It is as if Italy were not only the home of Art, but an immense and elaborate *objet d'art* herself." He wrote no less glowingly about the people: "The list of famous Italians is awe-inspiring." Barzini then goes on to fill half a page with the names of the notable saints, sinners, thinkers, musicians, poets, painters, military leaders, and scientists from Italy. The list starts with Saint Francis and ends with Toscanini, and in between are an amazing number of world-changing men and women like Galileo and Columbus and Michelangelo and Leonardo da Vinci and Dante. Even *The Italians*, which thoroughly dissects the Italian character and spirit, did not provide an answer. But it was not for lack of trying. Barzini directly asked the question: "Why are we the way we are?" His succinct answer: "I heard infinite theories and no conclusive answers." I pushed onward.

I read *Fontamara*, *Bread and Wine*, and *The Seed Beneath the Snow* by Ignazio Silone. His portraits of Italian farmers broadened my understanding of their lives, and their battles against the ravages of Fascism and Communism, but still the question of *why* remained unanswered.

The nearly thousand pages of Silone's stories were followed by the seven hundred-plus pages of *The Betrothed* by Alessandro Manzoni, and then *History*, a seven hundred thirty-four-page novel about the war years in Italy by Elsa Morante. I discovered that Italians write long books, but I got to the end of each still seeking an answer to my question of *why*. I followed Pietro's advice: I read Dante's *Divine Comedy*. Learning that Italians expect two judgments, one pass/fail, and the other distinctly graded, helped me to understand Italians better, but it still didn't give me an answer to my question.

I turned to other artistic expressions. While I worked, I listened to the rich, melodious love poems of Andrea Bocelli; the operatic genius of Luciano Pavarotti; the tango music of Astor Piazzolla, the master of the *bandoneon*; and the work of the incomparable Ennio Morricone, composer of the film score for *The Mission*, and other great films like *Cinema Paradiso*. Our lives, because of my immersion in Italian life and living, have changed in numerous ways. We eat differently. The food is local and fresh—*nostrano* as they call it in Tuscany. We get inspiration for celebrating Italian culture and food from Mario Batali, Michael Chiarello, and Giada De Laurentiis. I consider it a good thing when my food spoils—we are eating healthful food, not processed products that never die. We buy food for the day's meals and if we buy too much, we put what spoils into our soil. But I didn't learn only about food in Italy. I learned about people and families.

I hope to renew my friendship with my best friend from childhood, even though we live over a thousand miles apart. I would love to watch *Cinema Paradiso* with him, for it was with Rossy that I first climbed the narrow, steep stairs up to the projection booth of his parents' theater to watch the magic of film unroll in front of us, just as Salvatore did in Giuseppe Tornatore's lyrically beautiful film. Salvatore's friend operating the projector was Alfredo; our mentor was Ralph, and just like in the film, Ralph, by example, taught Rossy and me about serving people. I knew by then that Rossy was Italian, but now I understand, after seeing firsthand the entrepreneurial spirit of Italians, why his parents operated both the restaurant and the movie theater in our hometown. I would like to get together with him, to find out if he has ever visited his ancestral home—to find out what his parents told him about life in Italy.

I traveled to Tuscany with the idea of working alongside a people who, from what I could gather from reading about them, had created and preserved, even through the hardships of many wars, a way of life that rose to the level of art—the highest and best feelings to which men have risen—as Tolstoy defined art. I learned a lot about Italy and Italians during the seven weeks I picked olives and grapes, ate pasta and drank wine, but the ultimate voyage of revelation—*il viaggio della bella scoperta*—did not take place while I was in Italy.

A little over a year after my return from Tuscany, Annamarja's chiding for wasting my money on Rosetta Stone suddenly inspired me. She had told me to watch Italian television with subtitles. I preferred talking with Aurora, but I did watch *Sabrina*. I had seen the film often enough, and knew the dialogue well enough, that I could just listen to the dubbed Italian and keep my eyes off the subtitles. Or I could listen to the original English and read the Italian. Both were extremely helpful.

But I couldn't do that in America. Italian DVDs won't play in American DVD players. Finally Netflix came to mind. I wondered if they had a few American films dubbed in Italian. I found out that they don't. But to my great surprise and delight they have Italian films with English subtitles. When I first joined it was necessary to search through the list of foreign films from all over the world and pick out the Italian language films. I quickly discovered that Netflix has a rather large selection. Weeding through all of the foreign films to add Italian movies to my queue was time consuming, but worth it.

Annamarja was right; watching movies is a much more enjoyable way to learn Italian, more akin to how we learn to speak our native language. We hear it spoken and we pick it up. Within a few weeks I had waded through the foreign film list and had almost one hundred Italian titles in my queue. I called Netflix to thank them for their extensive selection of foreign films. As an afterthought, I asked the agent if she would mention to the executives for their next brainstorming session that people like me, hoping to learn a foreign language, would be grateful if they categorized their films into language groups. The young lady thought that was an excellent idea.

Within a month of my request, Netflix had Italian as a search refinement in its listings of foreign films. And I had another example of what I love about America—why I think many of the best companies in the world are in America. They are open to innovation, to providing customers what they want and therefore being rewarded for it. Netflix exemplifies what I mean when I say that we, each of us, are co-creators of companies and society by virtue of how we choose to spend our money. If we spend our money on local food—local farmers will provide it and we will grow communities with our values—an appreciation of good, healthful food. If we spend our money on processed foods, we send our money out of our communities and grow distant cities.

Netflix is national, but it has local distribution centers all over the United States, and because of that, even though I live far from a major city, I'm able to have, in the next day's mail, an Italian movie that I want to see. I've watched almost one hundred Italian films by directors like Rossellini, de Sica, Fellini, Benigni, and Tornatore. More than fifty Italian movies with English subtitles remain in my Netflix queue. As I watched movie after movie I continually asked, why is Italy unique?

Why did Italy give the world Saint Francis, who devoted his life to the least fortunate—the lepers, the poor, the downtrodden? Why in this land, do friends and strangers greet each other with the cheerful sound of *Ciao:* I am your servant? Why in Tuscany should I meet a woman who explained to me that our relationship with the land is connubial? *Perche in Italia la famiglia e sacra?* Why is the family sacred in Italy?

Each book I read and each movie I watched added to my understanding of Italy and Italians, but two movies gave me epiphanies about Italians and their character, because they took me back to an earlier time and showed a truth I hadn't seen, by revealing how Italians used to be. And in doing so, these films underscored for me the value of tradition.

The first was Roberto Rossellini's film *Era Notta a Roma*, which takes the viewer, as though in a time capsule, back to 1943 Italy. Hidden right at the end of the prologue was the answer I had for so long been seeking.

The sudden revelation helped me understand what Galileo meant when he said *All truths are easy to understand once they are discovered; the point is to discover them.* After reading Rossellini's prologue, I was seeing Italy in a profoundly different light—a way that helped me understand how Italians influenced the outcome of World War II. Italians were responsible for unleashing Fascism and Mussolini upon the world, but they also gave the world an extraordinary gift—a gift that Rossellini brought to the attention of the world almost before the peace treaties were signed ending the war. In his 1946 film *Paisan*, he hinted at what he expressed explicitly in his 1960 film *Era Notte a Roma* (American title: *Escape by Night*). The original version of the movie begins with the following words scrolling over an uncut scene of farmers and families on an Italian farm during World War II.

> On the 8ᵗʰ of September 1943 it was announced to the world that Italy had signed an Armistice with the allies who had landed in Sicily two months previously and who were now advancing up the peninsula towards Salerno.
>
> After the 8ᵗʰ of September 1943, thousands, tens of thousands of allied prisoners, British for the most part, who had escaped from concentration camps, wandered through Italy seeking asylum for weeks and months from north to south, mingling with the Italian refugees, asking for hospitality in the countryside and in the cities.
>
> No one denied us such hospitality.
>
> And on the outside walls of the houses where we were kept hidden were posters containing the communiqués of the German High Command, threatening with the death penalty anyone giving asylum or aid to Allied military personnel.
>
> Our lives were protected by the uniforms we wore.
>
> If we were caught the worst that could happen to us was to be sent back to a concentration camp.
>
> But for the Italians who helped us there was only one alternative—a firing squad.
>
> In spite of this, no one ever denied us hospitality.

None of these people ever acted for personal gain.
Many were not even definitely on our side.
I believe that for the most part their actions were guided solely by
a sense of Christian charity.

Bingo! Eureka! *Bella Scoperta!* What a Revelation!

I had never heard of this film. I *had* heard of Roberto Rossellini. He brought neorealism to Italian cinema, movies shot on location using real farmers, real soldiers. His movies are like time machines, preserving the attitudes of Italians during the war. Discussing her father's contributions to history, Isabella Rossellini revealed that he considered himself an agnostic, but at times she wondered if atheist would be a more apt description. That he was either shocked me, and made his assertion that Christian charity was the reason thousands of lives were spared, even more stunning. But with this revelation I now better understood the warmth that I felt when I walked through the door at Podere Paugnano. It was born of a commitment so deep that Italians were willing to die to extend hands of hospitality. No wonder I noted in my journal that first night at Giovanni and Giovanna's farm: *Their hospitality feels completely natural.*

Rossellini backed up my contention that what makes Italians unique is their willingness to give of themselves. He opened my eyes and showed me that Italians were willing to extend hospitality, even if it meant death. That is extraordinary. And Rossellini, although not a believer, saw it as a natural outgrowth of Christianity. *Galileo rides again.* Truth is easy to see once someone else points it out to you.

Why had I not made the connection?

The Roman Catholic Church is responsible for the qualities I love about Italy. Why had I not seen it? Was it because I was brought up Protestant that I did not see what was hiding in plain sight? Did the theological differences I have with Catholics prevent me from seeing the influence of the Roman Catholic Church upon the character of Italy? When I bicycled into the towns of Tuscany I had been hoping that by not overlooking the familiar I would eventually see the hidden.

On my first Sunday in Italy I suddenly saw old people as I had never before seen them. Now Rossellini had taken off my blinders so I could see the Christian—the Roman Catholic—character of Italy. Rossellini showed me what Galileo revealed to the world—*All truths are easy to understand once they are discovered; the point is to discover them.* I was lauding Italian graciousness and generosity, but not attributing it to the responsibilities of love and hospitality emphasized in the Bible, which every Catholic knows: *"Love the Lord your God with all your heart and with all your soul and with all your mind and with all your strength." The second is this: "Love your neighbor as yourself." There is no commandment greater than these.* Italians took these commandments to heart and made them tradition, so much so that they were willing to die to live them.

Again I thought of Galileo's truth when I recalled the greetings that Italians offer each other: *Ciao; I am your servant, your slave.* What can account for such sacrifice during World War II—at the risk of your own life? I know of only one thing: a commitment to Jesus the Christ: *What you do for the least of these you do for me.*

An interesting side note about Rossellini's *Paisan*—Italian moviegoers paid little attention to a humble film about what the Italian people had done during the war. Only after people from other countries began hearing of the film did the extraordinary story of Italian sacrifice come to light.

Another film that gave me eyes to see was *The Best of Youth,* an Italian TV miniseries. Told from the perspective of two brothers, viewers are immersed in their sometimes turbulent world for over forty years, beginning in high school in the 1960s. We get to know a deeply conflicted family weathering the storms of family life and the political upheavals of late twentieth-century Italy. In one of the early scenes, Nicola witnesses his parents fighting and squabbling. He overhears his father tell his mother that he has mortgaged their home to get money for a risky investment. An argument erupts that ends with his mother yelling, "Too bad divorce doesn't exist in this country."

Skip ahead thirty years to the end of the mini-series. Nicola, who is now a doctor, overhears another conversation between his mom and dad and discovers once again how they treat each other when no one else is around. He's shocked by how much his parents, who are now in their seventies, love each other. In private, he later tells his dad that he had no idea they loved each other. He admitted that he had carried a thought from childhood that they were always on the verge of divorce, and he had even wished they would divorce, thinking that was what his mother wanted. His dad responded, "No, we fought just to keep each other sharp."

Nicola, reflecting on the conversation with his dad, realizes what a great blessing his family has been to him. He also realizes how much his parents love him and each other, and their children and grandchildren. In that moment he comprehends how much he would have lost if he had gotten his wish—if his parents had divorced.

That touched me. I hit the search engines looking for information about divorce in Italy. I knew that Roman Catholics cannot get divorced. But what does the Italian government say about divorce? The movie was accurate—at the time of the squabble about the mortgage, divorce was not possible in Italy. But I was shocked to discover that getting a divorce in Italy, unlike most of the rest of Europe, is still very difficult. Three years is the quickest that a divorce can be finalized.

Marriage and family are honored. Italy is like it is because family is important in Italy. Marriage is seen, not as a contract between a man and a woman, but as a covenant between God the couple. Upon that covenant, I now believe, is built the special qualities that we celebrate as Italian.

I didn't see it coming. I didn't see it while I was in Italy. I didn't see it while Aurora was telling me about the connubial relationship between man and *la campagna* in Tuscany. I didn't even see it at Le Celle speaking with a gentle monk about the rain from God. I didn't make the connection while I was touring one church after another looking at beautiful Christian paintings. I somehow overlooked Roman Catholicism's influence on the things I most love about Italy and Italians.

I think of the good that I've seen in Italy and all that was done for me. And I realize that the hospitality of Italians, that quality that makes the world fall in love with Italy, was born of a very specific relationship of these people to God through a way of living which is built upon love.

Wendell Berry's words again come to mind: *It is not from ourselves that we will learn to be better than we are.* The first time I read those words, I thought Berry was speaking of learning from other people, that we *will* ourselves to learn, or that others teach us, if we are *willing*. But this time the thought comes to me without the word *will*—*It is not from ourselves that we learn to be better than we are.* I can't be certain that Berry had in mind that it was from the indwelling Holy Spirit that *we learn to be better than we are*, but I do know that Wendell Berry knows of mystery, of things being beyond human understanding. And that brings me right back to the Italians and what makes them unique.

The Roman Catholic Church, like few others within the Christian community, takes seriously the Biblical prohibitions against divorce. For instance, Roman Catholics have not fallen for the wildly accepted Protestant view that divorce is permissible if adultery is present in the marriage. The stability of marriage in Italy is a factor of Italian life that is rich in its ramifications for the sweet, but sometimes turbulent character of the Italian household. People committed to a lifetime of living together are going to see good times and bad times.

Another thing that struck me in Italy is that people are not shy about arguing—that even husband and wives argue and disagree. At first I found it off-putting, but the more I witnessed it, the more I found I preferred it to the tendency for married people to break off communication and get divorced. I wonder if the prohibition against divorce is the reason people argue in Italy. They know they have to work things out. They have to express their differences, expose their shortcomings, and accept them and those of their spouse. People and family are more important than the appearance of harmony.

Family is the foundation of community, and community is the foundation of society, and society is the foundation of country and civilization. Allow and even encourage the breakdown of family as our government and many others around the world are doing and the breakdown of society and even civilization will soon follow. We're supposedly doing it in the name of compassion, and we're suffering from the inevitable unintended but devastating consequences of social engineers who think they know better than God how a society should be structured.

I must remember that in this land, among these people, where I have found so much to my liking, so much to praise, was born Fascism, and having been nurtured in this land among these people, Fascism joined with Nazism and Socialism to create atrocities this world will never forget. I must also remember that very few in these societies spoke out against those abuses.

That's me in the corner, that's me in the spotlight, losing my religion, the band R.E.M once sang. For select countries across the globe, that could be true. And while America is not leading this trend, ominous signs abound. Calling things by their right name is difficult for those who object to restraint. Better-sounding words seduce. George Orwell's *Nineteen Eighty-Four* came and went, but what he warned us about is still with us. *Words are not for conveying truth, but for manipulating truth.* Abortion is called *choice.* Genocide is called *ethnic cleansing.* Pornography is called *adult entertainment.*

It is odd, though, that divorce is still called divorce. I guess no need was found for a euphemism for breaking up a marriage—no need for a sweet-sounding word. If the current trend continues it will no longer be hyperbole to say that almost everyone divorces at least once, if they live long enough. But not in Italy.

It may not be a politically correct suggestion but God may be blessing the families of Italy, and blessing all Italians because the government of Italy is not encouraging and abetting the breakup of marriages. The Pope, every Pope, starting with Peter, has faithfully opposed divorce. As a result Italians stay married, families remain strong, and society benefits.

In most countries of the world the divorce rate is nearly fifty percent. In Italy, by contrast, the divorce rate is under ten percent. Families also remain strong in Italy because the welfare system doesn't encourage unmarried parentage. One of every five families in Sweden is headed by a lone parent; in England it's one out of every ten. But in Italy only one family in every two hundred is headed by a single parent. The correlation between the amount of money paid for single parentage and the number of single parents is direct. Sweden pays the most, Italy the least. As the old saying goes, *you get what you pay for.*

If you're looking to establish a good society, a good community on this Earth—honor the ancient wisdom of the Bible, not just on marriage, but loving your neighbor as yourself. Italians are doing what the Bible and the traditions of generation after generation of forebearers have encouraged them to do.

Italy is what it is because of what Rossellini called *Christian charity*—a charity that is born in the Christian commitment to family. God created family as the foundation of humanity. If we allow that foundation to crumble, we do so at our peril. We deceive ourselves when we think we can create a perfect society. Man's record on perfect societies isn't so good. World War II was fought to get rid of one man's idea of a perfect society. We're better off sticking to the simple things that Italians pay attention to—loving and helping their neighbors. The summation of the Biblical commandments—that's what they do well. Italians have used those two commandments to create a society that has much to inspire the rest of us. Italians know that they are deeply flawed people. They too got swept up in that perfect society thing. But the things Italians get right—food, family, and hospitality—make them pleasant people to be around.

And that's a good foundation upon which to build a society. Many people say that hard times are coming. But I say if those hard times come, we'll have even more reason to celebrate *questa dolce mistero della vita italiana*—that sweet mysterious Italian life. It was during hard times that this vibrant way of life reached full blossom. If hard times come again, paradoxes will follow, and a philosophy of thankful stewardship will sweep over the land. Forgotten—almost overnight if people are hungry, if life gets down to its essence—will be the twin philosophies of materialism and consumerism.

Some will argue against the connections I make between God—and the Bible—and the Roman Catholic Church—and farming—and family— and food. I now see each as being in a unique *connubial* relationship with God—God and mankind joining to create the best that we can on Earth. God's will, it can be said with little fear of opposition, is that family is to be honored and that divorce is not recognized. Italy, because of the Roman Catholic Church, has honored life and family. And I'm going to stick my neck out and say that the *why* of Italy began with Peter's confession of *The Christ* and continues to this day because of the Roman Catholic Church. Italy is being rewarded, and we who have been to Italy are also reaping the benefits, *the good fits,* of a country that despite its failures, and the failures of the Church, is living a *connubial life married to the will of God.*

Pope John Paul II expressed Aurora's thought as *Creation was given and entrusted to mankind as a duty.* Put these thoughts with those of Jesus expressed in the *Lord's Prayer* and you have the essence of Italy, the reason the country stands out so delightfully on the world's stage. Compare that with the predominant materialistic mindset of the world, and the reason Italy is unique and attractive becomes apparent.

Italy, because of the teachings of the Roman Catholic Church, is taking care of family, land, and community: *the will of God, being done on earth as it is in heaven.* The result is a joyful delight of thankful stewardship, or as Ed Breslin wrote in *Drinking with Miss Dutchie,* his tribute to transforming love: *Christianity in its pure and true form is so beautiful it's breathtaking.*

Christianity pure and true: grace, charity, hope, faith, fellowship, sacrifice, stewardship, and love. People getting together to break bread and share their lives are my favorite memories of Italy—when you read the stories of Jesus you see the same thing. Jesus getting together with friends; his parables; his paradoxes; his first miracle turning water into wine for a wedding feast; dining with friends and strangers—*a glutton and a drunkard*—a friend of sinners. Jesus didn't fit the religious mold.

Jesus challenges and surprises. Even though the feeding of the five thousand involved a miraculous multiplication of bread and fishes, Jesus told his followers: *Gather the pieces that are left over. Let nothing be wasted.* Jesus also asked: *Who then is the wise and faithful steward?* Then He showed the world by example. The supreme Creator is the supreme Steward.

Jesus gave us a wonderful model when he got together with His disciples for the Last Supper, but we don't need to be Christians to recognize the importance of getting together with friends to offer our thanks for the food and the lives we share. Even though Jesus knew He would soon be killed on the cross, He took the time to celebrate Passover with those He loved. Jesus showed himself to be the supreme Servant— and Italians took it to heart. His *Ciao*, His commitment to servanthood, transformed the world. His willingness to die inspired a nation of people willing to sympathize with and participate in the suffering of the allied soldiers—and risk Nazi firing squads to do it.

What Jesus embodies, Italy at its finest embodies. Italians view life as a mystery, something beyond our limited understanding. Until we begin embracing mystery, it's hard to imagine that we non-Italians will learn the art of enjoying life the way Italians do. Italians have shown us how to celebrate life—a celebration that I learned is best enjoyed with family and friends. Did that pattern begin with Jesus? It's the best model I've found to explain the unfathomable mysteries of Italian life—their deep commitment to enjoying life. It's a long-standing tradition and I see no evidence of it changing. I'm convinced that a gene for *Celebrating the Sweet Life* is wound tightly in that mysterious double helix—deep in the strands of every Italian's DNA.

Epilogue

You can only see properly with your heart;
the essential is invisible to the eye.

ANTOINE ST. EXUPERY

🖋

Life is a long lesson in humility.

JAMES M. BARRIE

🖋

We must be willing to let go of the life we have planned,
so as to have the life that is waiting for us.

E.M. FORSTER

🖋

The essence of all beautiful art, all great art, is gratitude.

FRIEDRICH NIETZSCHE

🖋

In ordinary life we hardly realize
that we receive a great deal more than we give,
and that it is only with gratitude that life becomes rich.

DIETRICH BONHOEFFER

🖋

From His fullness we have all received,
grace upon grace.

SAINT JOHN

I think often of Aurora, especially on days when the willow basket
she gave me to remember the good times is overflowing or when
the sun lights up our late afternoon sky. I remember the evening
Aurora took in the beauty surrounding us on her Tuscan hillside and
declared it to be connubial—a marriage between God and man.

Siamo Alla Frutta

A year after I left Tuscany, I emailed Aurora to thank her for the great meals and wonderful memories. She wrote back, "Please, please, do not say so many kind things or I will not believe you. I know that Pietro was difficult." She repeated almost verbatim what she had said to me on the train platform the morning I left for Florence. I am amazed she does not yet realize how much I enjoyed being with her and Pietro and Joshua and Annamarja on her farm.

The olives had been picked and pressed, and, as Annamarja predicted, Aurora had turned over her farm to Pietro, Joshua, and Pietro's wife. But the story doesn't end there. Aurora did not let her dream of farming die. She has a new farm, on yet another side of Cortona, out in the wide Val di Chiana, where she has sun all day. She has asked me to come back to help her on what will be my seventh Italian farm. She wants me to help her decide what to build where. Pietro and his two bombs came immediately to mind.

"One for where you sleep James and one for where you..."

When I go back to Tuscany to help Aurora build sheds and pick olives, I hope that hearts will have softened, and Pietro will invite Aurora and me, and maybe Annamarja as well, to another *Feste Tuscanissimo*, one prepared in that domed, wood-fired Tuscan oven that *only the lucky farms have*. I would love to meet Pietro's wife and introduce her and Pietro to mine. I'd even like to cover my ears again as Joshua prances around the living room sing-songing dead roosters in the many languages he knows and a few languages he doesn't, and rebuild another Etruscan wall, while Pietro ricochets rocks around the yard with his noisy weed whacker, just to annoy me. It would be like old times.

I think often of Aurora, especially on days when the willow basket she gave me to remember the good times is overflowing, or when the sun lights up our late afternoon sky. I remember the evening Aurora took in the beauty surrounding us on her Tuscan hillside and declared it to be *connubial*—a marriage between God and man. With that one word Aurora sent me on a journey that eventually made it possible for me to *see with my heart what is invisible to the eye*—to comprehend why Italy and Italians are unique. It just took me a long time to discover the full meaning of what she was sharing with me.

Actually, that is not quite true. *Non e vero*. Truer would be that I am still trying to allow the wisdom she shared with me on that beautiful afternoon to shape my life. I'm still trying to absorb the benefits of *seeing* life as a *mysterious marriage* of God's grace and man's longing—a *connubial* relationship that leads to *thankful stewardship*.

Italians live those words. That's the key to Italian life.

The beauty of Italian life is not that it's perfect. The beauty of Italian life is that even when it seems hard, an appreciation for life shows through. Italians show gratitude for what they have. At least that's how it looks to people who aren't Italian. To Italians, they don't see anything quite so grand. They're just getting by as they always have, doing what they were commanded to do—*Love your neighbor as yourself*—benefiting from tradition. That's why in a country in which few know why they say *Ciao*, both coming and going, they nevertheless do. And for the same reason, they embrace friends and family, neighbors and strangers alike with an attitude of benevolent compassion. *I am your servant*, willing to sympathize in your suffering and your joy.

Grazie per Grazia.

Ciao!

*This beautiful door speaks to me of Italy in myriad ways. It's gorgeous, it's cared for, and it's flanked by greenery from nature. It's connubial writ small, as Aurora taught me to see. God and man getting together to create some of the most beautiful things and sights you are ever likely to see. Note the craftsmanship. Look at the bottom of the door. Usually finials are at the top and are ornate, but I'm calling that angled joint a finial. Even though it's at the bottom, it is a crowning achievement of love and craftsmanship.
This door says Italy to me.*

Friday parked in front of a farmhouse on the road to Aurora's olive farm sums up my Italian journey. The scene reminds me of the Italian people's love of the traditional. You know this isn't America—who builds a farmhouse over over a road in the USA? The house looks ancient, the road looks steep, and Friday carried me all over Tuscany—the photo does a good job of reminding me of the good people, the good times, and the good food I enjoyed in Italy.

About the Author

James Ernest Shaw lives and writes from small-town America,
along the shore of a beautiful spring-fed lake in the heart of
what John Steinbeck called *the prettiest state I ever saw,*
He and his wife Mardi divide their time between
their five children and eight grandchildren.

www.facebook.com/AmericanJourney
www.facebook.com/ItalianJourney
www.JamesErnestShaw.com

Made in United States
North Haven, CT
27 December 2022

30238250R00144